P9-DVJ-620

A Pioneer Gentlewoman in British Columbia

Recollections of the Pioneers of British Columbia

A Pioneer Gentlewoman in British Columbia is the second volume in a series of editions of important documents of the colonial and early provincial history of British Columbia.

The first volume is *The Reminiscences of Doctor John Sebastian Helmcken*, edited by Dorothy Blakey Smith. J.S. Helmcken was British Columbia's pioneer doctor, first Speaker in the legislature, and one of the negotiators of the colony's entry into Confederation.

A PIONEER GENTLEWOMAN IN BRITISH COLUMBIA

The Recollections of Susan Allison

Edited by Margaret A. Ormsby

UNIVERSITY OF BRITISH COLUMBIA PRESS
VANCOUVER

A PIONEER GENTLEWOMAN IN BRITISH COLUMBIA

The Recollections of Susan Allison

Canadian Cataloguing in Publication Data

Allison, Susan, 1845-1937.
A pioneer gentlewoman in British Columbia.

Includes index.
ISBN 0-7748-0039-9

1. Allison, Susan, 1845-1937. 2. Frontier and pioneer life—British Columbia. I. Ormsby, Margaret A., 1909– II. Title.
FC3825.1.A45A3 971.1'4'03'0924 C76-016022-8 F1088.A

Printed in Canada

This book has been published with the help of a grant from the Humanities Research Council of Canada, using funds provided by the Canada Council, and grants from

the Hamber Foundation

the Intellectual Prospecting Fund

the Leon and Thea Koerner Foundation.

CONTENTS

ILLUSTRATIONS

PHOTOGRAPHIC CREDITS

Plates 1, 10, 12, and 21 appear courtesy of Mrs. Elvie Sisson. Plates 2, 5, 6, 7, 8, 9, 19, 22, 23 are from the collections of the Provincial Archives of British Columbia. Plate 3 was provided by the National Maritime Museum. The Princeton and District Pioneer Museum, Princeton, supplied plates 16 and 17. Plates 11, 13, 18, and 20 came from R. N. Atkinson Museum, Penticton, and the sword illustrated in Plate 14, in the possession of Mrs. Dougal MacGregor, was photographed by Mr. Harris of the Atkinson Museum. Plate 4 is reproduced from Ernest A. Wiltsee, *Gold Rush Steamers [of the Pacific]* (San Francisco: Grabhorn Press, 1938); and plate 15 is reproduced from Frank Bailey, *Nicola, Similkameen and Tulameen Valleys. The Richest Section of British Columbia* (Vancouver: Ward, Elwood & Pound, c. 1913).

INTRODUCTION

On 18 August 1860, her fifteenth birthday, Susan Louisa Moir, in the company of her mother, her stepfather, and her sister Jane, landed from the river steamer at Fort Hope to take up residence in British Columbia. Already she was a seasoned traveller: before her fifth birthday she had made the long sea voyage from Ceylon, "the resplendent isle," to England; her nine years spent in and around London had been broken by annual excursions to Aberdeen, Scotland; and only recently she had completed a fifty-two day journey from Southampton to Vancouver Island.

For Susan's branch of the Moir family, there was nothing very unusual about travelling abroad to take up residence in a strange country. Since the days of John Moir, her great-grandfather, her family, which had originated in Sterlingshire, had considered Aberdeen its fixed place of residence. But her grandfather, William Moir, had left Aberdeen to join the 16th Regiment of Foot just before it was sent to Bengal and had later joined the Ceylon Regiment. Most of his life was spent at Colombo and Ratnapura.

William Moir's first wife was Ishbel Clarke, one of the six daughters of Lieutenant-Colonel Edward Clarke of Aucharroch, Angus, who in 1798 had entered the service of the East India Company. At her marriage Ishbel received Woodcote Lodge, near Colombo, as a gift from one of her brothers-in-law. Later, as an inheritance from her father, she acquired additional properties in Ceylon and India. When she died at Calcutta on 4 April 1817, aged only thirty-one years, her house and her lands fell into the possession of her husband.

William took a second wife eight years after Ishbel's death. On 17 October 1825 he married Louise, the eldest daughter of Lieutenant

Thomas Deacon, 16th and Ceylon Regiments, fort adjutant at Trincomalee from 1818 until 1823 and at Colombo in 1824 and 1825. Just before his second marriage, William resigned his position at Colombo as paymaster of the 2nd Ceylon Regiment, went on half pay, and entered the Ceylon civil service. He was appointed on 1 July 1825 agent for the District of Saffragam with headquarters at Ratnapura. Subsequently he became district judge, Colombo. At the time of his retirement on 1 May 1840, he had one son, Stratton, by his first wife, and three sons and four daughters by his second.

After his mother's death, Stratton had been sent to Scotland to be cared for by his aunt, Mrs. Jane Shaw. She saw to it that he received a sound Scottish education. In 1825, the year of his father's second marriage, Stratton Moir entered Marischal College, Aberdeen University. He graduated Master of Arts, Marischal College and Aberdeen University, in 1829.

Stratton Moir's most intimate friend at Aberdeen, James Skinner, a member of a famous Scottish Episcopalian family, was a few years younger than himself. Skinner entered Marischal College to take the Arts course in 1832, but the following year he transferred to the newly-established University of Durham, where he was a foundation scholar and later a fellow. Stratton accompanied Skinner when he travelled to Durham to study theology, and while there he met the Reverend George Hills, who in 1859 was named first bishop of Columbia. It was a matter of no little surprise to Bishop Hills, some thirty years after his first meeting with Stratton, to discover his widow living at Hope.

Stratton's occupation at the time of his 1833 visit to Durham is not known, but it is possible that, like his son after him, he was apprenticed in London to a banking house. Certainly he seems to have had the opportunity to meet frequently with his cousin, Alexander Rogers, a prominent London jewel merchant with business connections in India, who was also interested in investing capital in the coffee industry of Ceylon.

Stratton Moir's return to Ceylon was facilitated by his obtaining a position on a plantation owned by the Honourable Philip Anstruther, colonial secretary of Ceylon from 1833 to 1846. Anstruther's plantation was in the highlands of Kandy at Upper Bulatgame, Central Province. Though the area was at a fairly high elevation and the countryside was heavily forested with teak and other hardwoods, it was hoped that the cultivation of coffee there would prove very successful.

Before taking up his appointment, Stratton Moir was married at St. Pancras Church, London, on 4 April 1841, to Susan Louisa, daughter of Jan Mildern, a Dutch sea captain of Amsterdam. Their eldest child, Stratton, was born before the couple left London. Mrs. Shaw marked the occasion of her nephew's departure for Ceylon by the gift of a very old Bible. This token of her affection the Moirs reciprocated after the birth of their first daughter. The child born to them on 5 April 1843 at "Dhekinde," Ambegamoa, a plantation owned jointly by Stratton Moir and Alexander Rogers, was named Jane Shaw Moir.

For their third and last child, born at Colombo on 18 August 1845, Stratton chose his wife's name. Susan Louisa Moir was baptized at St. Peter's Church, Colombo, on 29 September 1845. One of her sponsors was Mrs. Rogers, mother of Alexander Rogers, and another was Bishop William Skinner, successor to his father as bishop of Aberdeen and *Primus* of Scotland.

When Susan was only four, Stratton Moir was taken ill, probably of malaria, and died suddenly. He left an unsigned will which named Alexander Gunn, clerk at Colombo for colonial duties for the civil branch of the Ordnance, as guardian of his wife and children. Gunn managed the plantations acquired by Stratton Moir and Alexander Rogers until 1854, when he discovered that Mrs. Moir had turned over to her father-in-law the deeds to her husband's properties and that William Moir was making very little provision for her support in England.

Mrs. Moir had returned to England after her husband's death to live with his cousins, Mr. and Mrs. Alexander Gordon of Bishopsteighton, Devonshire. Their daughter Jane was married to the Reverend George F. W. Mortimer, D.D., a distinguished headmaster, who at that time was head of the City of London School. Towards Mrs. Stratton Moir, the Gordons were kindness itself; and Dr. Mortimer was only too willing to offer her advice about the choice of schools for her children. A school in London was selected for Susan Louisa; there she received such good training in languages that she retained to the end of her life familiarity with Greek, Latin, and French.

As a widow, Mrs. Moir became increasingly dependent on the hospitality of her husband's relatives on the Clarke side of his family. Ishbel Moir's five sisters had all married well, and every one of them enjoyed the comfortable life of the upper middle class. They conformed to the habit of Victorian families of that class by offering shelter to relatives who returned home from the colonies and by providing love and compassion in time of their need. Mrs. Stratton Moir, however, was not without a sense of pride. As the income from her properties in Ceylon continued to dwindle, she began to long for greater independence than she could obtain as a guest. Marriage provided her only opportunity to attain her objective.

Just where she met Thomas Glennie is not known: possibly he had a connection with Ceylon, where the Venerable J. M. S. Glenie had been archdeacon of Colombo and King's Visitor. A gay and charming Scot, Thomas Glennie had already inherited, and squandered, several fortunes. Another legacy was left him in 1857. He had little difficulty in persuading Mrs. Moir to marry him. She also consented to emigrate with her daughters and to leave her son Stratton behind in London to learn banking.

It was not the arduous occupation of gold mining that attracted Thomas Glennie to British Columbia; rather, since he aspired to the role of country squire in a virgin country, it was the reports reaching the English newspapers of the need for permanent settlers in the gold colony and of the enactment there of measures to make land available on easy terms that aroused his interest. In preparation for pioneer life in the new British colony, Glennie booked first-class passages on the Royal Mail Steamship Line from Southampton. From London he arranged to have the family's household furnishings shipped round the Horn. These included Jane Moir's little rosewood piano; the silver candelabra which had once been used to provide light for imprisoned Episcopalians in their cells at the Gallows Gate, Aberdeen; and ornaments such as Chinese swords and porcelain figurines. For Susan's sake, the Bible which had been a present from Mrs. Shaw to her father, as well as her father's college books, were included. Portraits of the girls were painted; dressing-cases were ordered for them; and new wardrobes containing riding-habits were purchased.

Every experience on her voyage from Southampton to Esquimalt contributed to Susan Moir's anticipation of an exciting life to be spent in British Columbia. On the first lap of her journey, she found the shipboard passengers interesting; travelling across the Isthmus of Panama on the recently completed railway line, she was entranced with the beauty of the tropical forest and the exotic wildlife; at Panama and Acapulco her sense of history was aroused by evidence of Spain's past greatness in the Pacific; and her passage on the unsafe and overcrowded *John L. Stephens* was rendered memorable by a storm at sea. Her feeling of exhilaration continued during her short stay in the miniature colonial capitals of Victoria and New Westminster. And when in August 1860 she landed from the Fraser River steamboat to climb the riverbank to a stockaded wooden fort, she was excited at the thought of her family residing near this primitive post on the edge of the wilderness.

Fort Hope, the head of the navigation of the Fraser River at this time, was recommended to Thomas Glennie by Governor James Douglas. It had a beautiful location at a bend in the river where the silt-laden waters, finally released from rock-bound canyons, start to flow swiftly towards the sea. The Hudson's Bay Company's fort was flanked by a dark forest of conifers and overshadowed by snow-capped peaks, but there was arable land in its vicinity along the Coquihalla River and on "the Flat" below the fort, where the Company had planted eight acres of timothy as forage for its horses. A straggling town had grown up since the beginning of the gold rush in 1858, and a court house had been built in 1859. But far more imposing than the new false-fronted stores and the frame hotels were the heavy log posts of the palisade. Within that enclosure lived Chief Trader William Charles and the Company's servants, all heavily engaged in tallying the annual fur returns from the interior posts and making arrangements for the proper supplying of the needs of the fur traders in the Interior.

Fort Hope had come into existence in 1848. Its building was made necessary by the signing of the Oregon Treaty by Britain and the United States in 1846. With the 49th Parallel accepted by both countries as the boundary line between their territories from the Rocky Mountains to the Gulf of Georgia, it became necessary to reroute the fur brigades away from the Columbia River and have them converge on the Fraser. In 1846, A. C. Anderson, in charge at Fort Alexandria on the upper Fraser, was ordered to find a suitable route from Fort Kamloops on the Thompson River to Fort Langley. In May he explored the chain of lakes extending south from Lillooet to Harrison Lake. On his return journey from Fort Langley, he ascended the Fraser River as far as the Coquihalla, followed it for twenty-three miles, and then turned south-easterly to ascend Nicolum and Sumallo creeks as far as the Sumallo's junction with the Skagit River. Anderson's was certainly a passable, though a rather long, route through the hazardous Cascade Mountains.

Two years later Henry N. Peers was entrusted with the building of Fort Hope. Peers found a shorter route through the mountains, but one that was steeper and more dangerous. After he marked out a zigzag on Manson Ridge, however, it was decided to accept his route for the brigades. When Eden Colvile, governor of Rupert's Land, travelled it in

1849, he pronounced it difficult but suitable for adoption: "The only difficulties to be found on this route are a range of wooded hills that lie between the Similkameen River and Fort Hope. I crossed them with loaded pack horses in three days, although the road had only been opened that season. It was through some of the heaviest timbered land I ever saw. I measured one tree that was forty-two feet in circumference, and the avoidance of such trees as had fallen across the road necessarily consumed much time." Commencing in 1849, the brigades from the districts of New Caledonia, Thompson River, and Fort Colvile brought the furs annually by pack horse to Fort Hope; from there they were shipped to Fort Langley.

The last miles of the overland brigade trail passed through a beautiful parklike valley. There cascades threaded their way down steep mountain slopes to deep canyons; Douglas firs and cedars grew stately; and ferns and lilies carpeted the banks of creeks and shallow lakes. In this vicinity, Bishop Hills said, one might fancy one's self "in the wilder part of some cultivated domain in England."

Thomas Glennie evidently had the same feeling as Bishop Hills, for on 20 August 1860, two days after his arrival at Fort Hope, he chose a location on the brigade trail, two miles distant from the fort, for a pre-emption of 160 acres of land. At this lovely spot, where the grandeur of the mountain scenery must have reminded Mrs. Glennie of her view of Adam's Peak from her first husband's plantation in Kandy, Glennie prepared to have built on the banks of the Coquihalla River, "Hopelands," the manor house of his demesne. The substantial log house was to have something of the character of a hunting lodge in Scotland and be suitable for the furnishings which would arrive from England at the end of the year.

Meanwhile accommodation had to be found for the family. On their arrival, William Charles extended the hospitality of the fort to them. There they were comfortable, and in Charles they found a compatible companion, for he was a Scot who had been educated at the University of Edinburgh. Through his offices the Glennies discovered that the town of Hope contained a surprisingly large number of residents with an upper class background similar to their own. Peter O'Reilly, the gold commissioner and magistrate, who had a room at the new court house, was a Trinity College, Dublin, man. Judge Matthew Baillie Begbie, who visited Hope on official business, was a Cantabrigian. Lieutenant-Colonel Richard Clement Moody, officer commanding the Columbia Detachment of the Royal Engineers, had been stationed in a number of British colonies and had served as governor of the Falkland

Islands. The Reverend A. D. Pringle, a missionary sent out by the Society for the Propagation of the Gospel, had served as assistant curate at Christ Church, Paddington, London. Even commissioned officers of the Royal Engineers and professional men like the civil engineers Edgar Dewdney (who had accompanied the Glennies on the boat trip from New Westminster to Hope) and his partner, Walter Moberly, were representative of that type of Englishman referred to by Bishop Hills as belonging to "the better classes." It was a happy chance for the Glennies that this small town of five hundred inhabitants, where the chief occupations were the maintenance of the fur trade, the keeping of law and order in the mining camps, the supplying of the mines, and the opening of transportation routes, should have contained so many persons of their own sort.

While her mother and stepfather were making the acquaintance of men who were destined to rise to high positions in the government and administration of British Columbia, Susan Moir was discovering in the community such amusing characters as William Yates at the fort and Mrs. Landvoight, an educated Frenchwoman married to a storekeeper. Everyone Susan met, including the officers and servants of the Hudson's Bay Company, the native Indians, and the Mexican packers, aroused her curiosity and interest. By temperament she was admirably adapted to living in a pioneer setting where there was a mixture of races and of social classes.

Mrs. Glennie was not as adaptable as her younger daughter. Because there were a sufficient number of persons of her own kind to satisfy her need for companionship, she did not reach beyond that circle. In addition, her activities were restricted after she fell ill with Panama fever. Her husband's exuberance offset Mrs. Glennie's rather retiring nature. He was soon intimate with William Charles, Peter O'Reilly, and Captain H. R. Luard, R.E. They all enjoyed dances and other entertainments at the fort and found pleasure in riding and horse racing. To this group, Edgar Dewdney, then only twenty-five years of age, attached himself. Either because of his liking for Glennie or in order to advance his suit with Jane Moir, he was almost constantly in the company of her stepfather.

The gay parties that this little group of expatriates devised kept Mrs. Glennie from feeling forlorn. But she had reasons for feeling discouraged: it was not long before she realized that her preparation for pioneer life was singularly deficient. She knew almost nothing about the domestic arts: she had never learned to bake bread or to wash clothes with a scrubbing board. When the family moved into a windowless frame shack, she was unable to improvise any kind of protection against the penetrating cold of the high winds.

During these difficult months when Mrs. Glennie was experiencing the first hardships of frontier life, her husband refused to bridle his extravagant habits or to limit his social activities. His money was running out by the time that Hopelands was completed at the end of November. The decline of the family's fortunes from this time forth can be traced in the diaries of Bishop Hills and Peter O'Reilly. According to O'Reilly, the outlook for them was already "gloomy" when on 6 December, before their furniture arrived, they moved into their home. The arrival of Jane's piano on 22 January 1861 was Glennie's excuse for holding a dance. He soon found other pretexts for the same entertainment. On 8 February, O'Reilly complained: "Just as I was going to bed Glennie & Dewdney came in— G—— wanted us to go out & have a dance." Three days later Dewdney made a start on the wagon road he was to build part way to the Similkameen River. On this occasion Glennie turned the first sod and made a speech, and there was "Champaigne galore." Only a month later, a storekeeper in Hope who owned a pack train took out a summons in Supreme Court against Glennie for £800, and on 22 April he was served with a writ.

Finding himself in this financial embarrassment, Glennie made an attempt to farm the land. He had had the foresight to ship a plow from England, and in the spring he put it into use and planted crops. But his willow fence was too frail to keep out the bears and the cattle, and all his crops were destroyed.

On 3 January 1862 he received the certificate of improvement for his pre-emption. By this time a real crisis had been reached in his affairs. On the 17th, O'Reilly drove his sleigh to Hopelands, apparently with the intention of offering advice. On the 18th, Mrs. Charles drove out and brought the whole family back to the fort. That evening, O'Reilly wrote, Dewdney was "very spoony" and "old G—— doing the fine gentleman." On the 22nd, Dewdney and O'Reilly dined early and then drove to Hopelands to pick up the Glennies once more. "Mrs. and Miss G—— stayed at the Fort," O'Reilly wrote in his diary, "Old G—— took a bed at the court house. Tea at the Fort, & cards. Dewdney very sweet on Miss G—— old G—— became very confidential & kept me up till 3 a.m. to my great disgust." The following day, 23 January, an auction was held at Hopelands. O'Reilly, who attended it in the company of Charles and several other friends, "Bought the House & Place also the Piano for them—for the former I paid $80—

the latter $130." "Afterwards," he added, "drove Mrs. and Miss G—— out & sent . . . Meat bread &c &c."

Not even Mrs. Glennie's pride could now hide the fact that she had married a wastrel. Mrs. Charles and Mrs. Pringle comforted her at this time, but her friendship with Mrs. Charles became strained when on 5 March William Charles cut off the Glennies' credit at the fort. Even O'Reilly, who had been so forbearing, discovered on 8 March that "the G——s were by no means amicable. . . . What they are to do," he wrote, "the Lord only knows."

The friend who remained steadfast throughout this ordeal was Edgar Dewdney. He spent the winter of 1861 in Hope. With each passing day, he became more and more infatuated with Jane Moir. His romance was observed by others with amusement: in February 1862, Mrs. Charles laid a bet of five pairs of gloves with O'Reilly that Dewdney would be married within two and a half months; and towards the end of April she made another bet, this time of five dollars, that Dewdney would be married by the bishop. But Dewdney's ambition to take advantage of new opportunities developing in the colony restrained his ardour, and it was not until late in March 1864 that his wedding took place at Christ Church, Hope. Glennie was present on the occasion, but a few months later he disappeared, deserting his wife and her eighteen-year-old daughter, Susan.

At the time of Glennie's disappearance in 1864, Hope had changed greatly from the busy place it was at the time of his arrival. At that time, the mining and settlement frontiers had not yet destroyed the fur trade, and though the Hudson's Bay Company had lost its privilege of exclusive trade west of the Rocky Mountains in 1858, the fort was still handling heavy fur returns from the interior posts. Susan Moir never forgot the sight of Chief Factor Angus McDonald, dressed in buckskin garments and beaded leggings, leading the Colvile brigade in 1860 down the last stretch of the trail or the mad dash of the horses as they advanced to the Flat through a cloud of dust. The activity at the fort was intense during the following days as the furs were unloaded for shipment and the packs were made up for the return trip. The chief factors conferred at the fort and finally reached agreement on all the details concerning the operations of the coming season.

On the bars of the Fraser River, some miners were still engaged in panning gold, but hydraulic mining had begun, and the mining population was starting to disperse as parties headed up the canyon to Lytton and advanced beyond that point to the creeks of the Cariboo. The back-packing of supplies over rocky mountain ledges to the upper mines was now necessary, and the Mexicans and others who engaged in this occupation made Hope the place for assembling their tools and goods.

The great excitement at Hope in 1860 was the news that gold had been discovered late the previous year on the Similkameen River, south of the 49th Parallel, by a member of the American section of the North American Boundary Commission. A rumour spread that gold was also to be found farther north where the river flowed through British territory. Then it was learned that a discovery had been made at Rock Creek, a tributary of the Kettle River, some one hundred miles east of Similkameen.

Governor James Douglas was vigilant to avert the dangers of American occupation and economic penetration. As he told Bishop Hills, the southeastern portion of British Columbia had no natural obstacles to help prevent easy access from the American side, and it was consequently imperative to open up trade from Fort Hope. Only by this means could any movement of the Americans north to the British Columbia mines be intercepted. He arranged to have "Skiyou," a famous Similkameen bear hunter, explore a new pass to the Similkameen River, and he himself went to Hope on 5 June to question him. Bishop Hills observed the examination and was most impressed with Douglas's patience in extracting information. He was also impressed with the knowledge of the Indians: "Some of these Indians shewed remarkable cleverness in sketching out a map of the route [to Similkameen], marking the rivers, mountain valleys, passes & buildings."

The governor's dependence on this source for information greatly annoyed Colonel Moody and caused some criticism of Douglas in the press. But the Royal Engineers had only completed the construction of five miles of road the previous year, and, without doubt, Douglas shared the views expressed by his friend Donald Fraser in the London *Times* of 30 January 1860: "The Sappers and Miners, who were to have constructed all the bridges and to have made all the surveys of the public land, have made five miles of road and several bridges; but they have not made any surveys. At the rate they have hitherto progressed it would take 50 years to complete the road they have begun. . . . The fact is that soldiers cannot be expected to do this sort of work. The *im-*

pedimenta they carry with them, the costliness of their provisions and of their transport, the loss of time in drilling and squaring and scrubbing and cleaning them, make them the most expensive of labourers. They do their work well, it is true, better than civilians; but for all that it is a mistake to set them at it. Soldiers we want and must have, but a cheaper soldier than a Sapper and Miner or Engineer would answer our purposes better."

Having learned all he could from the Indians, Governor Douglas then called assembled miners and offered to stake a party if it would undertake a mining exploration. O'Reilly completed all the arrangements for this expedition on 26 June. It was to be led by John Fall Allison, an experienced miner who had been in California. Allison proceeded to the Similkameen forthwith and was able to report a month later that his party had prospected twelve miles up the north fork and had found diggings yielding five to six dollars a day with a rocker. Hydraulic mining of the gravel banks of the river, he thought, would yield still better returns. When this news reached Hope, three pack trains were made ready. On 6 August there was a great movement out of town of men, horses, and mules.

A few weeks later, Douglas returned to Hope to commence a tour of inspection of the Fraser mines. When he reached Lytton, he decided to ride 228 miles to investigate the Rock Creek area. His journey by way of Fort Kamloops, the Nicola Valley, the Similkameen Valley, and the southern part of the Okanagan Valley left him enthusiastic about the prospects for agriculture. He also observed that "The Forks" (Vermilion Forks at the junction of the Tulameen and Similkameen rivers) was well located for an agricultural and mining supply centre. O'Reilly was given orders to lay out a townsite just below it. As Douglas proceeded on to Rock Creek, he realized that the open country was inviting to American cattle ranchers and cattle drivers. And at Rock Creek he found what was virtually an American mining camp, supplied by mule trains from Oregon and Seattle.

On his return to Victoria, the governor made preparations to have "the Queen's Trail," as he called it—a mule trail seventy miles long—blazed from Hope to Vermilion Forks. Dewdney and Moberly obtained a government contract for this work. They were engaged in the enterprise while Colonel Moody was at leisure at Hope in August 1860, spending a holiday with his wife.

Moody, as chief commissioner of lands and works, could hardly believe that the governor had not consulted him or that he would make use of civilians while Sappers and surveyors were available for trail making. "The site of all towns as well as all wood trails or communications of whatever nature along our Continental frontier possesses a Military importance of the highest character . . . ," he protested. "I feel that I could not discharge from myself to anyone else whomsoever this important service."

Moody had further cause to be annoyed when, after Douglas's return from Similkameen, Sergeant William McColl, R.E., was ordered in October 1860 to survey a trail from Punch Bowl Pass on the Brigade Trail, down Whipsaw Creek (where the miners had now built sluices), as far as the townsite to which Douglas had given the name of "Princeton" in honour of the visit to North America of the Prince of Wales. Douglas responded to Moody's criticism by suggesting to McColl that he should henceforth request instructions from Moody, but he terminated the discussion of what were the most suitable localities for townsites, by the crisp remark that "people are not generally disposed to perch their houses on bleak mountains and inaccessible cliffs simply because they happen to be good military positions."

The road surveyed by McColl had a much better gradient than the Brigade Trail. Douglas now began to form a better opinion of the competence of the Royal Engineers. He complimented Moody on McColl's accomplishment and diplomatically suggested to him that it was probable that McColl's selection of a location for a townsite at Vermilion Forks was more suitable than O'Reilly's choice farther down the Similkameen River.

For his part, Moody forgot his pique and hurriedly pre-empted two hundred acres of land west of Vermilion Forks. Soon a land rush was on: Captain H. R. Luard, Sergeant William McColl, Sergeant James Lindsay, and Corporal Charles Sinnett, Royal Engineers, all filed claims for pre-emptions at Princeton. Charles Good, who had accompanied Douglas on his Similkameen trip (and who would soon become his son-in-law), had already pre-empted land, and Walter Moberly also filed a claim. Thus the two miners who had preceded Douglas to the area, John Fall Allison and John Marston, found themselves surrounded by properties which supposedly were being "proven up" by absentee landlords. Like the Similkameen Indians, for whom McColl had marked out a reserve on Douglas's instructions, they were left almost undisturbed.

These developments in Similkameen were on everyone's lips during Susan's first two years at Hope. Colonel J. S. Hawkins of the Boundary Commission showed her gold quartz picked up in the vicinity of the present Keremeos, and probably she was shown gold dust brought back from the Forks by McColl. Governor Douglas himself provided her with a description of the Similkameen Valley—it was "a paradise," he said, a country of open ranges covered with grass, shoulder-high. All the winter of 1860, as Dewdney and Moberly waited impatiently for the coming of spring, they talked of their plans to build in 1861 the first seven miles of the Hope–Similkameen Wagon Road. Captain J. M. Grant, R.E., let it be known that he would employ eighty Sappers and ninety civilians to continue the construction of the road from that point.

Susan was aware that the governor was having difficulties with miners around Hope, who protested his intention to tax them for using the wagon road, and she knew that the Reverend A. D. Pringle was aiding and abetting some of the Hope merchants whose preference was for a road to Kamloops; but the news in September 1861 of the governor's decision to discontinue construction of the wagon road came as a shock to her and to other members of the Hope community. By 1861 Cariboo had proved its superiority over every other gold region in the colony. McColl and other members of Moody's corps were able that year to make a careful examination of the Fraser Canyon and to establish the feasibility of building a wagon road through the canyon and beyond Lytton to Cariboo. The merchants of Yale, who in the governor's opinion were much more reasonable men than the merchants of Hope, were pressing hard for the construction of such a road. And Douglas himself was beginning to conceive a plan for building a great "North Road"—"The Queen's Highway"—which might some day be extended through Yellowhead Pass to Fort Garry.

At Yale, in 1862, the Royal Engineers began road construction. Here, where the Hudson's Bay Company's post had been less significant than Fort Hope, the town founded by miners sprang into prominence. Yale superseded Hope as the head of navigation on the Fraser River and stole from New Westminster the role of mainland supply centre for the placer miners and the road builders.

Gradually all the most intimate friends of the Glennies at Hope disappeared. Dewdney left to obtain survey work with Joseph W. Trutch, who had an important contract for building a section of the Cariboo Road. O'Reilly was withdrawn as magistrate. Landvoight acquired a pack train for the Cariboo trade. Colonel Moody and most of the Royal Engineers left the colony in November 1863. In 1864 Chief Trader William Charles was moved to Fort Yale, and in the course of the same year, the Pringles left for England. At Hope, the gay parties at the fort were over, and Susan was the only pretty girl left in the town.

Before departing from the colony himself, Thomas Glennie had obtained through his lawyer title to his property on the Coquihalla River and made arrangements to sell Hopelands. Mrs. Glennie was now homeless and almost without funds, though she still held property in Ceylon. Jane was living alone at New Westminster in 1865 since her husband had been awarded the contract to build the "Dewdney Trail," 220 miles long from Princeton to Wild Horse Creek in the Kootenay. She therefore invited her mother and sister to share her home, and they gladly accepted, for Jane was not only hospitable, but also warmhearted and deeply attached to her family.

Susan, now twenty, thoroughly enjoyed living in the capital city. As she listened on cold winter nights to the chimes of Holy Trinity Church ringing through the frost-laden air, her memories of her life in London were revived. She attended balls given at Government House and by officers of the Royal Navy; she made the acquaintance of "old Sappers" who had elected to remain in the colony after the disbanding of the Columbia Detachment; she met government officials like H. P. P. Crease, Joseph W. Trutch, and her old friend Peter O'Reilly; and she knew the women who were "society leaders." She became friendly with members of the merchant class, which at New Westminster contained a large component of Canadians with a distinct leaning toward "reform" politics. But, though she lived at a centre of strife, she did not take any interest in politics until after the union in 1866 of the colonies of Vancouver Island and British Columbia.

Susan, who was putting in time until her twenty-first birthday when she would inherit a little money from a great-aunt, obtained work as a governess by a stroke of good fortune during a visit to Victoria. As soon as she received her legacy she returned to New Westminster where she rented a cottage for her mother and tried to supplement her income by sewing and embroidery. Then her friend Mrs. Landvoight, whom she visited occasionally, suggested that she start a school at Hope. When the Dewdneys made plans to move to Soda Creek in 1867, she and her mother returned to Hope, rented the parsonage which the Pringles had vacated, and shared teaching responsibilities in the little school. This occupation was a distraction for Mrs. Glennie who had suffered another blow. In October 1866 her son Stratton, who, distressed by his mother's predicament, was on his way to British Columbia died of yellow fever in the West Indies.

Hope was now a quiet village—"played out," in the miners' expression. Sometimes traders and priests from the Okanagan Valley came over the almost disused Hope–Similkameen Wagon Road, which had been completed only for the twenty-five miles from Hope to Skagit Flats. Two or three times a year John Fall Allison drove cattle from his ranch in Similkameen over the road and passed through Hope on his way to markets at New Westminster or Yale. On one of these drives, Susan was introduced to him at Mrs. Landvoight's home.

The Similkameen country had captured Susan's imagination during her earliest days in the colony. Her curiosity about the area helped to lay the basis of friendship with a man who was twenty years her senior. When Allison discovered that she was fond of riding, he presented her with a cream mare, and sometimes when he was starting a return trip to Princeton, she rode out of town with him for a distance of ten miles.

Mrs. Glennie had ample opportunity to discuss a friendship that was ripening into a romance when Jane and Edgar Dewdney, who soon took a dislike to stock farming, came down from Soda Creek in June 1868. Several times that summer Peter O'Reilly passed through Hope on his way to and from the Interior, marking out Indian reserves in the Nicola and Similkameen valleys. His wife Cary, and her brother, John Trutch, sometimes joined O'Reilly at Hope, and while they were visiting there they often went riding with Dewdney over the wagon road. From the diary that O'Reilly kept that summer one gains the impression that the Dewdneys and the O'Reillys were certainly aware that Allison was thinking of getting married. This suspicion was confirmed when he travelled to New Westminster to obtain a license to marry Susan Louisa Moir.

On the evening of 1 September 1868, according to O'Reilly's diary, Peter and Cary O'Reilly dined with the Dewdneys, but "Mrs. Glennie or Miss Susan did not appear." The morning following was dank and misty, and the air was filled with smoke from forest fires. When the O'Reillys rode out with Dewdney to Anderson's Tree, it "came on to blow, a perfect hurricane." That night heavy rain drenched the woods. On 3 September, the Reverend Archdeacon Woods arrived by boat; and at the parsonage, "Miss *Moir* & Allison were married—quite private." Two hours after the ceremony Allison set out with his bride for Similkameen.

Had the impecuniosity of Mrs. Glennie and Susan been the prime reason for Mrs. Glennie giving her consent to the marriage? And did Susan accept Allison's proposal because she was now twenty-three years of age and had no other suitor?

John Fall Allison, the eldest son of Dr. Robert Allison and Sarah

(Briggs) Allison, was born at Leeds, Yorkshire, in 1825. His father left the position of house surgeon at Leeds Infirmary to migrate with his wife and children to Oriskany, New York, in 1837. The Allisons had relatives at Utica who seem to have been too optimistic about the benefits that the area would derive from the opening of the Erie Canal. Oriskany, however, was almost unaffected by the opening of this transportation route, and it remained a small village in which a woollen factory was the main industry. Dr. Allison took a position there and never achieved his dream of establishing a drugstore.

John Fall Allison obtained a good education, which included some medical training, but the other children were put to work in the mill before their schooling was completed. When his sister Elizabeth went to work in the woollen factory in 1848, Allison decided to join a mining company which was being formed at Oriskany to mine in the goldfields of California. He was a dutiful son who felt a keen sense of responsibility for his family and who was driven by a desire to promote their happiness and welfare.

The Oriskany Mining Company, a party of some ten persons, each armed with "a Carbine, one brace of Pistols and a Knife" and supplied with "Pick, Shovels, Crowbar, etc," sailed from New York on 26 January 1849 on the bark *Marietta* for Chagres. From Chagres the men took a small steamer up the river, and then, since there was no railway at that time, crossed the Isthmus of Panama with mules. Allison was in high spirits: "we hope to make about One million Dollars in Two years," he wrote his parents, but he admitted, "this is chimeral."

It took four months to reach Sacramento, and Allison did not arrive at the mines on the north fork of the American River until the middle of July 1849. He soon discovered that "mining is the hardest work I ever did. Imagine yourself in the bed of the *Oriskany Creek* digging up the cobble stones for six feet deep cemented together for ages by gravel, clay and sand and then carrying the dirt fifteen or twenty yards in the pails, throwing it into a washer and then rocking with one hand while you pour water with the other and working from ten to twelve hours a day, sometimes with wet feet and wet pants, and you may have some idea of gold digging." When the North Fork became crowded, he tried the dry diggings and then went to Sacramento to buy goods to establish a store at the mines. "As a company I exist no more"; he continued in his September letter, "every man has to work on his own energy." He had some success with this venture, but in 1850 returned to prospecting and mining. By January 1851 he was located in Sacramento with a business as a commission agent.

He now began to send money regularly to his parents. Some funds he retained for investment purposes since "I cannot bear dunning for money." "You must send little George to school," he wrote, "I will make up for the loss of his wages. I suppose Caroline has gone to school by this time. I hope William continues steady and is still in the Factory store." In 1852 he returned to mining and did so well that he encouraged William to join him. After William's arrival they went on a prospecting trip, "a tramp of one thousand miles," during which William discovered that "the getting of gold is much harder work than I expected to find it." But in 1853, when they employed Chinese on their claims at three dollars a day, they did so well that John made arrangements to visit his family in 1854.

He returned to California in 1855, and in 1857 he mined at Poor Man's Creek. Though he was able to send his family bank drafts in July, September, and November, his parents continued to be importunate. "You must positively give me the whole of the amount of your indebtedness for I shall never think of coming home until you are all clear of debt," he wrote his father in December. "I am able to pay anything you owe so do not be afraid to write the amount, but do not think me rich for I have too many *irons* in the fire to know whether I am worth anything or not. . . . I suppose you are considerably indebted to the O. M. Co. At what discount can you buy at the Store—pay for Cash. I want to make arrangements to settle all these matters."

It was at Poor Man's Creek in June 1858 that Allison heard about the Fraser River excitement. Still feeling compelled to find a means to provide more assistance for his family, he made up his mind to investigate the new discovery for himself. After a passage of seventeen days from San Francisco, he arrived in Victoria on 1 September.

The first mining season on the Fraser bars was now over, and many of the miners who were returning to California by way of Victoria were discouraged. But Allison was immediately taken with the country, and though his parents were begging him to return home, he decided to winter in Victoria. "I have spent my time agreeably in this City having a Church to go to and some society makes it feel more like home. I have been studying the Chinook Jargon and can now converse with the Indians," he wrote his parents; and he reminded them that "I have spent the best portion of my life in chasing after gold which has unfitted me for any other occupation, and to throw away the present chance appears to me like sacrificing all my past years of toil and giving up the prospect of independence in the future."

In March 1859 he was still in Victoria, "getting a little business posting books," but in June he moved to Trafalgar Flat, about three miles above Hope. There he built a ditch and commenced mining. "I like the location very well," he wrote home, "we are so near a cheap market. We have got a small Indian Canoe and can run down to Hope in half an hour. Steamboats are running regularly to Fort Hope, which puts us in communication with the World at large." When the rains started in September and the mountains were capped with snow, he went fishing one day for a food supply, "and caught about one hundred and twenty-five Salmon—sufficient to last through the Winter." The weather improved in October, and he was able to make five or six dollars a day.

In May 1860 he started out for Similkameen, but found there was too much snow in the mountains, so he returned to Fort Hope to wait for the Hudson's Bay Company's train to open the trail. While he was there Governor Douglas visited the town and arranged to have Allison lead a prospecting expedition to the Similkameen River. There Allison found diggings that he thought would yield him ten dollars a day, and he returned to Hope early in August with three horses to pack out a supply of provisions. On 2 September, he wrote to inform his parents that he was located on the south fork of the Similkameen, "or, as some call it, Allison's Fork, about seventy-five miles from Hope," and making from eight to ten dollars a day. "I think the diggings in this locality are much better than on the Fraser. There has been hundreds of men rushed in since we struck the diggings and hastily left declaring them a humbug. Such is always the case in gold mining, but I have considerable influence in this locality, not because I discovered it, but the indications are better and it has more of a California look than any other part of British Columbia I have seen."

When Douglas visited the area in September, Allison waited on him to inform him that he had discovered a new pass through the Cascades which would make a better road. He had discovered the Allison Pass, the route of the modern highway. Douglas authorized him to put a trail through immediately, and when he cleared a trail thirty-six miles long in four days, the governor thanked him for his energy and perseverance. Douglas intended at this time to make him gold commissioner and magistrate for Similkameen District, but miners who were disappointed in the Similkameen mines objected to this show of favour, and presumably the governor decided that the returns from this gold district did not warrant the appointment.

In the spring of 1861 Allison removed from his claim on the Similkameen River to his pre-emption near the townsite chosen by O'Reilly.

Since he was on friendly terms with the Similkameen Indians who cultivated crops of potatoes, he was able to obtain seed potatoes from them. He had taken up the 160 acres as a speculation, yet he had to admit that the country held attractions. "I think I have got the most desirable location for a farm in this part of the country, it is in the forks made by the junction of the North [the Tulameen River] and South forks of this river. Part of the soil is a deep black, the balance is a light sandy soil, but all fit for cultivation. There are thousands of acres of rolling hills around it that are the finest kinds of grazing lands. If I only had such a farm as this in any civilized country with my friends around me I should not wish for anything better." Though it was far from his intention at this time, Allison was to spend the remainder of his life at Princeton.

Near the river above Allison's and close to Vermilion Forks, the junction of the Tulameen and Similkameen rivers, was a large deposit of red ochre. This "red earth" was much in demand as paint by the Okanagan, Shuswap, and Blackfeet Indians, as well as by the Similkameens. They were constantly passing Allison's, and they frequently visited "Allison's Cave," which Arthur Bushby described as "a queer place—some 18 feet by 30 feet." Allison used it as a stable until his right to do so was challenged by later settlers. It was finally destroyed in the 1940's during the building of the Hope–Princeton highway.

Allison's existence was a lonely one, since most of the miners migrated to Cariboo in 1862, and the closest settlements of Europeans were at Hope and at Osoyoos, where a customs post was established by Douglas in 1860. The Similkameen Indians were his only companions, and though he accepted their companionship, he did not do so on a basis of complete equality. Sometimes during the long, hard winters, when the Indian express messenger brought mail only once or twice, he was driven by loneliness to undertake during a spell of moderate weather the seventy-five mile trip over the mountains to Hope on snowshoes. And it was the need for companionship that led him to enter into a partnership with an American by the name of Hayes, who was to assist him in turning his farm into a stock ranch.

During these early years, when the market for farm produce vanished with the exodus of the miners, government contracts supplied most of Allison's ready cash. He broke the news to his parents in November 1860 that he was unable to assist his father to establish a drugstore, but he told them that Douglas had promised that he would not be forgotten —"but scripture says 'put not your trust in princes.' " In July 1861, Douglas lived up to his promise by giving Allison a contract in the amount of £150 to construct a mule trail from Princeton to a point on Okanagan Lake opposite the gold mines on Mission Creek, and in November he was awarded another contract of £300 to improve the Princeton–Rock Creek trail and the Princeton–Kamloops trail. Later, in June 1864, at the time of the Wild Horse Creek excitement, Governor Frederick Seymour gave him a contract of £1,030 to improve the mule trail from the end of the Hope–Similkameen Wagon Road. The money was badly needed, since his family was now sending him "doleful reports" concerning "poor mother," and he was having difficulties meeting the competition on the beef market because of the American cattle drives being made to the Cariboo and the establishment of cattle ranches in the Thompson Valley. He was in the saddle all summer long, driving small bands of cattle to market at the Coast. On 23 October 1864, Bushby and A. N. Birch, returning from their investigation of the Wild Horse Creek mines, met him near the Summit "with his small train also a crowd of Indians—& their horses," and found him "very civil as he always is." Others found him equally civil: in the winter of 1865 he incurred considerable expense by hiring Indians to carry a destitute man who had frozen his feet over the mountains in a litter to the hospital at New Westminster.

By the time of the Big Bend rush in 1866, Allison and Hayes had accumulated a considerable stock of cattle. But their hope of obtaining a good market tumbled when the diggings did not turn out well. Once more Allison made cattle drives over the Hope Mountains to New Westminster and Yale. One of these trips to Yale was made in August 1868, and it was on this occasion that he made arrangements to marry Susan Moir. From Hope he sent a short, hasty note to his mother to inform her of his intention. In November he wrote from Similkameen to his brother George to ask him to deliver to her a photograph of his wife.

At the time when Mrs. Allison, riding sidesaddle and wearing her long habit looped up to a button on the side, started on her honeymoon trip, only one other European woman had crossed the Hope Mountains. Mrs. Marston had been so terrified in 1860 that she had dismounted and walked the trail all the way to Similkameen. Mrs. Allison had no fear of danger—as she and her husband started from Hope at dusk, she was confident that the pack train, led by Cockshist, the well-known Indian guide who had served Dewdney and O'Reilly, as well as Bushby and Birch; Johnny Suzanne, the Indian packer; and Yacumtecum, the Indian bell-boy, would lead her safely up the switchback on the mountains. At Lake House that night, when she and her husband sat round the campfire listening to the Indians tell tales about the Big Men Of the Mountains (the Sasquatch) and the Monster of Okanagan Lake (Ogopogo), she felt exhilarated at the thought of the wild, free life she would now live.

That her only neighbours would be Indians with whom she could not communicate since she had not yet learned Chinook, that only an occasional passerby would stop at her home during the four long winter months, and that she would never see her mother again unless she recrossed the treacherous mountain trail, failed to dismay her, for she patterned her behaviour on that of her mother, who had accepted all her disappointments with composure and dignity. Not even the first meeting with Hayes, her husband's partner, who showed his resentment of the termination of Allison's bachelor existence by objecting to Mrs. Allison's dressing for dinner, "a habit I was drilled in as a child," upset her. His rudeness was driven from her mind by the pleasure she had derived from her ride through the red rhododendrons of Skagit Flat and down the trail by Whipsaw Creek and the Tulameen River to the roomy, high-ceilinged, rough-hewn, log house that her husband had just had constructed.

She had little companionship from her husband during those first months of marriage. A fortnight after their arrival at Princeton, Allison started with his pack train for Hope, and he made another trip before snowfall. In November he and Hayes took their five hundred head of cattle over the trail to Okanagan Lake to "Sunnyside" (Westbank) to winter. She busied herself during these absences by adding feminine touches to her home, and it was only when she had her first call from an Indian woman and they both sat in strained silence that she realized how imperative it was for her to learn Chinook and how dependent she was on the Indians for companionship. But her interest in the Indians was not fully aroused until the following spring when she saw the Similkameens from Chu-chu-ewaa parade past her home as they left their winter quarters. As she watched this array of handsome, stately horsemen, she realized that these people were quite different from the Flatheads she had observed at Hope. She determined to learn something about their customs and to record their folklore and their legends.

During her first winter at Similkameen, Mrs. Allison's domestic duties were not heavy since Allison had made everything snug for the cold weather. He had time to spend with her since he had no cattle to care for, and she had time to join him in hunting and trapping wild animals. With the coming of spring, she discovered that more was expected of her than the completion of normal household duties: Allison had a trading post where gold dust was the medium of exchange. She was expected to serve in the store, to operate a primitive post office, and to keep the accounts. The account books that she kept during these early years indicate that she found these occupations tiresome—the books are full of jottings of stories, based on her family's experiences in Ceylon, and of notes on Indian customs. For her writing became a substitute for human companionship.

Mrs. Allison's duties as the wife of a rancher living in a remote and isolated district seldom visited by Europeans included not only the burdens of housekeeping, cooking, fur trading and bookkeeping, but also the responsibilities of bearing and rearing children. Between 4 July 1869 and 28 August 1892 she gave birth, without medical assistance and with only her husband and an Indian woman in attendance, to fourteen children, all of whom lived to maturity. Her Victorian upbringing must have prepared her emotionally to accept maternity as one of her obligations, but she seems to have been unprepared emotionally, at the time of the premature birth of her eldest child, for the pain of childbirth. This pain she endured stoically, while admitting that she did not have the endurance of Indian women. Her stoicism was taken for granted by her husband, who had great respect for her strength of character. But like many other Victorian husbands, he did not concern himself too gravely when she experienced miseries during her pregnancies. Thus in 1874 he was able to write in this cheerful strain to his parents: "The children are all well, but I am sorry to say Susan is not at all well. She is not able to move about much, but I hope she will be all right again after her next confinement which we expect in about six weeks."

As her brood of children increased, Mrs. Allison was able to secure some release from her household duties by employing Indian boys and girls to perform certain tasks. This contact with the young Indians facilitated her acquaintance and growing friendship with the older Indians, and once she mastered Chinook, she was able to invite the patriarchs of the Similkameen tribe to her home. Clive Phillipps-Wolley, visiting at Allison's in 1887, found "the younger Allisons" whiling away the long evenings with story-telling, "the mother collecting the wild fairy legends of the Indians, and dressing them in familiar language for her children."

During the first years of his marriage, Allison was confident that his prospects as a cattle rancher were favourable. When a Pacific railway was promised as a term of British Columbia's union with Canada in 1871, he envisaged the development of a much larger market on the Mainland. The gold rushes to Wild Horse Creek and Big Bend had been short-lived, and though he had driven cattle to these markets, he had not benefited greatly from them. The construction of the Canadian Pacific Railway, however, would create a large local market for beef. So he set out to improve the quality of his stock by importing "Red Oak," a shorthorn bull, from California in 1872. His concentration on the production of thoroughbred stock did result in his beef—"Similkameen beef" as it was called—becoming famous on the coast market. But the expansion of his herds necessitated the acquisition of more property and more grazing rights. During the 1870's he went into debt to accumulate nearly 3,000 acres of land. When, in 1874, railway construction was delayed by the business depression and the change in federal policy after the Liberals came into office at Ottawa, he was forced to tell his parents he could offer them no help: "I am very troubled about you for I know that you need assistance, but at present I am not able to collect a dollar. Business is fearfully dull at present, a general gloom prevails over the community about the uncertainty of the Canadian Government carrying out the terms of Union with regard to the immediate construction of the Canadian Pacific Railway.... We have all been looking forward to the building of the road as an opening for the sale of our cattle and produce." In 1875 he ran in the election for the provincial legislature as a "reform" candidate pledged to obtaining the fulfilment of the Terms of Union, but his name was left off the ballot at Cache Creek and other polls, and he was not elected.

However well watered the rolling, grass-covered hills of the Similkameen country, cattle ranching in the remote district was a precarious occupation. In the lower Nicola Valley where Allison grazed some of his cattle, the bunch grass grew ten feet high in places in the 1860's; but the continued grazing caused it to become shorter and shorter. For winter feeding, hay was a necessity, and it was for this reason that Allison had his cattle driven in November to Sunnyside on Okanagan Lake where there were excellent hay meadows. The hot summers of the southern Interior left the forests on the Hope Trail tinder dry: the conflagrations of 1868 and 1869 marked but two of the summers when for weeks at a time it was impossible to drive cattle to the coast market. The worst hazard of all was the bitter cold which often came in the last six weeks of winter. The dangers to the cattle of this intense cold at a time when the snow on the hills lay two or three feet deep had been known to the stockmen of Oregon and Washington for some time and had led them to diversify their operations. But it was only after Allison experienced four hard winters—1869-1870, 1873-1874 (when he lost fifty head of cattle), 1877-1878, and 1880-1881 (when he lost half his herd)—that he began to engage in mining operations once again. But even after his partnership with Hayes was shattered in 1879 following a dispute arising from the oral agreement they had originally made and after Hayes had obtained in the courts compensation of $3,000, Allison was still enlarging his stock farm by acquiring the properties pre-empted by members of the corps of Royal Engineers and by other purchases. This he did in the hope that the completion of the Canadian Pacific Railway would be followed by the settlement of the interior valleys and the creation of a market nearer at hand.

In June 1881, following his decision to sell his Okanagan property and to move his family to Princeton, he was forced to write to his mother: "I was very pained to hear that you have suffered so much during the past Winter, and more grieved to know that perhaps I had added to your suffering by my neglect. I have put off writing month after month with the expectation of being able to do something more for you than merely send a letter. We have had two very severe Winters in this country and lost the greater part of our stock; that would not trouble me much if we had a market for the remainder. I could sell but few last season and this year have not sold a hoof yet. I have got badly involved but hope to be able to work through it. I did hope to be able to do something for you this Spring, but I have just got a letter from the Bank stating that Notes due me deposited there were not paid, and that I shall have to give an extension of time. It places me in a very bad position as I have debts to pay within a month or so to the amount of five or six thousand dollars."

Until the hard times of the 1880's, Mrs. Allison was content at Similkameen, which in the days of her early marriage was, as she and

Phillipps-Wolley agreed, "A Sportsman's Eden." She gloried in the abundance of nature and in the success of her garden and of her homemaking activities and found time to cultivate her interest in botany and Indian folklore.

During those early years at Princeton she still had the opportunity to see her mother and her sister, who often paid visits to Hope. On three occasions she crossed the mountains. On her trip over the mountain trail in 1869, when her baby Edgar was only one month old, she experienced at Skagit River the searing flames of a forest fire. Her second visit to Hope began on 28 October 1870, very late in the season, and the trip was accomplished during a blinding snowstorm. On this occasion, she planned to stay in Hope until after the birth of her second child, and this she did, not returning to her home at Princeton until May 1871. On her departure from Hope she was sadly missed: "Susie has gone home, & I miss them very much," Jeanie Dewdney, who was childless, wrote to Mrs. O'Reilly. "Little Edgar was very fond of his Aunty, so much so that 'Grandma' was a little inclined to be jealous, & devoted herself to the baby [Wilfrid] in consequence. 'Sweet, mild and intelligent,' that is Granny's idea of Wilfred." The third visit paid by Mrs. Allison to Hope took place after the birth of her daughter Beatrice at Keremeos in January 1872. The difficulties of travelling the Hope Trail on horseback with three young children were enormous, and it is not surprising that Mrs. Allison did not again attempt to travel across the mountains until the 1890's when she went to Victoria to visit her mother who had fallen at Government House and broken her hip.

What to Mrs. Allison was "a perfectly ideal life" opened for her in November 1873 when her husband suggested that they take up residence the following spring on their property in the Okanagan Valley. The events of the next nine years would have discouraged a less serene person: their log house was not completed at the time of their arrival in November, and there was no domestic water; deadly rattlesnakes coiled themselves in every crevice in the house and even in pots and pans; shrouds had to be sewn for Indians who died of the grippe; there was every likelihood of an Indian uprising in the Okanagan Valley in 1876; her husband had a strange accident in 1877, from the effects of which he never fully recovered; and she was threatened, while alone with the children, by the wild and outlawed McLean boys, the murderers of Johnny Ussher. But in her old age, the most vivid memories of these years were of the night round the campfire when Johnny McDougal told his story of Ogopogo; the time when her husband was rescued from an ice floe; her contact with an European woman, Mrs. Eli Lequime; and the visit paid by Jeanie and her husband, Edgar Dewdney, M.P. Above all, she remembered the idyllic summers when the children were small and were able to spend hours fishing in the reeds along the lakeshore, watching the ants and taming the wild deer.

Four of her children were born during these happy years. When Bishop A. W. Sillitoe, first bishop of New Westminster, called at Sunnyside on his return trip from Penticton to baptize the seven children on 23 September 1880, he was surprised to discover that the four little ones had only twice before seen Europeans. For Sunnyside, twenty miles on horseback from Penticton, and nearly two miles across Okanagan Lake from the Mission of the Immaculate Conception, was the first home to be built on the west side of Okanagan Lake.

The first of the calamities after their return to their Princeton home befell the Allisons during the dreadful winter of 1880-1881. The snowfall that winter was so heavy that its weight crushed the roof of their house. Allison had earlier lost half of his herd on the dissolution of his partnership with Hayes, and he had suffered further losses during the intensely cold weather; he was also finding it difficult to raise the money to satisfy Hayes's claims against him. This further disaster, coming "at these dull times," seemed almost too much. Writing to his mother to explain why he could not send her money, he said, "On my arrival here I found our house broken down by Winter snow—the roof caved in. I had to put my family in the milk house until we got a roof on the house again. We moved in a day or two ago and are now comfortable. You must not think we are suffering for want of food. We have plenty to eat and drink, but it is hard work to raise money to buy boots and clothes for the children at present."

As a helpmate, Mrs. Allison was now invaluable to her husband. She had learned many skills since the days of her spinsterhood when she had whiled away hours by stitching fine tucks on petticoats three yards wide. Now she could not only make clothes for her children, but also make moccasins, braid straw for hats, and strand and braid lariats. She had learned long ago to bake bread, and she could now cure fish and dry venison. With the help of an Indian boy, she could plough and plant a garden. Though she disliked keeping accounts, she ran the trading post and there served the Indians and cowboys with sugar, blankets, and tobacco. She had long since learned how to deal with common ailments, and, having picked up some medical knowledge from her husband and the Indians, she was constantly being consulted about remedies for illnesses and called upon for nursing.

Though she did not love the Similkameen as she did the Okanagan, she made her home a happy place where every visitor, Indian or European, was welcome. And no longer was she so isolated—the establishment by the Hudson's Bay Company of a small post at Keremeos in the 1860's to permit the transfer of goods from Fort Colvile and Fort Okanogan to British soil had been followed by a handful of pre-emptors settling in its vicinity. Henry Nicholson and his partner Barrington Price, who built a grist mill at Keremeos, were generous with help in time of distress, and she found Mrs. W. H. Lowe and others equally helpful. Mrs. Thomas Ellis of Penticton, who always went to the Coast for her confinements, she frequently saw. Nor did she lack for news and comments from the outside world. However hard up the Allisons might be, they subscribed to the coast newspapers and to English and Scottish journals. And however busy Mrs. Allison was, she did not neglect her correspondence with her large English and Scottish connection, especially with her Gordon, Mortimer, and Jellicoe relatives. Occasionally, too, she received letters concerning property she had inherited in Ceylon, property that she did not sell until 1928.

Mrs. Allison's qualities as a true pioneer woman were demonstrated on the occasion of the second calamity at Princeton. On 1 April 1882, a year after the family's return, during her husband's absence, her home and everything in it, including Mrs. Shaw's Bible which her father, Stratton Moir, had taken to Ceylon, were destroyed by fire. Mrs. Allison saved from the flames only the photograph of her brother, Stratton, her dressing case, and "a small piece of bacon, and an open sack with about fifteen pounds of flour." Her reminiscences illustrate how inventive she was in this emergency, and a note written many years after the event illuminates her character: "That month I learned two lessons that have lasted me through life. First, that money in itself, is valueless, and second, that contentment is invaluable." The dressing case contained one hundred dollars, "But the gold did not feed us when we were hungry or clothe us when we were cold. I also found that when the children's minds were active they did not notice the hunger so much. The old Bible was hunted for stories and when it was exhausted I told them stories I could remember . . . and so was able to interest the children sufficiently to make them forget their troubles."

The education of her children she had to undertake herself. During the winter of 1880-1881, the winter that ended so disastrously for the Allisons, two of the girls and one of the boys were sent to Mrs. Glennie's school at Hope. Jane had left early in 1881 to join her husband in Ottawa, where during a visit he was offered, in addition to his appointment as Indian Commissioner of the North-West Territories, the office of lieutenant-governor. After her departure, Mrs. Glennie's health deteriorated, and in 1884 she moved from Hope to Regina to be near the Dewdneys. Thereafter, the Allisons were able to send a child or two for a year or so to a boarding school at New Westminster. They did try to find a teacher who would conduct a school on their ranch, but Mrs. Allison provided most of the instruction for her children. This she did in a relaxed and happy atmosphere, for one of her great achievements was to create a home in which there was harmony and comfort.

One of General W. T. Sherman's aides at the time of his call at Allison's in 1883 has left an account which illustrates her successful adjustment to the pioneer life: "Allison's place was a comfortable dwelling with a few outbuildings. In one of the latter was a small store. Allison was at Victoria but his courteous wife received us with hospitality. She was a rosy cheeked woman of about 25 [*sic*], born in Ceylon, and she had 10 children, healthy handsome urchins, which goes to show that the more distant and difficult of access the place, the more prolific are the human inhabitants. Residing here she appeared cheerfully happy and contented in her isolated home."

The third and worst calamity at Princeton occurred in 1894, the year of the great floods in British Columbia. By that time, Allison had increased his holdings to 5,000 acres and expended much money in increasing the number of his ranch buildings and his miles of snake fences. To visitors descending the trail along the "broad blue river between bold mud-bluffs" and riding through the bull-pines of the last upland, Allison's seemed, for the Interior of British Columbia, to be a model pioneer home. Allison, who admitted that he was "not able to stand the rough work and hardship I formerly could," was beginning to feel his age. The loss of his home and thirteen farm buildings in the flood was therefore a terrible disaster for him. The cost of reconstruction forced him to mortgage his lands, and since a host of new problems, including grasshopper plagues, were making cattle ranching even more precarious as a livelihood, he began to give more and more time to mining ventures.

On the prospecting trip in 1860 when Allison found placer gold on the Similkameen River, he also discovered coal and copper pyrites. Long after the gold miners departed for Lightning and Williams creeks, he remained confident, since he had found coarse gold, that the country was rich in minerals. Consequently, for many years he employed a few men to mine. The Chinese shared his confidence, and very few of them left the area. And after the decline of Cariboo, a few miners came each season, but no further rush to the area occurred until 1885.

The coal that Allison had discovered he used for domestic purposes. He had the impression that the coal-bearing area was extensive, and this later proved to be the case in the Princeton–Coalmont region, but he did not have the capital to bore for lignite. No serious work to investigate the seams was undertaken until after Allison's death when the Vermilion Forks Mining and Development Company was organized.

The copper deposits interested him most of all: he believed that there was a very wide mineral belt running through the country containing vast deposits of copper "all peacock and rich sulphur which carry a percentage of both silver and gold." After James Jameson, who had packed for the Hudson's Bay Company, brought his family over the Hope Trail in 1884 and saw an outcropping of peacock copper seven miles up the Similkameen River from the Forks and after "Volcanic" Brown was told of this discovery and staked a claim on Copper Mountain, Allison staked two claims opposite the mountain on Friday Creek. He appealed to his brother-in-law, Edgar Dewdney, who had maintained an interest in mining (as in other speculative endeavours), to assist him in interesting an American company, but his ore proved too low-grade to attract the investment of capital.

Allison's discoveries laid the basis for the great mining boom of the 1890's in the Boundary country, which resulted in the rise of the mining towns of Hedley, Fairview, Camp McKinney, and Greenwood. The mining of that period was financed by companies supported by heavy capital investment, advised by experts, and equipped with sophisticated machinery.

That these developments would take place had first become evident with the Granite Creek gold rush of 1885. An intimation of a rich gold strike came in 1883 with the discovery of heavy nuggets near the Tulameen River and with the subsequent bitter dispute between two Chinese mining companies, which left Allison, endeavouring to settle the dispute in his role as justice of the peace, the loser in a lawsuit. But it was not until the autumn of 1884, when he was shown heavy nuggets from Granite Creek, a tributary of the Tulameen River and twelve miles from Princeton, that he appreciated the importance of the discovery. That winter he packed in supplies in anticipation of a strike. News of what he was doing reached the ears of four American cowboys camped on his ranch. With the coming of spring, Johnny Chance staked the discovery claim.

The Granite Creek rush attracted companies of miners from Cariboo—men who knew all the techniques of lode mining. This knowledge they needed, since the richest area, five miles from the mouth of Granite Creek, was located in a deep gorge. Despite the difficulties of extracting the gold, between 5 July and 31 October 1885 an amount worth $90,000 was taken out, and Thomas Elwyn, sent by the government to inspect the area, reported confidently, "I believe that the discoveries on Granite Creek will lead to the opening up of an extensive gold-field—a gold-field in fact which, from its accessibility and close proximity to farming districts, producing beef, flour, vegetables, oats and hay, will be of more benefit to the Province than any, with the exception of Cariboo, hitherto discovered." Allison, who was appointed assistant gold commissioner on 9 April 1885, could do no more than employ ten men to work his claim.

By the autumn of 1885 there were between 400 and 500 Europeans on the Creek and between 150 and 200 Chinese. Seven stores, three of them kept by Chinese, two restaurants, two licensed houses for the sale of liquor, and a butcher's shop were opened. The following year almost every inch of the creek was staked, buildings sprang up everywhere, and a road was opened up from the Nicola Valley to avoid the difficult canyon trail from Allison's. Allison had a good market for beef the first winter, but in 1886 when gold worth $203,000 was taken from the creek, Nicola cattlemen offered him stiff competition. By 1887, though the diggings still produced substantial amounts of gold, the mining companies, with their advanced technology and powerful pumps, had extracted the heavy gold. As late as 1890 Allison employed miners, but his operations were on a small scale and yielded only four dollars a day a man. One of the ironies of this gold rush, which took place almost on his doorstep, was that he was aware that the gold was mixed with platinum—a white substance which the mining companies discarded. But he had neither the capital nor the equipment to exploit his knowledge to the full. From that time forth, with some encouragement from Dewdney, he pinned his hopes on his copper claims near and on "The Big Hill."

The pioneering period in the Similkameen Valley came to an end with the gold rush to Granite Creek and the emergence of a town there replete with saloons, restaurants, and gambling houses. Before it came into existence, the Allisons attempted to capture the provisioning of the mines. Mrs. Allison's participation in this effort was later described by a churchman who went to the camp: "I well remember the first time I met Mrs. J. F. Allison, or rather, the first time I saw her. I was coming towards Princeton and she was riding side saddle to Granite Creek. Behind her came a number of pack horses loaded with beef which she was taking to Bob Stevenson's camp. Behind the horses was riding one of the boys. . . . I remember at the time thinking of the courage and endurance of a refined and educated woman like her to make her home so far out of the way from the comforts and conveniences of even the farming districts nearer the larger centres. She was riding on quite serenely and appeared to be enjoying the ride and the beautiful scenery, and at the same time keeping an eye on her pack-train."

By 1886 merchants had established at Granite Creek large stores which could be supplied by goods freighted by the Canadian Pacific Railway to Spence's Bridge and packed from there, and beef was more easily obtainable from the Douglas Lake Cattle Company in the Nicola Valley which had expanded its operations to supply the work crews on railway construction. Professional men, lawyers and a doctor, made their appearance at Granite Creek, and, though most of the population had disappeared by 1888, there remained in the southern Interior a residue of miners, merchants, and professional men. By 1894 Allison's, the pioneer home and the supply centre, was beginning to take a back seat to the village of Princeton. And the family, which during the 1880's had infrequently enjoyed visits of the Indian Commissioners, Dr. G. M. Dawson of the Geological Survey of Canada, and big-game hunters from the "Old Country," now began to have more visitors and to make the acquaintance of English and American mining engineers and capitalists. And when, in 1892, Edgar Dewdney returned after a long absence to British Columbia to serve as lieutenant-governor of the province, he was instrumental in directing attention to the area. "Dewdney is on leave at Montreal, with a possibility of his going to England," O'Reilly informed John Trutch in July 1896, "he is hand & glove with some American mining capitalists who have gigantic schemes, which they are anxious to float—& hope to make use of our friend, & his position, in connection therewith. E. D. is just as fond of speculating as he was in the early Sixties." The raising of capital by Dewdney, however, was not accomplished by the time of Allison's death on 28 October 1897.

Beginning in 1890, when his eldest son struck out for himself, Allison was handicapped by a shortage of stock hands. The competition for the beef market had become keener since much larger ranches had emerged in the Okanagan and Nicola valleys. These operations had the advantage of being closer than his to rail transportation. In an effort to meet this competition, Allison began to drive cattle 112 miles through the Nicola Valley for shipment by rail from Spence's Bridge. The Hope Trail then fell into disuse.

Mrs. Allison longed as much as her husband for the coming of the railway. Eighteen months after her husband's death she wrote to his brother George: "You ask about our Railway. Well, every year we are promised one, but as yet we are about one hundred miles off Spence's Bridge, our nearest Station, but if our Copper Mines turn out anything like we hope we *must* have a line through soon." Not until 1909, however, did the Great Northern Railway reach Princeton, and the Canadian Pacific Railway's Kettle Valley line was not completed until 1914. By that time, Allison's properties, some of which Mrs. Allison virtually gave away, were much reduced in extent.

Allison was laid to rest on his own property at the foot of Castle Rock. He had outlived his mother by only eight years, and he left behind him a widow, who at the age of fifty-two was still a vigorous woman. His two eldest sons had married, and in the spring following his death his daughter Rose married S. D. Sandes, a young English mining engineer who was interested in the deposits on Copper Mountain. Mrs. Allison took such a liking to Sandes that she allowed him to have the original pre-emption to lay out as a townsite. But this venture, like the one promoted by a company founded by Dewdney to lay out a townsite on the old Luard property, failed to succeed.

It was a great comfort to Mrs. Allison to have Jeanie and Mrs. Glennie return from Ottawa to British Columbia. Jeanie had lived a very different life from her own since the evening in 1881 when she and Edgar had been invited to dine with Sir John and Lady Macdonald. Jeanie was comfortable in the world of politics, and, as a very partisan Conservative, she was as quick to condemn "that horrid old Gladstone . . . the many headed monster," as any other Liberal. She had enjoyed her role at Government House at Regina as much as she enjoyed being chatelaine at Cary Castle in Victoria. But however much she was inclined to choose her friends at Ottawa and Victoria from among Conservative families, she remained, as she had been as a young woman, kind to her relatives, friends, and acquaintances.

"The Dewdneys are getting settled in Castle Carey," O'Reilly reported to John Trutch in December 1892, "the house was in a wretched state, a number of men have been at work putting it in order. She is to be seen every morning in the town, about 9 o'c. shopping, marketing is more correct. He drives about a good deal in a sort of tea Cart & is generally accompanied by Louisa Allison—the Coachman wears a light drab fashionable livery & cockade. Changed times for Ned, you will say. Mrs. Glennie is also of the party. She looks wonderfully well."

A year later, O'Reilly sent a further report: "The Dewdneys get on fairly well, they generally have some one staying with them, at present Carey Castle is full—the party consists of Mrs. Glennie, Miss Allison, Mrs. Walter Dewdney, two Dewdney nephews & one niece—you will see that he is taking care of his relations—but already there are murmurs of discontent at the absence of entertainments at Gov't. House; there have been two or three small dances—but '*no Ball*'!" Balls were given in the course of time, and in the meanwhile the Dewdneys were wonderfully good to the Allison girls. When Louisa, who lived with them for over three years, was desperately ill with typhoid fever in August 1893, they provided "2 nurses, & 3 Doctors" who "strained every remedy to the utmost."

The hospitality that the Dewdneys provided for her daughters and the opportunities they arranged for them to meet eligible young men were appreciated by Mrs. Allison. But she was also practical enough to wish her daughters to obtain training of some sort. "Elfreda is learning typewriting and stenography in Victoria," she informed George Allison in 1899, "I think it is so nice for girls to be able to get their own living if need be and a good stenographer is sure of good pay." Another daughter trained as a nurse at the Royal Jubilee Hospital, and a third became a schoolteacher, travelled to Japan, and there married a young Englishman. It almost seems as if Mrs. Allison was determined to see that her daughters should become aware of the limitations of pioneer farm life.

During Dewdney's term of office, he and the Allison children travelled the Hope Trail many times. Thus, in May 1895, O'Reilly informed John Trutch, "Edgar, with his niece & two nephews, have gone to Similkameen over the Hope mountains, to spend a month with the

Allisons. Mrs. Dewdney remains to do the honours at Gov't. House & to take care of her Mother, who is, I am glad to say, much better [after breaking her hip], and will not I think, make a die of it this time." And in October 1897 he wrote, "I think you have heard that Louisa Allison accompanied by Elfreda & Harry went off to the Similkameen a month or two since, & now we hear the former is returning. We had been told that she was to spend the winter there, as her lungs were affected—& she wd require the *greatest* care if she remained here. The old lady is wonderfully well, & they are getting rid of the dogs—only one remains, & the parrot! but the latter now has to live in confinement (his cage) as he nearly broke the old lady's finger—by biting it!"

While some of her daughters were enjoying the entertainments at Government House and adapting to the social life of Victoria, Mrs. Allison was not only managing what remained of her husband's cattle ranch, but also performing her duty as a grandmother. On one occasion when an epidemic of measles broke out at Princeton, she found herself turning her home into a hospital for the care of two sons, their wives, three grandchildren, and two daughters of her own. To her assistance came "Our Louisa," "the daughter and sister of an Indian chief . . . clean, delightfully clean, a good Catholic, and a thorough housekeeper." Louisa performed every duty until one beautiful moonlight night when she slipped out of the house and did not appear again until morning. Mrs. Allison was fully aware of what was going on during Louisa's "nocturnal wanderings," but she kept the knowledge private. They parted, when the sick were better, on the best possible terms.

Despite her equanimity on this occasion, Mrs. Allison was deeply concerned about the degradation of the Indians. She put her thoughts down on paper: "Their civilization is very much retarded by their passion for strong drink for in spite of the stringent Canadian laws, the Indians in the interior of B.C. can get all the Whiskey they want—and they do get it, the settlers are all too indolent and apathetic to try to put an end to practices that may eventually bring ruin on themselves as well as demoralizing the unfortunate Savages." She recognized that the Indians possessed a singular degree of acuteness and penetration, but at the same time that they were "very childish, confiding and sensitive." As her reminiscences make clear, she had great respect for the Roman Catholic missionaries, who she thought had unfailing sympathy for the Indians.

"The priests possess great influence with the natives and it has been said that they are inclined to exert it in a rather arbitrary manner," she wrote, "but it must be acknowledged that they always throw their influence on the side of decency and order. The Indians have many peculiar habits and customs that must be very disgusting and shocking to their instructors whether Catholic or Protestant, viz., swapping their wives and selling their daughters, to say nothing of the loathesome practice of exhuming their dead every now and then and dressing the mouldering remains in new garments and holding a feast or potlatch in their honour. The Indians' religion is purely emotional, and they will join in religious services with great fervour, but they cannot carry it into their daily life; they will refuse to eat meat on Friday, or to work on Sunday, but think nothing of lying or petty stealing. Under the influence of the priests polygamy is dying out, and few of the men have more than one wife at a time, but their domestic relations are decidedly complicated owing to their propensity for trading their wives—sometimes for new ones, sometimes for horses. There seems to be no real love or affection amongst them save in some rare instances between father and son or mother and daughter, though they always mourn and lament over their dead relatives, and pay their debts in a most exemplary manner; superstition no doubt has a great deal to do with this, as they are horribly afraid of the Spirits of the dead. The Indians are inveterate gamblers and will often gamble away every rag of clothing they possess, even the garments they are wearing, and leave themselves in a state of utter destitution."

Within two years of her husband's death, she prepared for publication a long narrative poem of fifty-two printed pages. *In-Cow-Mas-Ket*, she said, was part of her reminiscences, "for it is an account of the lives, manners and customs of some of the Similkameen Indians as I knew them in the 60s, 70s and 80s, while they were still a people. I may say a passing people. Now they are nearly all gone, just a down-trodden remnant, whose land is coveted by some of their white neighbours.... The White man has much to be ashamed of in his treatment of the rightful owners of the land." Allison had always been scrupulously fair in his dealing with the Indians, particularly with regard to their land rights, and as early as 1875 had asked the provincial government to recognize the "not unreasonable demands" of the Indians. Mrs. Allison shared her husband's attitude, but her feeling for the Indians was much deeper than his: from the first days of her marriage she was fascinated with the folklore of the Similkameens and with "their own beautiful religious ideas."

In-Cow-Mas-Ket, she said, was criticized by some of her friends as "bad poetry, neither rhyme nor blank verse," but this work, like its companion "Quinesco," which was not published, contained the folklore as given her in Chinook by the Similkameen chiefs. "These legends are hard to translate from the Chinook," she wrote, "so much depends on the gestures of the original narrator." And in her introduction to her "Tales of Tamtusalist," a collection of ten Indian tales, she stated, "in giving these tales to the public I have called them translations but who can translate accurately a language that is in part voiceless, for Indians convey their meaning by gesture and facial expression as much as by word spoken. The mind of the listener must be en-rapport with the mind of the narrator to give their full meaning. I have, therefore, written these tales from the impression received by my mind from the Indians' mind."

The style of these works, whether poetry or prose, reflects a literary mode which was popular in Mrs. Allison's youth. The lasting value of her production lies in the fact that she recorded, albeit in a rather old-fashioned style, the experiences of the Similkameen Indians before they came into contact with the Europeans (*In-Cow-Mas-Ket*); the life of Quinisco, the great bear hunter who was famous in the days of Sir James Douglas; and the legends of the Similkameens as preserved by Tam-tu-sa-list, the wisest man of the tribe, who obtained them from his grandfather.

By 1902 Princeton had been surveyed into town lots and was a village of log buildings. There were three general stores, several Chinese restaurants, two hotels, and a blacksmith shop. Mail arrived weekly by the stage and mail line from Spence's Bridge. Copper claims were being worked on Copper Mountain, and Montana interests had started to develop the Nickel Plate gold mine at Hedley. Prospectors from the Boundary and Cassiar districts roamed the countryside.

Though there were many business matters to be attended to, Mrs. Allison found herself with more leisure than she had had at any time since her marriage. Eight of her children were married and established in homes of their own. Of these, two sons and three daughters lived in the Princeton area; two daughters resided in England; and Rose had moved with her husband, S. D. Sandes, to Texada Island where he was employed by the Vananda Copper Company. Only six children remained at home, and the youngest of these was ten years old. As the pace of her life slowed down, Mrs. Allison seized the opportunity to concentrate on her writing.

Indian life and folklore, subjects which had interested her from the beginning of her life in the Similkameen, absorbed most of her attention. She also wrote a number of sketches of Indian women whom she had known before there was much contact with white men. Princess Julia, the last of the hereditary chieftains of the Similkameens, had died in the autumn of 1901, and possibly her tragic death and her funeral, which had elements of both Christian practice and Indian custom, provided the inspiration for this work. Short stories, based on the most dramatic incidents in the life of John Fall Allison as explorer, prospector, and cattle driver were also written. And as the supernatural held an interest for Mrs. Allison, she set down on paper Indian tales of mysterious forces, ghost stories based on certain experiences of her family in Ceylon, and tales told her by superstitious miners.

Many of these sketches and stories she sent for criticism to Clive Phillipps-Wolley, an established author, who had obtained from her material on the Similkameen Indians which he incorporated into his book, *A Sportsman's Eden*. He seems to have given her little help either as a critic or as a friend who was in a position to assist her with placing them for publication. Since she had few contacts outside British Columbia, she did not know how to find a Canadian publisher, and so most of her work, apart from what appeared in the *Similkameen Star* when it commenced publication, remained in manuscript form. Otherwise, in addition to *In-Cow-Mas-Ket*, she succeeded only in having one paper published. But it stands to her credit that this paper on the Similkameen Indians was accepted for publication by the British Association for the Advancement of Science.

During the years when Mrs. Allison did much of her writing, the transition from cattle ranching to mining took place in the Princeton area, and both the quality and the flavour of life changed. For some years after the prospectors made their appearance in numbers in 1898, the society was predominantly one of men. The community was now visited by Presbyterian and Methodist ministers who travelled from the Nicola Valley to hold services in the bar-room of a hotel. "Whenever service was to be held, the proprietors of the hotel, Jim Wallace or J. H. Jackson, as it might happen to be, would go in the bar-room and tell the boys that they would have to polish off their drinks," E. E. Hardwick wrote. "Sale would be held up while the service was on, in which all the patrons of the bar would join with the regular congregation, and they usually chipped in generously with the collection." The annual celebrations which started on Dominion Day and continued through the Fourth of July were marked by foot races in the morning, horse races down Vermilion Avenue in the afternoon, and card games of poker, blackjack, and solo in the evening. Flags, including a Hudson's Bay Company flag (though the post at Keremeos had been closed in 1872 and no trains went through to Hope after that date), were flown. On Dominion Day in 1899 the miners fired a royal salute of twenty-one sticks of dynamite which they had placed in trees and timed to explode in regular succession. There were one thousand miners, prospectors, cowboys, and ranchers in town and "whole families of Indians in all the hues of the rainbow." The "klootchman's race," featuring competition between Princess Julia, Princess Agnes, Chin Chin, and Ahkat, was so colourful that it was photographed for the London papers. A race course was later laid out on the hill, and "card" horse racing became as popular as football and baseball.

The Vermilion Forks Mining and Development Company, an English company which engaged in gold and coal mining, was partly responsible for attracting a number of young English mining engineers to the area. The Waterman brothers, who were connected with this endeavour; the mining recorder, Hugh Hunter; and several professional men with an English background provided Mrs. Allison with the kind of company she had not known since her early days at Hope. Dewdney, whose interest in speculative mining ventures was as great as ever, was a frequent visitor at her home; he often brought news of the Allison children who had left the area as well as information about what the O'Reillys called his "wild mining schemes."

It was Dewdney who received the news of the first death to occur among Mrs. Allison's children. On 5 December 1904 Sandes informed him by telegraph from Vancouver of the death of Rose aboard the *Cassiar*. The funeral was held the next day. Shortly afterward Sandes took his infant son to his family in England and himself proceeded to Rhodesia.

Two years later Dewdney telegraphed Mrs. Allison on 28 January 1906: "Your mother died yesterday. Wife cannot last many days."

While they were at Government House, Jane and Edgar Dewdney, O'Reilly admitted, had "filled the bill" well: ". . . pretty hard work it must be—they are asked everywhere—Dinners, dances, musical societies &c &c—& they I think never refuse," he wrote John Trutch in 1893. When, after the death of Sir John A. Macdonald, Lady Macdonald and her invalid daughter spent the winter of 1893 in Victoria, Jane did everything possible for her friend. On the occasion of the visit in 1894 of Lord and Lady Aberdeen, the Dewdneys took rooms in Victoria so that the governor general and his lady might have privacy at Cary Castle. On this occasion they entertained at a state ball, held in the Drill Hall. On the conclusion of his term, even those old friends who were overly critical admitted that Dewdney had been a satisfactory lieutenant-governor. To Cary O'Reilly, the new régime of Sir Henri Joli "appears very funny & though many condemned the late incumbents, & stigmatised their entertainment as mean yet they are now avenged for the present royal family are 'total abstainers,' and *lemonade* & *ginger ale* are served with dinner!"

After Dewdney's retirement, Jeanie lived quietly at Edgehill, the fine home Dewdney had built on Rockland Avenue. Much of her time she spent in the company of the younger Allison daughters, who had been invited to share her home while attending school in Victoria, and in nursing her mother. Little hope for Mrs. Glennie's recovery had been held out after her fall at Government House in 1897. In January of that year O'Reilly had informed John Trutch that "Old Mrs. Glennie is of course confined to her bed with no hope of being able to walk again." But by 25 March Mrs. Glennie was progressing favourably, "the bone of her thigh which it was thought would not unite, has knit, & she is again able to move on Crutches. Wonderful old Lady, 84 [*sic*] Years!" She was well on the way to recovery that autumn. In 1905, when she was ninety years of age, Mrs. Glennie became frail, and Jeanie herself fell ill.

O'Reilly, who himself was far from well, and would, in fact, die before the end of the year was shocked to hear how ill Jeanie was. "You will be sorry to hear that Mrs. Dewdney (Jeanie) is not at all well," he wrote to his brother-in-law, "they don't wish it known, *so dont mention it, please.* We have always had the warmest regard for her—much more so than for him." Ten days later he wrote again to John Trutch: "Now I must tell you a sad bit of news. In my last I mentioned that Mrs. Dewdney was very unwell. Now I can tell you, on the authority of Dr. Davie, that she has cancer in its worst form. He says she cannot live over the Year. For some strange reason they dont want it known, so pray dont mention it where by any chance it would come back to Victoria. She was always been a good woman, so far as I could see & she was always a friend of my beloved Cary. I am deeply sorry for her."

Mrs. Glennie's death, at the age of ninety-one, came suddenly in January 1906. Dewdney inserted in the paper a notice which referred to her as Mrs. Susan Glennie Moir. The day after her funeral, Tuesday, 20 January, Jeanie, "a daughter of the late Stratton Moir, Esq. of Aberdeen, Scotland, who settled in Ceylon, where Mrs. Dewdney was born," died at Edgehill. Her funeral was held at Christ Church Cathedral, Victoria.

Mrs. Allison, now sixty years of age, was the sole remaining member of her family. All her ties with the past were being shattered; not only had she lost her mother and sister, but also many of her first friends in British Columbia. Mrs. O'Reilly, "Cary," had died in 1899; "Joe" McKay in 1900; Sanders in 1902; Sir Joseph Trutch in 1904; and Peter O'Reilly in 1905. Only Edgar Dewdney, on whom she had relied for business advice after the death of her husband, remained. Within three years, however, Dewdney travelled to England, and while there, he married. On his return his attention was focussed on his own relatives, rather than on the relatives of his first wife.

Changes also occurred in Mrs. Allison's immediate family circle. Her son Jack (John Stratton) was killed while prospecting in the Queen Charlotte Islands in 1908. Her second youngest daughter, Angela, married that same year, and her youngest daughter, Alice, married in 1911.

With two of her children dead and others dispersing to other parts of the province, or to England, the old home became empty. Very little of Allison's lands remained: much of his property had been sold to Keremeos cattlemen such as R. L. Cawston, Thomas Daly, Richard Lowe, and Frank Richter to pay his debts. Other lands were disposed of imprudently by Mrs. Allison, who had never been inclined to concentrate her attention on financial matters. Some revenue which she did obtain from land was unwisely invested. Almost nothing remained of the stock ranch, and unlike so many of the old-timers in the southern Interior who had founded cattle ranches and later disposed of their holdings to syndicates promoting townsite schemes, she was prohibited by the remoteness of Princeton from sharing in this boom. In the course of time, however, a subdivision was marked out on Allison's Flat, about a mile above the Fork, and she decided to leave the old home and to build a small house there.

Because of its proximity to Hedley Camp on Twenty-Mile Creek, Princeton benefited in some respects from the gold mining boom which occurred there after the turn of the century with the development on Nickel Plate Mountain. In 1894 Dewdney had held three claims on the mountain, but he permitted them to lapse. After 1903 the Daly Reduction Company operated the gold mine and the stamp mill. By 1904 production was so great that each month two gold bricks were sent under escort to Penticton for shipment to the assay office in Seattle. During this period the Princeton–Hedley area was oriented eastward. A wagon road replaced the portion of the old Dewdney Trail between Princeton and Keremeos. By 1903 there was daily stage coach service from Hedley to Penticton. A stage from Princeton to Hedley connected with Welby's stage line. By 1904 Hedley had electricity, and by 1910 it boasted a hospital and a volunteer fire brigade. The first railway station was built at Princeton after Spokane mining interests induced the Great Northern Railway to extend into the area. On 23 December 1909 the first train, the Great Northern Railway train from Oroville, Washington, arrived at Princeton. It would take five more years before, with the completion of the Kettle Valley Railway, Princeton would be re-oriented to Hope.

Though Princeton remained a small town, it was affected in many respects by the growth of capital investment and the beginning of industrialization in the Boundary area. It says much for Mrs. Allison that she was able to adjust to these changes. They also stimulated her to return to her writing to recount her experiences as a pioneer.

In 1900, when she published *In-Cow-Mas-Ket*, she had used a pseudonym, "Stratton Moir," the name of her father and her brother. In 1923 when she wrote a series of articles for the *Princeton Star* (*Similkameen Star*) on the "Early History of Princeton," she published under her own name. This was also true after the founding of the Okanagan Historical Society in 1925, when she published several of the Indian legends in its *Reports*.

The writing of this period came to the attention of Cecil O. Scott, editor of the Magazine Section of the *Vancouver Daily Province* in the late 1920's. Scott was anxious to preserve the memoirs of pioneer settlers, and he was impressed with the quality of Mrs. Allison's writing. After her eightieth birthday in 1925, she began to spend the winters with one of her daughters in Vancouver, and in 1928 she moved to Vancouver. At Scott's persuasion, she undertook to write her recollections. They were written quickly, without reference to documents or notes, but with some reliance on the short stories she had written years before. Commencing on 22 February 1931, they appeared in thirteen issues of the *Vancouver Sunday Province*. Immediately they attracted wide attention, not only for the flavour of the pioneer period which they managed to convey, but also for their literary quality. They have continued to hold interest and have appeared in shortened form, as in *Canada West Magazine* (Winter 1969–Winter 1970), or as the basis of newspaper articles.

In 1954, Barbara Pentland, composer, and the poet Dorothy Livesay collaborated to produce a one-act chamber opera, *The Lake*. It had its premiere on CBC Wednesday Night early in March. The setting of the opera was the Allison log cabin at Sunnyside Ranch in the autumn of 1873, and the theme, the danger that John Fall Allison exposed himself to from the Lake Monster when he decided to cross Okanagan Lake, just prior to the birth of his fourth child, to obtain winter supplies.

Though Mrs. Allison was dubbed "The Mother of the Similkameen" and was beloved in the Princeton area, recognition in her lifetime came chiefly from the Okanagan Historical Society and the Similkameen Historical Society. Her last years in Vancouver were lived quietly and with little contact with the community. Like her mother before her, she broke her hip, and like her mother she recovered from the accident. She returned to the sun-drenched hills of the Similkameen to celebrate her ninetieth birthday in August 1935. Then she became frail. On 1 February 1937, at the age of ninety-two, she died in Vancouver, and on 3 February she was buried on Allison property below Castle Rock, at the side of her husband.

The manuscript of Mrs. Allison's "Recollections of a Pioneer of the Sixties" was deposited with Major J. S. Matthews at the Vancouver City Archives. Several transcripts had been made by that time, some with considerable editorial revision, and these found their way to various depositories, including the Provincial Archives. The present edition is based on the holograph copy in the Vancouver City Archives. Since Mrs. Allison was inconsistent in spelling names, particularly Indian names, reference has been made to transcripts made by members of her family. On the whole, however, this edition is based on the original manuscript.

Mrs. Allison had a poor memory for dates, and occasionally her memory, at the age of eighty-five, failed her when it came to identifying individuals. Errors of historical fact have been indicated in the notes.

The recollections are the only account we have of the life of a pioneer woman in British Columbia. Other women, such as Mrs. Augustus Schubert, had remarkable experiences, but none of them left a record of life in the pioneer period. Not only because they enlarge our knowledge of social conditions in the pioneer era, but also because they are a first-hand account of the development of the southern Interior of the province, her recollections constitute an important historical document.

Mrs. Allison remains our only authority on the life and customs of the Indians of the Similkameen region. As she says, her account is based on her impression of their life and customs, an impression gained from the stories that Indian chiefs told her and from the customs she observed. Up until this time, the archaeological evidence has not been fully examined, and until that is done, our knowledge of the Similkameen people must rely on Mrs. Allison's impressions. In this volume, there have been included two stories, one having to do with their superstitious beliefs and the other dealing with their folklore.

Mrs. Allison, with an instinctive feeling for romance and drama, concluded her recollections with the closing of the pioneer period. She long outlived that period, but she was never so happy again. After that time, there were no great adventures, no proud and undefiled Indians, and no virgin country. In her last years, the influences to which she was exposed in her first years became strong, and she became absorbed in studying eastern religions. At her death, it was said, "she sought a faith that was broader than creed."

Margaret A. Ormsby

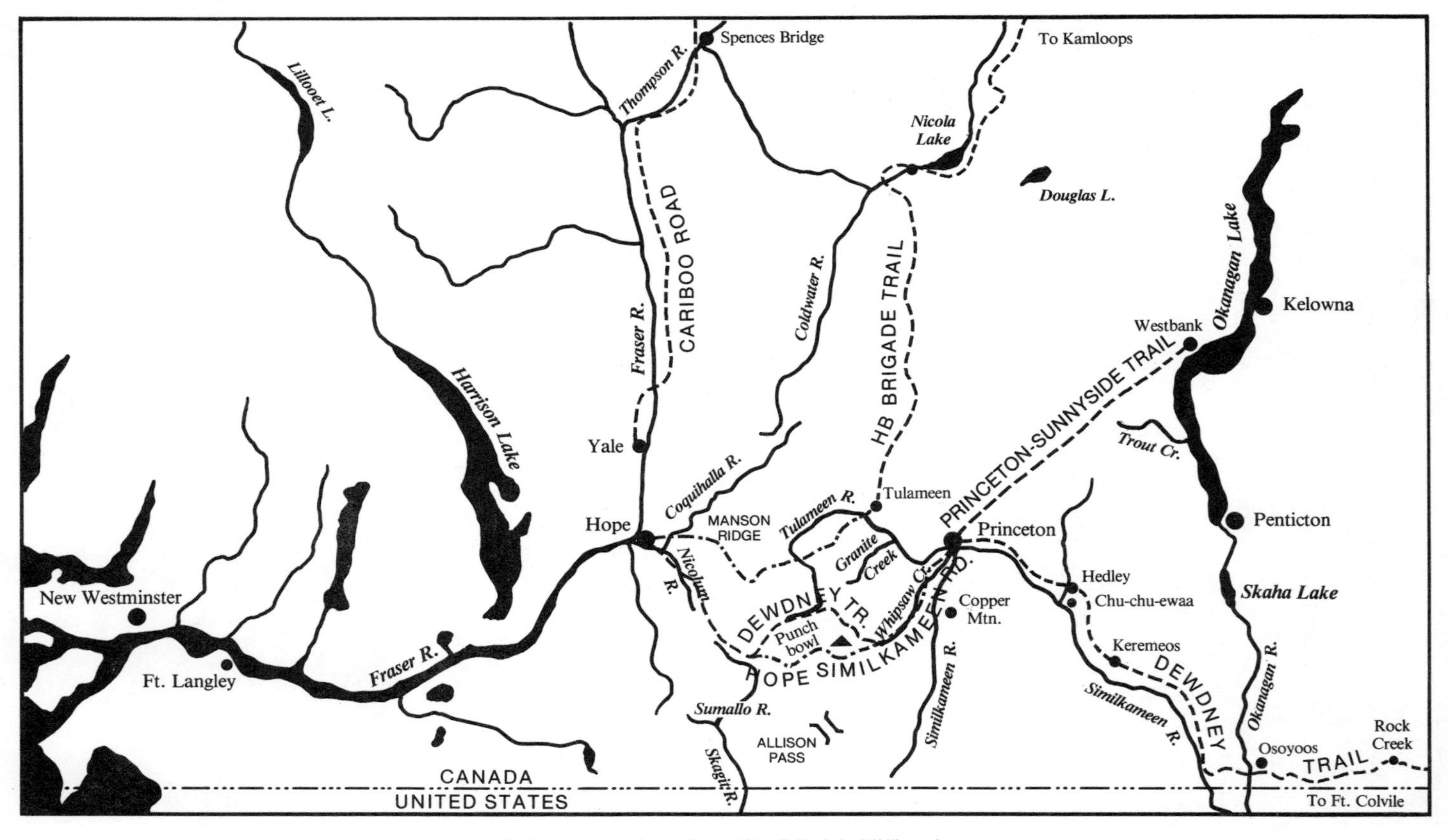

Southwestern British Columbia, Showing Major Trails of the Mid-Nineteenth Century

Some Recollections of A Pioneer of the Sixties

In 1860 there was great talk in England of the Fraser River and its gold bearing sands. It had taken the place of California in the minds of English people. I say English people because I was living in London at that time. I am Scotch and I feel sure that my countrymen were there mining while we Londoners were talking about it.

Well, anyway, my stepfather [Thomas Glennie] who had almost got through a fortune left him by his uncle made up his mind to emigrate to the golden shore of B.C. My mother would not leave her girls, so as we were young and keen for adventure we insisted on going with her. It was agreed that we should but that my brother [Stratton Moir], who held a position with May Matheson and Company in the City, should stay there until we were settled on a farm somewhere in B.C. I think we had all seen farms but that was all we knew about them.

In June, when England was at her loveliest, we left London from the Euston Station and journeyed to Southampton. We were to travel by the Royal Mail route and were at once driven to the wharf where we boarded a waiting tender which deposited us all on board the *Atrato* (Capt. Wooley [Woolley], Commander). After a short delay, we had just time to bid goodbye to my brother and friends, when we started off. We stood on the deck watching and waving till friends and "Chalky Cliffs" faded to nothing. Then we went to our cabins.

My memory of the voyage on the *Atrato* is dim but it was very pleasant. The *Atrato* was a floating palace—I have a distinct recollection of the beautiful stained glass in the stateroom windows. My sister and I shared a cabin and our window had the Empress Maud with such lovely hair. My mother and her husband were directly opposite. There was a missionary and his bride going out to work among the Coast Indians. I believe the name of Tugwell became well known and that they did good work. There was a young fellow, too, named Mofort—the other passengers only went as far as the West Indies. Capt. Woolley was a good host and kept the ship's passengers in good humour. As my sister and self were among the few who did not suffer from sea-sickness we came in for a good share of attention. I don't think we ever missed sitting down to table and Capt. looked after us and a pretty Creole heiress who was on her way out to Jamaica in charge of her parent who often had to keep to his cabin. In the evening an old darkie used to take his banjo and sing plantation melodies to us. We did not go quite to Jamaica. Another Mail steamer met us and took part of the mail and many passengers, including the Bishop of Demerara [Antigua]. We saw the distant form of St. Vincent with St. Pierre and Mount Pele then behaving very quietly with just a tiny cloud of smoke. Then we swept into the beautiful harbour of St. Thomas where the *Tamar* (Capt. Wolcot) met the *Atrato* and carried off and on her passengers. We were very sorry to leave the good ship and her captain.

The *Tamar* was a much smaller steamer than the palatial *Atrato* but Capt. Wolcot looked well after the comfort of his passengers and we had on the whole an agreeable voyage to Colon. The July weather was most terribly sultry and the air round us was shimmering the day we landed in Colon or Aspinwall, as the Americans called it, and when there, we got into the quaintest concern with a funnel shaped smoke stack that was called a train and crawled across the isthmus to Panama, but I really think we were glad to go so slowly, it enabled us to enjoy the sights. The air was dank and heavy, there was a drizzling rain, and as we passed through the narrow cut through the dense jungle we watched and were watched by the curious monkeys that slowly followed the train, swinging from branch to branch. Every now and then a mother monkey with her baby in her arms, clinging to her like a little human, would watch and jabber at us. Then our attention was called to the parrots, beautiful grey and green birds, swinging on tree branches and darting in and out of the dense forest. I must not fail to mention Chagras [Chagres] River—how shall I describe it?—a wide sluggish stream of liquid mud—a river of peasoup creeping onward [*sic*] to the Pacific. The yellow muddy Chagres was certainly a fitting setting for the apparently inert crocodiles that lay sunning themselves on its banks. I have called the disgusting creatures crocodiles, but they may have been alligators. I remember that I did learn at school the difference, something about teeth and hind legs, I think, but they were such loathesome looking scavengers I did not feel drawn toward them to investigate—no close quarters where they were concerned. The train was near enough.

We had been troubled with mosquitoes ever since we landed, but now they were rained upon us and no way of escape—if they had been sent to plague Pharoah instead of frogs, his heart would have softened at once I am sure. What with the stench, heat and mosquitoes we were utterly exhausted when we landed at the hotel in Panama.

The hotel had been a Spanish palace. It really was beautiful with its marble pillars and the grand stairway, but mosquitoes followed us up those marble stairs and into our rooms. Mosquito bars would not keep them out, and they sang for us night and day. The first thing we wanted when we got our rooms allotted to us in the hotel, which we were told was full of guests, was a nice clean cold bath. Well, we were told we could have what we wanted but not to use too much water as water was rather scarce. The bath was grand—marble—but the water was simply filthy!! Thick, muddy and warm; we could get no better—the best water was kept for drinking!—and bad enough it was, so perforce we had to use wine or coffee. I never forgot the horrors of that bath. Between dirty water and mosquitoes it was torture.

The heat was still intense though there were punkas at work in the halls and dining-room, but when the sun went down it became cooler and we and some other strangers thought we would go for a stroll and see the city. We noticed when we left the hotel that four or five men seemed to detach themselves from nowhere and follow us round. When we attempted to walk out of city limits a man stood in front of us and told us that we were taking great risks, and must return to the city. There were bandits around and we would be in trouble. So after that we confined ourselves to city limits and seeing the grand old buildings—the magnificent cathedral, and the crumbling old wall, and thinking of Sir Francis Drake, Queen Elizabeth and the men of Devon. I think I never was in a small place with such a mixed population and the costumes of the coloured ladies were most varied and gorgeous. We managed to drag through ten days while waiting for the U.S.A. steamship, the *John L. Stevens* [*Stephens*], to come and pick up mail and passengers.

The wharves were a curious sight. We saw piled everywhere round us iron tanks about eighteen inches long and four or five inches through, most singular looking things which, upon enquiring, we found contained quick-silver destined for the gold mines in California, and so heavy I could not lift one though I tried. Just before we left Panama we managed to contract Panama fever, so we were glad to get away from the historic place and embark on the U.S. mail steamer.

The Pacific steamers were not to be compared with those on the Atlantic. The accommodation was poorer, and those we were in did not seem to be as clean and well kept.

It was a very sultry day when we left Panama and the barometer was falling. The Captain (Pierson) [*sic*] said there was every indication of a gale, which was not a pleasure to look forward to as the *John L. Stephens* was known as the "floating coffin." Towards evening there was a terrible storm and the ship seemed to be tossed about hither and thither helplessly. At midnight the storm was at its worst. There was one terrific crash which seemed like the crash of doom. The *John L. Stephens* shuddered and seemed to settle down—down as if going to the bottom of the ocean. Cabin doors were thrown open and all the passengers turned out, some with hastily snatched wraps, some with next to nothing on, swearing, cursing or calling on the saints to save them; I really think that the Tugwells and ourselves were the only calm passengers aboard. The captain and the seamen were cool enough, they were used to tropical storms and now they had their hands full quieting the passengers and clearing the decks. A bolt had shattered the main mast to splinters and passed down through the bottom of the ship. The carpenters and crew had hard work to keep the ship floating. We were told next morning that we should have to make for Acapulco for repairs.

The storm had cleared the air and we spent a pleasant day at Acapulco. Looking down into the deep clear water of the harbour we saw swarms of lovely fishes. These we were told were Parrot fish. I don't know that they are edible but they were beautiful. They had noses like a parrot's bill and were coloured red, green, blue and gold. It was great fun to watch them frolicking about gleaming in the sunshine. Then a small fleet of Indian canoes came out from Acapulco with baskets of shells and coloured coral for sale. When the passengers threw money into the water the Indians would dive and redeem the coin. They also had pearls for sale. Altogether we spent a very pleasant and amusing time.

The voyage after that was uneventful except that we passed a small island that looked like a hat thrown into the ocean. The Spanish had named it "Sombrero" and about fifteen or twenty people lived on it and manufactured saltpetre. These people signalled our ship as she passed to enquire if the Southern States had seceded from the Union yet. This was not long after [*sic*] the election of Abe Lincoln. One of the officers on the *Stephens* was a southern gentleman named Selim Waterberry, and he was very much stirred up. He thought as they had been allowed to hold slaves that the government should at least have bought them from their owners as they were their acknowledged property and it was not treating the South fairly.

Well, we were only too glad when the crazy old ship reached San Francisco and we were able to crawl out of our "floating coffin." We were fevered and ill, all four of us, and could not leave San Francisco for quite two weeks. We had just one drive out to see the roses at the Mission and it was worthwhile enduring the drive for the glorious sight. The gardens were well kept.

It was near the first of August when we left on the *Otter* [*Oregon*]. I think she was a Hudson's Bay Company ship. She carried the mail and went up the Columbia River, touched at Portland, then a very small city. It may have been that the buildings were far apart, but it did not look like a city, but the orchards were to be admired. We did not investigate as we were afraid of getting lost and the boat leaving without us.

Our next stop was Victoria. That, too, did not look very much like a city—Government Street existed in all its glory and we put up in either the Oriental or Occidental Hotel. I think that Mrs. M'Kean [McKeon] was the proprietor, but really I was still too ill to take much notice. One thing I do remember was the lovely walks to Beacon Hill in the cool of the evening. Here we lost sight of the Tugwells. They went at once to the post of duty.

My stepfather had letters to James Douglas and called and presented them. The Governor advised him to proceed at once to Hope and take up land there. He said as Hope was the head of navigation it certainly had a bright future before it. The *Otter* would take us to New Westminster and we would find a steamer run by Captn. John Irving [Captain William Irving] that would take us on to Hope. We liked Victoria but as Mr. Douglas advised, and my stepfather thought that he was in a position to know, so [we] resolved to take his advice.

While in Victoria, we were trying to rest after the long journey so did not meet many people. Though Victoria was quite a city, to us it seemed very small. Government Street existed and some others, but I don't remember much about them. Mr. Cridge had been there for years with his wife and family and we also met some Hudson's Bay Company people, people always hospitable and kind. We were introduced to Mr. Charles Good, the Governor's secretary. The Governor himself was a genuine Douglas, kindly and urbane in manner—"A glove of velvet on a hand of steel"—one of the wisest and best Governors we ever had, if he was arbitrary. Dr. Helmcken ever helpful with good advice.

The few days we were in Victoria we went for walks in the evening all over the city and up to Beacon Hill. We enjoyed the scenery and we saw other people doing the same. We also met romance in the shape of a queenly Indian woman who wore a blanket round her shoulders like a Royal Robe and over the blanket hung two long ropes of black braids, such magnificent hair. We were so impressed by her grace and dignity that we inquired who she was. The answer was "Oh, she's not an Indian. It is A—— going to meet her L——. Her father has forbidden them to meet. Everyone knows how they do manage to meet except her father." So you see, even in the sixties Beacon Hill was a romantic spot—Romeo and Juliet. Another romantic spot was the old Bastion, which was still standing in what is now Bastion Street —all was peace in the sixties, but it spoke volumes.

We went on the *Otter* (Capt. Mowat [Mouat]) to New Westminster, where Captn. Irving's boat, the *Reliance*? was waiting to start up the Fraser River to Hope, then the head of navigation.

Westminster seen from the river was nothing but a few huts and tents. We did not know that the real town was on the hill hid from view and that Sapperton, or the Camp as it was called, was really a stirring little place and we could see it from the boat landing. Capt. Irving was very kind and introduced us to many of his passengers. The first we met was Edgar Dewdney, a young English surveyor and engineer from Devon, Mr. Newton, who was going up to join his wife and family on a holiday, Judge Begbie, Mr. Bushby his clerk of the court, and many others.

It was my fifteenth birthday on the 18th of August when we landed in Hope, such a charming, busy little place it seemed to us, nestling in the mountains and Ogilvie's Peak towering above it. We ran joyously up the bank and on top waiting to meet the boat we met many who proved to be life-long friends. First, there was Mr. Wm. Charles, in charge of the Hudson's Bay Company Fort and Offices in Hope. With him was his factotum, Wm. Yates, one of the most amusing characters I ever met, P. O'Reilly, the Stipendiary Magistrate and Judge, who was there to meet Judge Begbie, Colonel Moody, Captns Luard and Parsons, Drs. Seddle [Seddall] and Oliver, Sergt. Lindsay, and Corp. Howse, all R.E.'s. Of townspeople there we saw George Landvoight, J. Wirth, hotel proprietor, Wm. Sutton, Wm. Teague and many more than I can mention and we were hastily introduced to nearly all by Captn. Irving and Edgar Dewdney. It was quite a relief when we were carried off by the ever hospitable Wm. Charles and introduced to his wife and sister-in-law, Miss Birnie, and to one who became a very dear friend, Joe M'Kay [McKay], a Hudson's Bay Company Chief Factor, also the Honble. E. N. B. Portman, a young C.E. just returned from Similkameen, also Walter Moberly, who was anxiously waiting for his partner, E. Dewdney, who had a contract from Governor Douglas to build the Hope Similkameen Wagon Road. This was to be started without delay.

Colonel Moody his wife and family were living at the Court House and with them was a very pretty girl, Miss Jessie Nagle. We soon got to know all the ladies. There was a French lady, Mrs. Landvoight with whom I afterwards became great friends, a Mrs. Sutton, a Mrs. Pemberthy and, of course, Hope had to have a beauty—Miss Sally Grey was really lovely, and she and Jessie Nagle were the belles of Fraser River for some years.

Mrs. Landvoight told [me] that by the time she and her husband reached Hope two years before that their money was all spent and they had nothing left but a sack of flour, a can of jam and a can of lard, and a small iron stove with a drum, a tent and some blankets. Otherwise, they were flat broke and amongst strangers, but she had an inspiration and put up the tent and stove and baked tarts and pies with the jam and sold [them] for twenty-five cents per slice. She made three dollars the first day—after that she could not make pies fast enough for her customers and soon added a cup of coffee—another twenty-five cents—and soon they were able to start a small store which now was a big one. She was a brave lady and did all she could to build the little town of Hope.

Hope really was a flourishing little town and had good prospects for continuing so. There was a pretty little church and parsonage, Court House, Hudson's Bay Company Fort and Store, hotel, saloon, two stores, butcher shop, blacksmith's shop, and lots more things that I have forgotten. Oh, yes, I remember the sawmill; they were laying on water for town use and had a pile of huge cedar logs which were lying by the mill. There was a water-power carriage that drew the logs up to a huge auger, which bored through them and came out at the other end red hot. We had never seen anything of the kind done before and were highly amused watching it. This was one of the sights with which our hospitable friend, Wm. Charles, entertained us. Another was within the Hudson's Bay Company stockade—There was first of all a gun, a small cannon, mounted ready to fire. Now it was an occasional salute but formerly it had been used to overawe the Indians. It made noise enough. Then there was the Store and the houses of various employees of the company, including his own. Aparajos and pack saddles innumerable [were] piled outside the different buildings and posts firmly planted in the ground to tie the horses when required. We stayed a few days with this kindly gentleman till we could find a place for ourselves.

The first house we occupied in Hope was a light timber frame with a lumber roof—lined and partitioned with cloth and paper. It was divided into two with this light partition and a blanket hung over a pole served for an inner door. Sheets served for window blinds. I can well remember how airy it was, the high Hope winds almost raised the roof. Opposite was a stable with a fine horse that belonged to a man named Shannon. I believe he used part of it as a house. Next door was John Wirth's Hotel, and he was kind enough to allow us to use his well.

None of [us] knew how to wash clothes. We had a tin bath tub that we brought out with us that we used for a wash tub and as we were ignorant as to the use of wash boards, we bent over the bath and rubbed with our hands till they bled and our backs felt broken. As we always wore white embroidered petticoats we had rather a bad time on washing day. Another difficulty was baking bread. At first Mrs. Charles was good enough to bake for us but we could not impose too long. We got a sack of flour and a can of "Preston and Merril Yeast Powder" and when we went by directions managed to make fairly good bread, at least my mother did. We younger ones sometimes forgot to put in the baking powder and once in a hurry grabbed a can of sulphur by mistake and did not find out till the bread began to cook and we began to choke and splutter with the fumes. Then a man named Kilburn told us to use sourdough and bake in a skillet and when once we got on to that and did not let the bread stand too long we made a great success.

From the doorway of our shack we could see the Hudson's Bay Company's Post and watch the pack trains come in from Colville, Keremeos and other places. Sometimes there would be a grand stampede and the pack trains would disrupt. Horses and men could be seen through a misty cloud of dust, madly dashing all over the Hope flat, lassos flying, dogs barking, hens flying for safety anywhere. Suddenly the tempest would subside as fast as it had arisen, the pack boys would emerge from the clouds of dust leading the ring leaders in the stampede. These Hudson's Bay Company horses, though called "cayooses," were most of them splendid animals, hardy and enduring, with lots of good horse sense. Mr. McKay told me that they really were descended from the Spanish Barb brought to America over three hundred years ago by the Spaniards and left to run wild had spread all over the continent. It is possibly quite true. They were quick, hardy and enduring.

In the early days we had no roads, only rough trails mostly those used by the Hudson's Bay Company and Indians—with no attempt at grades. In crossing the Hope Mountains the Hudson's Bay Company Brigade always took twice as many horses as were needed and went well armed. The horses were taken to enable them to negotiate "The Slide" on Mansen's [Manson's] Mountain where they invariably lost half their horses. There was no road, the trail ended at the top of the Slide and the horses were driven over the bank and once started had to go on sliding to the bottom. A few of the horses who had been used before had learned to brace themselves and went without being forced to go, and usually came through without accident. Coming back it was easier on them. Sometimes some of the Blackfeet came over, too.

While Col. Moody and the Sappers were in town we had a gay time but they left the week after we arrived. The town was still busy, for there were at that time miners on the Fraser River Bars, Sappers outfitting, and hunters and fishermen. The Nicalome [Nicolum] and Silver Creek abounded in trout.

I shall never forget my first sight of a Hudson's Bay Company Brigade train coming in from Colville. I had gone for a stroll on the Hope–Similkameen trail. There were still a few berries and I was getting a "feed" when I heard bells tinkling and looking up saw a light cloud of dust from which emerged a solitary horseman, the most picturesque figure I had ever seen. He rode a superb chestnut horse, satiny and well groomed, untired and full of life in spite of the dust, heat and long journey. He himself wore a beautifully embroidered buckskin shirt with tags and fringes, buckskin pants, embroidered leggings and soft cowboy hat. He was as surprised to see me as I was to see him, for he abruptly reined in his horse and stared down at me, while I equally astonished stared at him. Then, as the Bell Boy and other horses rode up, he lifted his hat and passed on. I never met him again, but was told he was a Hudson's Bay Company Officer in charge of the Colville train and that he said he was never more surprised in his life than to see a white girl on the trail—he had lived so long without seeing anyone except Indians.

Soon after this the Rev. A. D. Pringle's wife and children came out from England. She was a young woman of twenty-five and a very good mixer so we soon had a nice agreeable community. Mrs. Pringle was kind enough to invite me over to the parsonage where we spent an afternoon once a week reading French together.

There was a pretty little church at Hope (it may still stand) endowed by Miss Burdette-Coutts [Burdett-Coutts]—she also supplemented the minister's salary. We went to the church every Sunday and when the congregation was dismissed most of us adjourned to Mr. Charles' home or the Court House. Some of the men went fishing and when they returned their fish stories were edifying.

Adjoining Hope was an Indian Village, one very long house containing several families, rather a smelly place as they dried fish on the roof. The Indians made baskets, blankets, and rugs—some of them worked in silver making the large Mexican dollar piece into amulets and rings. The Baskets were very costly and were useful as well as pretty. They were watertight and took a long time to make, some of them months even of hard work; they were used for many purposes. We wondered when we were told that they were used for cooking till one of them explained that they did not use them on or over the fire, but filled them with water into which they threw red hot stones till the water boiled, when they covered [them] tightly and kept it boiling till the food was cooked. Baskets also were used for the babies, long narrow baskets in which they lived night and day till old enough to be strapped on a stick and have their heads flattened as was the custom with the Hope Indians. The Blankets they made from the hair of their dogs—and wove many pretty patterns in them by dyeing them with native roots and herbs.

The Hope Indians lived mostly on fish which they dried for winter use, also berries with which the country abounded. Wild geese, too, came over in flocks in the fall. Wm. Yates had a wild gander with a broken wing for many years, much to my terror. No one could pass him with impunity, but with Yates he was quite tame. Mr. O'Reilly had a pet cub, a young black bear that he brought up on a bottle, but the little fellow soon got that he liked Mr. O'Reilly's sugar, butter and candles better than his bottle and bread and milk.

The fall of 1860 was very pleasant and we thoroughly enjoyed it. Mr. Dewdney, when he could find time, took us for long rides on the new Hope–Similkameen Road. We went as far as the fifth crossing of the Quealla or Coheekalla [Coquihalla] as some called it. I am not sure how it should be spelled, but I know it swarmed with spent salmon. These rides were pleasant though the trails were rougher than any road I had ever ridden on and my poor old habit got many an ugly tear. Mr. Dewdney was always beside my sister but I had to struggle along the best way I could, sometimes losing the trail in the brush, but the horse, better used to it, always found it again.

My stepfather soon found a small piece of land which he pre-empted and Mr. Kilburn got out the logs and made ready to build a house—four rooms and a lean-to kitchen, verandah and real windows—most of the shacks out of town had none. It was a great novelty to go out into the forest to watch Mr. Kilburn and E. S. Van Horn, who worked for him, felling trees. The ring of their axes as they alternately fell on the tree trunks had a sort of musical rhythm and then when they shouted "Look Out," to see the giants totter and sway, then a sharp crack just before the crashing fall; to us it was blood curdling to see the men who were expert axemen just stand aside and watch the fall, while we were in terror lest they should be crushed under the tree. These trees were limbed and cut into logs the right size, then dove-tailed at the joints. The house was to be up and finished by early spring—meantime we occupied our cloth and paper lined shack.

Mrs. Charles was a charming hostess and her pretty little daughter, Mabel, an infant a few months old, was an everlasting delight to her guests. We had many good dances at the Hudson's Bay Company house. My mother, who had a lovely voice, sang the old pathetic English and Scottish ballads so she was able to contribute her share to the general amusement. So the first winter passed.

With spring Hope woke up to life and activity. As head of navigation it really was an important place. Now we went to our new house. The things we had sent round the Horn arrived in due time. My sister's little piano, a plough, lamps, crockery and many other things, all useful and even ornamental for the house. Our beds were made of round poles and we used blocks sawed off small logs, with a branch for a handle left on each for seats. Of course, these were heavy but they answered our purposes. We had a nice big sitting room the whole length of the house. There was a huge fireplace round which six or eight people could sit and enjoy themselves. On the mantelpiece we mounted some old silver candelabra and an ornamental clock, a few pictures on walls and a mantel, also some Chinese swords and other little things we valued on the walls. These, with our old home curtains, deer skins on the floor, and we really had a homelike, comfortable sitting room. We soon had a garden fenced with willow poles and in the open we were foolish enough to plant carrots, potatoes and oats—I say foolish because as soon as the carrots grew to be any size the Black Bears came at night and dug them up and ate them.

This spring we were visited by Capt. Hawkins and a young man named Hastings of the Boundary Commission. They had some pretty gold quartz rock they had brought from near Keremeos and spoke most enthusiastically of the country, the abundance of game and fish—it was a pleasant visit though short. We were only two miles out of Hope on the old Brigade Trail, and used to walk to Hope once a week for our mail and we had many visitors.

On May the 24th Hope celebrated the Queen's birthday with races. People came from outlying districts, Op[p]enheimer from Yale, Saunders [Sanders], the Magistrate of Yale, Bouies [Buies], Jack and Jim, Teague and Lawrence, and many, many others. It was then I first saw Similkameen Indians, and in contrast to the Hope Flatheads they stood out with lustre. I had noticed how very ugly the Hope women were, with the exception of one who on enquiry proved to be a Thompson woman called Lallipetticoe, she stood apart in her loveliness from the other women. I never saw but one woman, white or coloured, that was as beautiful—that was long afterwards, and she, too, was a Thompson woman.

Moberly and Dewdney had a small house and stable near the race track. Their pack horses had been sent to Similkameen for the winter in charge of some Indians and they had kept an Indian boy, Little George, with them for a helper. Him they trained to act as jockey for their horses and rigged him out in regular jockey clothes, of which he was immensely proud—possibly the first "white man's clothes" he had ever worn. A grandstand was erected for the visitors or anyone who cared to occupy it. I don't remember the winners. I only remember it was a jolly good time—and as usual [was] topped off with a dance at the Hudson's Bay Company house.

Governor Douglas and his men in attendance rode out to the Similkameen and inspected the road. He was a fine, far-seeing man. He called in to see us and told us what a paradise Similkameen was—Mountains covered with tall grass which could be converted into wheat fields or ranges for large herds of cattle and added with a Scotchman's pride "there were thistles and heather growing in places."

Hope could not be beat for beautiful wild flowers. There was a beautiful Nefolium lily that sprang up as soon as the snow went off and another small lily like a star, Linnear Borialis, Tiger Lilies, Dogwood, and a small plant like a miniature dogwood and bore a small berry. It was known as the Partridge berry. I am a poor botanist but it seemed to me there was an infinite variety of flowers.

Lots of people outfitted at Hope for a journey to Carriboo [Cariboo]. The two Trutch brothers were working on the construction of the Cariboo Road. Cariboo was in everybody's mouth. The Hope ladies got up a picnic to Silver Creek, we went too, and while enjoying lunch Walter Moberly joined us with Mr. Robert (Bobby) Stevenson and Charles Oppenheimer who could do nothing but talk of Cariboo. They were going up for the season's work there.

On Governor Douglas' return trip from the Similkameen there was a very stormy interview between him and the townsmen of Hope. They wanted him to hurry the construction of the Hope–Similkameen waggon road, and he said that he could not, nor could it be finished unless they would agree to pay a toll of half a cent on the pound. They foolishly refused. The Governor then stopped all work on the road, made Yale the head of navigation—and turned his attention to Cariboo. It was a dreadful blow to Hope, though the people there really deserved it. It would have amounted to nothing to pay that small tax and have the benefit of a good waggon road and avoid Manson's Mountain and its horrors. After the first soreness was over Mr. Douglas agreed to open a good pack trail through to the Similkameen.

My friend, Mrs. Landvoight had very bad rheumatism and the doctor recommended her to go to the Hot Springs. It was rather a rough trip and as she hated to go alone she invited me to go with her. I could have danced for joy, I was so anxious to see more of the country. It all was so new and strange after having lived in London so I most readily accepted her invitation.

We took Captn. Irving's boat down the river as far as Harrison and then went in the *Douglas* as far as Douglas on the Harrison Lake. Douglas was then the terminal point of the Cariboo Road and was beginning to drop owing to the recent activity of Yale. There was a magistrate and constable resident. One hotel [was] kept by some people named Hanna. There we went and were made very comfortable by kind Mrs. Hanna who told us we would find the next day's journey very trying, the roads were so rough and she told the truth, for as we bumped along in the four horse stage we both felt that we would much rather have been on foot. On the road that day I saw a sight I had never seen before. It was a huge van or truck, I don't know what it should be called, drawn by sixteen oxen crawling along the rough uneven road—teamsters swearing and whips cracking. They were taking machinery to Cariboo.

The Hot Springs we went to were about twenty miles out from Douglas on a ranch owned by Mr. Stein, an Irishman, and his young wife who had been Miss Fanny Morey, one of the Sappers' daughters. Mrs. Landvoight had forgotten to notify her that we were coming and the poor little woman was surprised and altogether unprepared. However, she made the best of it, cooking trout and grouse. Her house was clean and comfortable. We went to see the Hot Springs. It just gushed out of a solid rock from a round hole like an auger hole and would cook an egg in three minutes or less. At its source there were open ditches to convey it to the baths, which were rough wooden affairs in a large shed partitioned off. We sampled them at once for we were both tired and dirty and found them refreshing, but the water was very nasty to drink. The Roaring River was a beautiful and romantic spot. We often walked to it and sat near the cool water during the heat of the day, taking our crochet or embroidery with us to help pass the time when too lazy to explore—books, we had none.

Every day the ox teams would pass one way or the other and Indians on horseback would gallop by. Mrs. Stein said that they were not friendly—the Fountain Indians she called them, better looking than the Hope Indians but they were not as fine looking as the Similkameens. We put in a month or six weeks bathing in the hot water regularly. Mrs. Landvoight felt much better and was anxious to get home again. So back to Hope we went, rattle, bang over the rough road.

Matters in and round Hope seemed gradually to get worse and worse. Mr. O'Reilly left Hope [June 1862]. Gov[ernor] Douglas thought that Mr. Sanders could come down to Hope occasionally. Judge Begbie continued his circuit, so that was that. We managed, though everybody was sorry to lose Mr. O'Reilly who had been kind and helpful to all. Then Mr. Charles and the Hudson's Bay Company still helped all they could to help Hope and the trail was soon made over the mountains. Pack trains continued to arrive and traders as they established themselves bought their goods in Hope. That saved upcountrymen about a week or ten days that trading with Westminster would have taken.

In 1864 my sister married Edgar Dewdney. It was the first [*sic*] wedding at the little Hope church. Mr. O'Reilly, the Charles', and Landvoights were present besides our own family. We had a lunch at the Hudson's Bay Company after which my sister and her husband left on the old *Reliance*, Captn. Irving's boat, for New Westminster.

I was the only girl in Hope now and felt rather lonely though there was lots of work and hard work at that. Not long after this Mr. Pringle brought Miss Annie Moresby up from Westminster as governess for his children, but she had not been in Hope six months when the Yale Magistrate swooped down and carried her off as Mrs. Sanders—that was the second wedding at the little church. Then it was decided by those who had the say in such matters that it was not worthwhile to keep the church going for us and the Pringles vanished from the scene and the parson from Yale came down, I think, twice a month.

We struggled on for another year, things getting duller and duller. Mr. Charles was moved to Yale. I visited Mrs. Charles at Yale the year the Alexandra Bridge was completed, rode out to see it with Mr. Ross, Hudson's Bay Company. Everyone was talking about the wonderful bridge. I know it was a wonderful ride over those bluffs with the Fraser boiling below. I had never been on such a road in my life, but the bridge did not [*sic*] seem so wonderful. It seemed a great mystery how it ever was thrown over the rocky Canyon of the Fraser. That was wonderful and a great credit to those who built it. The names of Joseph and John Trutch ought certainly to be remembered—that was only one of many things they did for B.C. We had a somewhat late lunch at an inn near the Bridge and it was dark when we rode back to Yale and I was glad not to see the dangers of the Canyon when I was getting tired.

There were several accidents during the construction of that road, one to Mr. Tingley who was driving his bride out to see it. The horses shied at a wheelbarrow carelessly left on the road, [and] went over the bluff, buggy and all. Mrs. Tingley and the horses were killed and Mr. Tingley [was] seriously injured. When the bridge was finished Mrs. Joe Trutch, justly proud of her husband's work, went to Yale to see it, visiting Hope on the way. Then I had the pleasure of meeting one who afterwards filled most graciously the position of first lady in B.C. Petted daughter [*sic*] of the Surveyor General of Oregon, she always was ready to face any hardship and make the best of everything. I can remember visiting her in the early days at Government House at New Westminster, when she put me in an armchair of which she had several, so comfortable and well padded, made out of a sugar barrel. The furniture for Government House had not arrived and she made them with her own tiny hands for present need—Lady Trutch was one woman in a thousand. But I am getting a little ahead of time for Sir James Douglas was still Governor when the Alexandra Bridge was built.

Shortly after this my mother's health failed and as Mr. Dewdney had lots of work at Cariboo my sister asked us to go to New Westminster and stay with her. Cariboo was then in such a rough state Mr. Dewdney would not take her to Williams Creek. We were thankful to go.

There, as in Hope, we met many friends, Judge Crease and his family, our old friend, Mr. O'Reilly and his wife, formerly Miss Trutch, sister to Joe and John Trutch, Mr. Pooley, Mr. J. Fisher of the Bank of B.C., Mr. and Mrs. Prichard of the Penitentiary—lots of old Sappers who had made their home in New Westminster.

While large ships could not reach New Westminster the small ones did. Everyone looked forward to the coming of the gunboats. It meant lots of gaiety for the young people. The *Chameleon* [*Cameleon*] and the *Sparrowhawk* generally ran to Westminster when in the vicinity. The *Alert* tried it but grounded.

There were lots of girls in Westminster at the time of which I write. My friend, Miss Jessie Nagle, was teaching in the Public School and her pupils were devoted to her. Our society leaders were Mrs. Trutch, Mrs. O'Reilly, Mrs. Crease, Mrs. Black, Mrs. Dickinson [Dickenson], and Mrs. Webster. I can't enumerate them all [as] it would take up too much space. We had a gay time in the winter trudging through the snow and slush, holding up our long skirts, all the way to Government House and occasionally to a dance on board the boats. Everyone was good natured making allowances for the shortcomings of their neighbours. Certainly the people of Westminster were an agreeable community till there were certain political changes that threw us all into disorder.

John Robson, our premier, and Frank Barnard were our champions in the struggle for the capital. We thought Westminster was quite as important as Victoria. It did most of the business and shipping to the upper country. I think the thing we felt proudest of was our chime of church bells. Mr. Pooley, then a young man, and J. Fisher, H. Nagle and other young fellows used to make the evening lively by rendering "Home Sweet Home," "Rousseau's Dream," "Nearer My God to Thee," on the bells. These bells were the gift of Miss Coutts. Westminster justly considered itself an important place. The church was represented by Rev. Archdeacon Woods, the Methodists by Ebenezer Robson. Columbia Street had a brick building erected by Mr. Holbrook. Clute and Major had an emporium at which you could buy a needle or a blanket or anything needful. There were lawyers and doctors—two at any rate, Dr. Black and Dr. Oliver. Dr. Black was considered one of the best doctors on the coast. He had been a doctor in the Crimea during the war.

With all her great advantages [the] Hudson's Bay Company['s] capital got the best of New Westminster, and Victoria was chosen capital, though many felt that it should have been Westminster, Langley or Kamloops.

About this time there was some trouble with the Chilcotin Indians, I don't exactly remember what, a murder, I think, and the chief refused to give up the offenders. However, it was our men in office who grasped the situation like men of mettle and sent volunteers from Westminster and two gunboats up to the scene of action and the situation ceased to be a menace. There was joy in the city when the volunteers returned in safety with the prisoners.

Shortly after I went to Victoria to visit Mrs. Charles, whose husband had been removed from Yale to Victoria, and after a few days I met her sister, Mrs. J. M. Wark, who was looking out for a governess for the children. I was fortunate enough to secure this position. There were four children. Mrs. Wark was living on Bastion Street in a roomy house next to Dr. Tewso [Tuzo]. I was there for rather more than a year and treated with the greatest kindness and consideration. At that time I met and became great friends with Agnes Anderson, who afterwards married Captn. Gaudin. We spent much of our spare time together. I was waiting there until I should attain the age of twenty-one, which then seemed to me to be an almost venerable age. An old grand-aunt had left a few thousand dollars which I was to get at that time. When I did get it I hit the trail for New Westminster where I had many friends and I rented a small cottage on Royal Avenue near a house built by [the] Nagles. Captn. Irving had a mansion there, too, and the three very dissimilar houses were at that time the only ones on Royal Avenue. Clarksons were close by, also my sister and Mr. Dewdney's two sisters and his brother, Walter, who had just come from India. I tried to add to my small income by doing fancy work but did not make a brilliant success but I enjoyed nearly every hour I spent there as I had so many friends—the Dickensons, Blacks, Homers, and others whose names are commemorated in the Vancouver streets and have passed into provincial history.

I used to make visits to Hope to see Mrs. Landvoight; at her house I first met my husband, J. F. Allison, also many of the old fathers, many of them I should say [were] such good, self-sacrificing men. One I never can forget, Father Grandidier. Father Pandosie [Pandosy], too, though I saw more of him afterwards at Similkameen. Mrs. Landvoight thought that if I moved up to Hope and started a small school I would do well. At that time there were no public schools at Hope or Yale. In the spring of sixty-seven Mr. Dewdney broke up his home in Westminster and with my sister and his sister, Mrs. Lethbridge, went up to Soda Creek. My mother and I gave up our cottage and went to live in Hope at the now vacant parsonage. Here we started a small school.

I do not remember the year in which Captain Louis Agassiz came to Hope but I remember his coming. It was after Mr. O'Reilly and Cregie, the constable, were removed. It was found that Hope could not do without a constable and Government Agent of some kind, so a good selection was certainly made when Captain Agassiz was established at the Court House. Captain Agassiz was a fine-looking man and physically fitted for the job, and broad minded enough not to embroil himself in little local disputes. His family then consisted of four children, Florence, Arthur, Jean and James. They were nice hospitable people and we spent many delightful evenings playing cards or enjoying social chats. The children, too, were nicely brought up—each child had his little task to perform everyday and did it cheerfully. They lived at Hope until the Captain took up a ranch down the river near the Harrison Springs. I think this was afterwards purchased by the Government and is now the Experimental Farm or it may be the Agassiz townsite.

In my spare time I used to take my work to Mrs. Landvoight's and the two of us sat in the shade of her verandah and sewed. I can remember one task we set ourselves—white petticoats were always worn in summer and we would not be behind the fashion so we got white linen and started each to make one. They were three yards wide, no petticoat was less, and had twenty-one tucks and a hem, all hand sewing. We also had good times in the summer evenings when the Clarkson girls visited Hope. Miss Mary Clarkson was engaged to C. J. Major who was then running Mr. Landvoight's business for him. When the girls came to Hope we had long rides out to the swimming pool Mr. Landvoight made by putting a dam in the creek flowing out of "Bishop's Lake," the property of Bishop Hills. When the girls were not there C. J. Major was my escort in long rides on the Hope–Similkameen road. Mr. Allison brought in a cream mare for me to use and we often rode out as far as Lakehouse [Lake House] (then the property of E. Dewdney) with him on his return trips to the Similkameen. One evening lives in my memory and more than in my memory. I can feel the effects of it even today. Mr. Allison had lingered till it was getting dusk but Major and I thought we would have time for a quick short ride with him. But we went a little farther, and a little farther, till we found ourselves at Lake House. Mr. Allison had to make Powder Camp that night so he continued on his journey while Major and I started home again. Well, we went the pace, fourteen miles without drawing bridle. But just as we turned to the race course a tree which had partly turned over caught me full on the chest and dragged me off the horse, my skirt hung on the horn, and I was dragged for a mile to Landvoight's stable, the horse kicking me in the side. When the skirt had torn off I managed to rise with Major's help—went to Mrs. Landvoight's house, had a very hot bath, went to bed and got up next day feeling crumpled up and very sore. Fortunately, my mother was not there or I would have been forbidden more rides. It took some fully two weeks to get about as usual; I have never been the same since. I had such good health before. Cream Kate was spoiled. She would never let a man mount her after that without a great fight, though she did not object to me. Horses are queer creatures if you study them. They have their own characteristics.

My mother and I started quite a nice little school. Mr. Yates sent his little boy, Mr. Hunter sent his girls, and Bill Bristol, who was then Similkameen mail carrier, sent his daughter, and some children were sent from Yale. I did not like teaching but it helped out my small income.

Mr. Allison, when we were married, would have liked my mother to live with us, but she had heard such wild stories of the Similkameen and the horrors of the trail that she would not think of it, but kept on the little school.

I was married in September, about the eighteenth or the twentieth, I am not sure which. My husband went to Westminster and got a special licence from Governor Seymour, and Archdeacon Woods came up to Hope to marry us. My sister and brother-in-law were visiting in Hope at that time. Also Mr. and Mrs. O'Reilly, so they and of course, Mrs. Landvoight were present at the parsonage when we were married.

Then began my camping days and the wild, free life I ever loved till age and infirmity put an end to it.

On the journey out we rode the two Kates, Cream and Grey. My husband sent the three packboys on ahead to fix camp. (This was over the Hope–Similkameen Trail.) As the three boys will often appear in these memoirs, I may as well pause and introduce them—Cockshist was cargodore, that is, he looked after the packs and cargo generally, storing it under shelter when removed from the horses and assigning each horse its load. Johnny Suzanne was packer. Cockshist assisted in the actual packing but Johnny had to round up the horses, mend saddles, see that the ropes were dry. Yacumtecum or Tuc-tac as he was then called was bell-boy and cook. He led the leading pack-horse with the bell when the train started and cooked meals when in camp. We left town just at dusk and in a little over an hour reached the Lake House where we found the tents up and a blazing log fire and Yacumtecum cooking. In the tent a canvas was spread over the floor and a bed made of "mountain feathers," Spruce branches, and a buffalo robe. A wash basin [was] mounted on the box. Outside, there was the most delicious smell of grouse cooking. I went to the creek and washed and did up my hair in the darkness and when I regained the camp Tuc-tac had spread a canvas in front of the fire with fried trout, grouse, bacon and bannock. That [was] washed down with tin cups of delicious tasting tea. We sat and talked till late, the Indian boys sitting with us and telling us stories of the place. Here, Yacum-tecum said, one of the Big Men (giants) lived and had been often seen. Cockshist said they also lived on the Okanagan. This led to talking of the creature now called the "Ogopogo." The Indians did not say "Ogopogo." They looked on it as a superhuman entity and seemed to fear it, though none of our boys had seen it nor did they want to. When we were all sleepy we retired for the night but were up with daylight in the morning in order to get the packs over the Skagit Bluff in the daylight. Tuc-tac had the same savory meal ready for us and we were soon on the second day. About noon we stopped at the Cedars for a hurried bite then on up the zigzag to the Skagit. Here we met a coloured man, a fine strong fellow. He stopped and spoke to my husband, who said that he was Richardson who was then removing some slides off the Skagit Bluff. Mr. Richardson assured us there was not even a stone left on the Bluff and added that we would still see some of the flowers for which the Skagit was famous though the best blooms were over. Then we proceeded on our respective ways. Mr. Richardson was right, the Skagit Flat was lovely. The rhododendrons were lovely still though not at their best. I think by the general colouring that there had been a touch of frost. The packboys paused to tighten their packs before we got to the Bluff. Mr. Allison told me to follow the packhorses closely and he would keep behind me in case of accident. We crossed without mishap. We kept slowly on till we came to Powder Flat, now rechristened by the pioneers of the "Nineties" as Cayoosh Flat. We called it Powder Flat from the circumstance that one time [when] my husband and his partner were packing out the camp caught fire and there was a rush to throw the blasting powder into the creek. There was gunpowder, too, but it was in cans and not much danger. It did not even get wet in the creek. As I said the place is now named Cayoosh Flat and the mountain back of it is called Spencer Mountain. Then it had the Hudson's Bay Company name and was called after one of their Chief Factors.

Well, that was my second camp. It was no time before the boys had the tents up and everything comfortable, but the mosquitoes were simply unbearable. They beat against the tent like a hailstorm and as for eating supper, we could not do it without swallowing as much mosquitoes as food. It was worse even than Panama, except one could bathe the bites in clean cold water. I was glad when we started the next morning and got out of that miserable place. That day we reached the "Nine Mile," took off the packs and had a grouse lunch. One of the boys went a little off and got a deer. Then we went on again and were at the Similkameen ford by six. We forded the river and in a few minutes were home.

My husband had just finished a new log house—large and comfortable. There was a store attached and Indians came from miles with skins and furs. It was rather a costly affair to build in those days as all lumber had to be cut with a whipsaw and cost seven cents per foot. A man named Fitzgerald did all the sawing for Allison and Hayes. Mr. Allison had the whole building double-floored, sealed and partitioned with lumber—it was expensive. This was by no means the first house in Princeton which, by the way, was two miles from the present city. My husband and his partner had built as soon as Governor Douglas had located the townsite. Also Captain Marsden [Marston], a miner, a man named Young and several others had small cabins on the river bank. In fact there had been a nucleus of a thrifty little town but Cariboo and Rock Creek proved a powerful magnet to draw everyone away. My husband and Mr. Hayes stayed as they had just purchased eighty Durham Shorthorns from a man across the line who was anxious to get out of the cattle business. Mr. Hayes had a good supper ready for us the day I first saw Princeton, though he did not approve my dressing for dinner, a habit I was drilled in as a child and has always stuck with me to some extent. As I did not object to his coming to table in shirt sleeves I did not see why he objected to my habits, but I think he half forgave me when he found I could milk cows and was not afraid to go into a corral full of cattle.

As it was getting near snow-fly when the Hope Mountain was closed and all travel stopped with horses or cattle, my husband could only spend two weeks at home, most of the time seeing to the horses and rounding up the cattle for another trip with beef for the Westminster market, so I was virtually alone. I had a visit from an Indian woman, a niece of Quinisco, the "Bear Hunter" and Chief of the Chu-chu-ewa Tribe. She was dressed for the occasion, of course, in mid-Victorian style, a Balmoral petticoat, red and gray, a man's stiff starched white shirt as a blouse, stiff high collar, earrings an inch long, and brass bracelets! I did not know my visitor seemed to think she ought to sit upright in her chair and fix her eyes on the opposite wall. I think "Cla-hi-ya" was the only word she spoke. I was not used to Indians then and knew very little Chinook. I felt very glad when her visit was over. I know now that I should have offered her a cigar and a cup of tea.

I amused myself the best way I could during the ten days my husband was away. The first thing I did was to hang white curtains in the dining-room windows. Mr. Hayes said they made the room dark, he also did not like a tablecloth and said oilcloth was good enough. I thought he was unreasonable at the time and for as long as I had someone to wash for me, but when I had a lot of children and had to do my own washing I agreed with him oilcloth was good enough.

When I looked around my bedroom I thought it would look better with a toilet table. There was a plain wooden table about three feet long and two wide standing under one of the windows. I thought that would do, so hunted amongst my belongings and found some pink stuff with which I covered the table and over the pink gathered a white muslin skirt and threw a white dimity toilet cover over. This, with a fairly good mirror, made a beautiful toilet table. I also made a large pin-cushion of pink and white and as the room was already nicely papered I hung my pictures on the wall. When my husband returned he was delighted with the changes I had effected.

Then began a busy time. It was now the first of November and the cattle and horses had to be driven to their winter quarters. My husband and his partner had about five hundred head of cattle to move that winter and a big bunch of horses, I don't know how many, I had not yet been introduced to them all. It took three or four busy days to gather them all and start them down the Canyon. Some of them would come back but the older ones just hit the trail and quietly grazed down the river and on to Okanagan, where their winter range was. It was a long journey in those days—but later, instead of going by Penticton and the lake, my husband cut a much shorter trail for his own use by Trout Creek. Of course, it was rough but answered his purpose.

When the bustle had subsided my husband set to work to make us comfortable for the winter, sawing logs that lay on the flat near the house for winter firewood. Then he hunted up what planks were left from house building and old tea boxes from which to make a desk, bureau, rocking chair and other articles of furniture we couldn't bring out. My sister had given me her old piano (the first one to enter B.C.) [*sic*] but as it could not then be packed over the Hope trail I left it with my mother. So we made the most of the few things we could get.

We were soon shut in by snow, our nearest neighbour at the Hudson's Bay Company post at Keremeos, forty miles down the valley. There were no white settlers at Nicola, which place was named for the Great Head Chief, Incola, who claimed jurisdiction over the tribes of the Similkameen, Thompson, Shuswap, Okanagan, and even Kamloops. He died before I came into the country—but his memory was warm in the hearts of all the tribes he governed.

The Indians had gone to their winter quarters, either Nicola or Chu-chu-ewa. I found lots of amusement in making little things to make the house look pretty, and watching my husband carpentering. If he made a chair or couch I would make a covering for it. Then when Christmas came we gathered oregon-grape leaves for holly, and roseberries judiciously sewed in through the leaves looked like the berries. Snow berries took the place of mistletoe and [we] had a jolly little Christmas dinner all to ourselves.

As the weather got colder and the snow deeper my husband began putting out bait for the wild creatures. When the river froze I used to go with him on the ice, where it was easy going. He would take a very small piece of bacon or small lump of lard and put a few grains of strychnine in it, roll it up and put it in a can and off we would go. When we came to what he thought was a good place he would throw the bait some distance off from our trail lest the creatures should smell man on it and avoid it. I have often thought since, how beastly cruel we were. The wild animals then were that and no more to me, but now that I know them and have learned to love them I think and feel altogether differently, but in those days I did enjoy hunting.

One morning my husband went out earlier than usual and came back quickly telling me to hurry and come out with him and see what he had got. He took his hand sleigh, and when about a quarter of a mile from the house, we saw an immense black wolf lying stiff and stark and two more a little distance apart and later on my husband found three more gray wolves belonging to the same pack. The wolves then ran in packs of from ten to twenty. Another time he got a wolverine near the house in an old Indian cache. His tracks led to his hiding place. Wise in his death, poor thing. Coyotes were harder to find. They would run for miles after eating the bait; sometimes they vomited and then ran on as well as ever. We got numerous foxes of all grades, and a few nice fishers. One time a wolverine had been robbing my husband's traps. The fox tracks and tufts of fur indicated that he had stolen many foxes. My husband rose early thinking to get ahead of the robber—to his disgust he found one fourth of a valuable Black Fox left under the "dead fall." This portion he afterwards sold for eighty dollars.

This all was day work; the evening was spent either in good reading or carpentry. The combination desk and cupboard was a work of art—the panels were made of tea-box boards, the rest was rough lumber which we covered by glueing wrapping paper over them to hide the roughness and then varnished the whole affair with the same glue which we had made from cow and deer feet. On the whole the effect was not bad. I had brought many good books out with me. Some of them were from my father's college library so on the whole our time was well spent.

We were most agreeably surprised one day when we heard a knock at the store door and when my husband answered it he found standing there a man from Rock Creek known as "Russian John" with his little dog, Towser, at his heels. He brought them both into the house where I was. John looked well and hearty but poor little Towser was footsore and weary having travelled two or three miles for every one his master had trod. Towser soon made great friends; he too was a Russian. I left the men to talk Rock Creek and Cariboo and went to bed. But next morning Towser was so glad to see me that John who thought the poor little feet would never make Hope gave him to me. I was glad for he would be company when alone. John went on to Hope with his snowshoes.

The next break was Bristol Bill who brought our mail and passed on to Osoyoos and Kootenay. The winter soon passed. About March that year the Chinooks began to blow and the snow melted gradually, leaving green grass all over the range. Then the Indians seemed to awaken from their winter's lethargy and the whole of the Chu-chu-ewa tribe started out, some to the mountains, some to hunt, and some to visit friends at Nicola and Coldwater. Now I got my first good look at the Indians, my husband telling me their names as they passed on horseback. First rode the Chief Quinisco's two brothers, fine looking men dressed in buckskin shirts and leggings of embroidered cloth. One

Plate 1. Susan Moir, born in 1845 at Colombo, Ceylon, spent most of her childhood in London and Aberdeen, Scotland. Her portrait was painted in London before her departure in June 1860 for British Columbia in the company of her mother, her stepfather and her sister, Jane.

Plate 2. Jane Shaw Moir, born in 1843 at "Dhekinde," Ambegamoa, Ceylon, was educated in London. Her portrait was painted there before she sailed with her family to British Columbia. After her marriage to Edgar Dewdney she lived for many years in Ottawa and Regina but returned to British Columbia in 1892 to be the chatelaine of Cary Castle, then the official residence of the lieutenant-governor of the province.

Plate 3. Susan's "floating palace," the Royal Mail Steamship Company's paddle steamer, the *Atrato*, on which Mr. and Mrs. Glennie and the two Moir girls sailed to the West Indies on the first lap of their journey to British Columbia. Their passage was smooth, unlike the scene shown here as the *Atrato* comes to the aid of *Rover's Bride*.

Plate 4. The "floating coffin," the *John L. Stephens*, one of the overcrowded ships on the Pacific Mail Steamship Company's run from Panama to San Francisco. Susan was exhilarated by the furious tropical storm she experienced while travelling on this ship.

Plate 5. Edgar Dewdney, the young English civil engineer whom Susan and Jane met on board the river steamer carrying them to Hope. He was just beginning in 1860 to make his name as a trail-maker and road-builder. After his marriage, Dewdney became prominent in political affairs. He was appointed Indian Commissioner for Manitoba and the North-West Territories in 1879, and lieutenant-governor of the North-West Territories in 1881. Later he served in the federal cabinet as minister of the interior and superintendent of Indian affairs. In 1892 he was appointed lieutenant-governor of British Columbia. A kindly man who had no children of his own, he was generous to his own and to Jane's nieces and nephews.

Plate 6. From the deck of a Fraser River steamer, Susan on 15 August 1860 caught this view of Fort Hope, the townsite of Hope, and the Indian salmon cache. At Hope, her family found accommodation first in the fort and then in a rented light timber frame house, so airy that "the high Hope winds almost raised the roof."

Plate 7. Susan's first home in British Columbia. Soon after a log house was completed for her step-father, this painting was done by Edgar Dewdney who was already courting Jane Moir. "Hopelands" was situated two miles east from Hope on the Hudson's Bay Company's Brigade Trail to the Interior. Glennie's wilderness home stood on the north bank of the Coquihalla River.

Plate 8. The "pretty little church," designed by Captain J. M. Grant of the Royal Engineers, built in 1861 and consecrated on the first of November by Bishop George Hills. Here on 23 March 1864 Jane Shaw Moir was married to Edgar Dewdney. Christ Church is the oldest Protestant church on the mainland of British Columbia still standing on its original site.

Plate 9. John Fall Allison, English born and American educated, who mined for gold in California, Fraser River, and Similkameen River, explored the Cascade Mountains for trails, found copper and coal in the Similkameen Valley, and became the pioneer cattle rancher in that region of British Columbia. He was photographed about the time of his marriage to Susan Moir.

Plate 10. Susan was photographed in New Westminster in 1867. Probably it was a copy of this photograph that John Fall Allison had sent to his mother in Oriskany, New York, to break the news to her that he had taken a wife in September 1868.

Plate 11. Sunnyside, Mrs. Allison's Okanagan Valley home from 1873 until 1881, where she lived a "perfectly ideal life." This log house, located at what is now Westbank, was the first European habitation to be built on the west side of Okanagan Lake.

Plate 12. Granite Creek, only twelve miles from "Allison's," was the scene of a gold rush in 1885 that drew miners from Cariboo. In the aftermath of the rush a residue of miners and professional men settled in the Similkameen Valley. The rush marked the end of the pioneering period.

Plate 13. "The sweetest, most generous lady in the upper country," Mina Wade came from Ireland in 1872 after her marriage to her sweetheart, Thomas Ellis, who had left Ireland originally in 1865. Ellis was the pioneer settler and stock rancher at Penticton. After 1895 when he absorbed into his holdings the land belonging to the Haynes Estate, he was known as "The Cattle King of the Okanagan Valley." While Mrs. Allison was residing at Sunnyside, she considered Mrs. Ellis, who lived some thirty miles to the south, to be a close neighbour.

Plate 14. Visitors at "Allison's" were rare, but a number of them were distinguished men. In August 1883 General William Tecumseh Sherman, of Civil War fame, called on Mrs. Allison while making an inspection of American military posts south of the border. The General was entertained when Mrs. Allison yielded to his insistence that she parade her small children in their nightshirts and was impressed by her son, seven-year-old Jack (John Stratton), who not only rode the General's horse but raced to deliver "despatches." The sword that Sherman presented to the boy is now in the possession of Mrs. Dougal MacGregor, Summerland.

Plate 15. "Colonel" Robert Stevenson, a Canadian who joined an American military expedition to mine at Rock Creek in 1860 and who, when Susan Moir first met him in 1861 at a picnic near Hope, "could do nothing but talk of Cariboo." After spending many years mining in Cariboo, Stevenson turned his attention in the 1890's to the coal lands and the copper deposits in the Princeton area. He was part-owner of the "Sunset Mine," one of the best copper claims on Copper Mountain.

Plate 16. A Similkameen Indian, one of Mrs. Allison's neighbours at her first home in the Similkameen Valley.

Plate 17. An Indian statue presented as a gift to Mrs. Allison by her Similkameen Indian friends.

Plate 18. "Our kind neighbour" at Keremeos, forty-five miles distant from "Allison's." Barrington Price, an Englishman, pre-empted land at Keremeos in 1873, founded a cattle ranch and operated a grist mill which was built in 1877. Mrs. Allison found him and his English partner Henry Nicholson "very nice gentlemen with a strong taste for brandy." She was grateful when in 1882, after the fire which destroyed her home and all her possessions, Price brought her flour and other provisions.

Plate 19. John Carmichael Haynes, posted as collector at the Osoyoos Customs House in the 1860's, was a "near neighbour" of Allison. A young Irishman who came to British Columbia in 1858, Haynes entered government service. He had many duties, the most important of which were as customs and revenue collector at Osoyoos in the southern Okanagan Valley and as justice of the peace for the Osoyoos and Kootenay districts. The pioneer settler at Osoyoos, he accumulated twenty-two thousand acres of land for a cattle and a horse ranch. In 1888, after being taken ill on the Hope Trail, he died at "Allison's."

Plate 20. Cattle belonging to "Judge" Haynes being rounded up on the bunch grass covered hills of the southern Okanagan Valley for the drive over the Hope Trail. Allison's cattle in summer roamed an area in the Similkameen and Nicola valleys of a similar character. For wintering they were driven to Sunnyside on Okanagan Lake where there were natural hay meadows.

Plate 21. Within four years of the flood in which the Allisons lost their home and fourteen farm buildings, and within a year of Allison's death, a town had emerged near the forks of the Similkameen River across the river from "Allison's." The townsite, promoted by the Waterman brothers, bore the name that Governor James Douglas had chosen in 1860 for a proposed townsite.

Plate 22. Mrs. Allison, aged forty-eight, with eight of the youngest of her fourteen children. This snapshot, now faded, was taken at her home near Princeton by S. D. Sandes, who married her daughter Rose in 1898. Rose, mounted on the horse, is holding Mrs. Allison's last child, Alice Olivia Ashwick (later Perkins, then Wright).

Plate 23. The Allison's third house on the Similkameen River. Though they sawed the house in half in an effort to save it from the disastrous flood of June 1894, the Allisons lost it as well as thirteen other farm buildings and were forced to make their home in the stable.

of these men like Quinisco was a great hunter and utterly fearless. His name was Tatlehasket (the man who stands high), the other [was] Incowmasket—he was supposed to be the peacemaker of the tribe. And then came a lot of young men like Cockshist and Johnny Suzanne, all these were armed with rifles (old style), then two or three more of the Chief's brothers and their sons, last of all the women, children and boys such as Tuc-tac. Very last rode Quinisco himself with Topes and Whylac.

They crossed the ford, then camped across the river.

At the time I am writing of the tribe living at Chu-chu-ewa were under Quinisco, as the Bear Hunter, and numbered nearly two hundred (today I doubt if they number ten). Quinisco gained his name as a hunter from the courageous way he hunted and attacked grizzly bears—he would go out quite alone, armed only with his knife and follow them up until they stood at bay. Then, without waiting for them to charge, he would rush on them and plunge his knife into them while they were hugging him. That is how his brother, Shla-wha-lak-an, described his method.

The women of the tribe wore a garment something like the ladies wear today, cut like a Victoria chemise, and the foot of the garment which reached below the knee, cut in tags and fringes. This dress gave them a certain dignity and grace that was absent when they tried to dress like white women. The women were not as friendly as the children—the children flocked around and I got lots of help with my housework from them.

On washing day one or two boys would come and get the water, fill the tubs and scrub on the washboard. If they took a fancy to any garment such as my stockings they would wring them out and bring them to me and ask for them. If I gave them, they would draw them on wet and wear them home triumphantly. These little fellows learned to clean knives, polish stoves, and were a great help and amusement. I missed them when they went away—there was no keeping them, they were like wild birds.

As the summer advanced the pack-trains came and went as usual from Colville, Kootenais, Osoyoos, and Keremeos. One noon on the third of July Mr. Tait rode in from Hope where he had breakfasted and asked my husband to lend him a horse to ride on to Keremeos to the Hudson's Bay post there—laughing and saying "Breakfast at Hope, lunch at Princeton, and supper at Keremeos—not a bad ride for one day."

I thought that I would hurry lunch for him and picking up an empty water bucket I ran down the bank to the river and back again, put on the tea kettle and soon had lunch ready. But as soon as Mr. Tait left I was all doubled up with pain—I did not know what to do. I called my husband and he came with the only two medicines we possessed, Castor Oil and pain killer. I swallowed both and then exhausted by the pain fell asleep only to wake again worse than ever. My husband, alarmed, left me and ran to the Indian ranch returning with one of Quinisco's sisters, Suzanne (the mother of Johnny), afterwards married to Tom Cole, so we will call her Madame Cole. She smoothed up my bed and suggested "whiskey" which I swallowed. I think I would have swallowed anything to get rid of the pain. About nine o'clock next day my baby was born two months too soon, the first white child born in the Similkameen Valley. I had intended going to Hope for the event but Mr. Tait's wonderful ride stopped that for at least a month. It really was a wonderful ride, over a hundred miles of mountain road in one day.

Suzanne was very good to me in her way—though I thought her rather unfeeling at the time. She thought that I ought to be as strong as an Indian woman but I was not.

It was about this time I first really became acquainted with the girls. They came to see the baby. There was Lily, Yacumtecum's niece, Sibyllakim, Cosotasket's girl, Marie, and a host of others. I tried to keep Lily with me to look after the baby, but in a few days she wearied and so went back to her people. Suzanne was a perfect treasure and so was her boy, Hosachtem, and I always feel grateful when I think of the kindness I received from them—they have passed away long ago.

As my husband had business in Westminster that August I thought I would take the trip with him. The baby was now a month old and I got one of the women to make me a birchbark basket to pack him in. It was a very comfortable little nest and my husband said he would carry it himself. As we needed only take one pack horse with a tent and food for three days we thought we could make the journey without help. We were told that there were fires on the road when we started. My husband thought the fires might not be bad though the air was full of smoke. When we made the "Nine Miles" it grew unpleasantly thick. As we neared Powder Camp we found the trees were blazing on both sides of us. My husband handed me the baby to carry and went on leading the pack horse. Poor pony he did not like the fire and had to be dragged along the road. My husband wanted to turn back but I, not knowing what was ahead, said "go on" and we pushed on until it became clearer. Near Skagit we met a man on horseback who stopped to speak to us. He said "turn back while you can, no one can get through that fire, the Skagit is boiling." But as the smoke and fire behind us looked far worse, we told him we would try it, and that he had better hurry if he wanted to get through. So we parted. He had not exaggerated. When we got to the Skagit we found the timber on both sides of the creek (which here is smaller) on fire. The rocks were red hot and the water was boiling or at any rate it seemed like it. We dared not stop but hurried on thinking to get out of it. When we reached the Cedars Pony and the other two horses had to be blinded. The whole forest seemed to be on fire [and] the heat was almost unbearable. The smoke was suffocating and we kept a blanket wrapped around little Edgar's basket. To add to our misery a huge cedar crashed across the trail. I held the three horses and baby while my husband tore the bark from some of the cedars lying near and made a bridge on to the top of the cedar, over one side and down on the other, then led Nelly and Pony over this bridge with the third horse. The bridge caught fire and his leg was badly burned, but we did get over, and a little farther we got beyond the fire. We were afraid to camp but too exhausted to go farther that night. We left our dangerous camp early next morning and reached Lake House where we camped and took our ease and rested till next day.

My mother was getting quite alarmed about us when we arrived at the old parsonage. There was no one able to get through to the Similkameen for days.

Hope seemed the same as usual, if anything quieter. I visited my mother for a month or six weeks during which time the trail had been cut out and fallen timbers cut away. The Indian boys brought in our pack-train and as the freight had arrived by boat from Westminster we started back home again.

Now began a busy time. My husband had sold a bunch of steers for the Westminster market and had to collect them and after driving them over the mountains ship them on the old *Reliance* to Westminster. Then he returned to get in our winter wood and coal. The coal he dug out of a hole he had made in the bank across the river where he used to put it in sacks and pack it through the river in that way. He said he had burned coal since '59 [1860] and that he had taken samples of it to Governor Douglas, who said that in England, when tested, it was pronounced a remarkably good quality of lignite but not worth anything for commercial purposes. Perhaps not then, there was no Vancouver and little or no shipping. However, Mr. W. Waterman discovered this same coal in the later '90's and made a mine of it.

At the end of October Sebastian Lotario came down from Roche River with a nice little bag of gold dust (the first I had seen). The old man was making for the coast where he said he would buy a sloop and trade with the Northern Indians. He said that he had a bank on the Roche that he drew from whenever he was broke and got a good start every time. He would hold Edgar and was so pleased when the baby smiled.

I did not dread the coming of winter though now the baby tied me to the house for he was a great amusement and I had dear little Towser and Lily who said she would stay the winter. Towser was a wonderful little dog. He would fetch and carry slippers and when the baby cried Towser would rush off to comfort him the moment he heard the cry—and the crying would cease. I wondered how Towser managed to quiet the baby and watched to see. This is what I saw—Towser's tail wagging while with nose and paw he rocked the cradle!! Whether he learned it from his former master I can't say but I know that is what he did. The winter passed much as the former one had except that I kept plenty of medicine on hand, and had more work to do. We had a jolly little Christmas as before. Shortly after Christmas some of Lily's people came and she bawled to go with them, so she went. Then we had a visit from Cosotasket—Medicine Man and Hunter—he and one of his wives were going to hunt and set traps. My husband had gone to look after his baits at the time and told me to keep Towser from following him. He was with me in the house when Cosotasket unfortunately left the kitchen door open and little Towser followed Mr. Allison's tracks and got some of the bait and died. I did miss poor little Towser and so did Edgar who had grown attached to him.

I think it was in '69 that Mr. Ellis bought cattle to stock his ranch at Penticton. He, too, got them across the Line. Mr. Haynes had a bunch of thoroughbred horses but for some reason they did not do as well as he had expected, and he and Mr. W. Lowe went into cattle. Just common stock. He said a steer was a steer but he found out later that the breed made a difference in value and weight. Joe McKay came through on business of some kind. I think he was then Indian Agent, but I am not sure. We were always glad to see him, he was such a well informed man and always posted in the latest events. It was like getting a magazine or newspaper, and what he said was always reliable. There was a Chinaman mining on the river—I think he did very well though he said he only made two bittie a day. There was a Scotsman, William McKillop, he was between Vermilion Forks and Roche River.

I had an old school atlas of my father's in which the Similkameen River was marked, also Roche River only there it was called Rogue's River. Perhaps it was made from some of old Hudson's Bay Company maps. I never thought to ask Mr. Joe McKay.

Frank Richter sometimes passed with his pack train and also Mr. Theodore Kruger.

In those early days we were well off during the summer—we could always send our pack-trains over the Hope Mountains for groceries or anything we needed. The Similkameen River and its tributaries gave us trout, Dolly Vardens and Greyling in abundance. We had heavy crops of Saskatoons, raspberries, strawberries, huckleberries, in their season. Wild roots and vegetables for those who knew enough to gather them, and for those that desired meat there was deer, bear, grouse, wild chicken and ptarmigan. In short, the place was then what Phillips Wooley [Phillipps-Wolley] afterwards named it, "A Sportsman's Eden." But if we neglected to get all we required we might feel the pinch of want. Perhaps our flour, sugar, or salt would give out—just try bread or fish or vegetables without salt and you will understand. It was nothing to do without sugar. This winter was nearly the same as the last and then began the eventful Seventies.

Some Recollections of A Pioneer of the Seventies

I remember the winter of '69-'70 was very pleasant and the end of February the soft south wind began to blow and melt the snow on the flats and the "Big Hill." The ice on the river was rotten, water running over it, and a channel opened up in the middle. We used to sit on the veranda and enjoy the sunshine and warmth. Some Indians had wandered up from Chu-chu-ewa and were camped on the flat. On the night of March first the wind veered to northward and the thermometer fell till we had forty below zero. In the morning we found long icicles hanging over the windows and from the roof and felt the cold all day long, but the fires blazed in the outer kitchen where we had both a fireplace and cooking stove, and in the big fireplace in the dining-room. My room was always warm with a cheerful fire in the stove. We passed the coldest day in comfort.

But next morning we were surprised to see smoke under a tree at the other side of the river. Then we saw an Indian lead a horse down to the water's edge and cross the slush ice returning almost immediately carrying another Indian and a pack. They did not stop at their camp but came straight directly to the house. It was Poo-la-lee, our Indian mail carrier, with the soles of both feet frozen. He had struggled on till he came to the river and had refused to cross unless the mail came too. Mr. Allison took him in and we gave up the kitchen to him and his friend who doctored his poor feet. This was done by applying red hot coal to the soles of his feet. What he must have suffered and without a moan, but we broke the law and gave him two or three good drinks of whiskey. The faithful old man insisted on going into Keremeos the next day with his mail. He had agreed to make Osoyoos at a certain time. When he left I went into the kitchen to clean it up after the doctoring and I found in the fireplace two leather soles—yes, soles of human flesh—that after the burning were cut from Poo-la-lee's feet!! But though seemingly cruel the treatment was effective, for the Indian did not seem any the worse the next time I saw him.

About the middle of the month Cosotasket came from the mountains with a quantity of furs—my husband said he had at least five hundred dollars' worth. Some he traded with him, the rest he hung in a tree till he felt like going to the Hudson's Bay Company post at Keremeos. Cosotasket said that that year he only had a few martens as his favourite trapping ground at the Skagit was spoiled by the fire. The martens always climbed up into the trees to escape and perished instead. Cosotasket at that time lived mostly in the mountains and was known among the tribesmen as the Mountain Chief.

In his spare time that spring, my husband split pickets for fencing a garden as we had brought our raspberries, currants, asparagus, artichokes, and gooseberries in the fall and kept them in the cellar buried in sand. They were in fine trim for planting. Then he made a large "under shot" water-wheel like the Chinamen used in mining with coal oil cans nailed on the flanges—primitive but effective. This was to irrigate the garden.

Mr. Hayes, my husband's partner, brought the cattle back from the Okanagan and in May my husband went to Penticton to trade some animals with Mr. Ellis, which he drove back with him on his return, also half a ton of flour made by Manuel Barcelo in a very primitive mill like a huge coffee mill, and then screened through several sieves. It was not very nice but very wholesome.

I was rather put out about help that year as both Johnny Suzanne and Yacumtecum or Tuc-tac thought that they were too old for housework. Then a boy of Tatlehasket's came from Kamloops where he had been at the Rev. Good's Mission. He was warranted to be capable of doing any kind of housework and, indeed, I found him all that could be wished for. I could depend on him for everything. He was kind and gentle—at least I thought so. My garden grew well. It seemed an ideal spot for small fruits—of course, I had no berries that year but the bushes could not have done better.

One of the Indians camped near the house was very sick and called in a doctor. They promptly made the night hideous with a tomtom and chanting, varied by yells and shouts. I was dying with curiosity to see what was going on, so when it got dark enough to hide me from sight I crawled out and, screened by a log fence, watched the proceedings. In the centre of the camp there was a blazing fire, and a little distance from the fire lay the sick one. With a mat separating her from her patient stood the doctor—a very powerful one, I had been told. She sang and swayed from side to side without changing her place, making gestures with her hands, filling her mouth with water which an assistant passed to her, and spitting. She seemed to get very excited and hot but I got cold and cramped watching and went into the house. I was told that she had removed a snake from the body of her patient and the patient was expected to recover. I saw the woman after in our store—such a nice looking, pretty woman. I could hardly believe it was the frenzied creature I had watched in the night. I told one of the young women that I had watched and she said I ought to have come over and sat with the others.

This year I first made acquaintance with Ashnola John, or, as he was better known in Westminster, Captain John. My husband possessed a treasure. A Henry rifle was then considered the last word about guns, and as a marked favour he lent it to some of his Indian friends. John had borrowed it to hunt and when he came to the store to return it, [he] brought a haunch of venison. I foolishly asked him how much he wanted for it. I did not know gun etiquette demanded a haunch for the use of the gun. John asked a big price and I told him to keep it. Then began an argument that got somewhat heated. He wanted me to take the meat but pay twice its value. Then he roared at me, stamped his foot, pounded with his fists on the counter. I was so astonished that at first I did not know what to do—then I remembered that to give him a dose of his own medicine might help, so I roared at him and stamped my foot and pounded the counter. John was as astonished as I had been—he stood back, looked at me and burst out laughing. "Take the meat," he said, "we are friends. Allison is my friend and you are my friend." Ever after we were the best of friends. I used to write his business letters for him for many years and one still lives in my memory. It was to Mr. Vowell (I think). John said to tell the Governor that there was an insect or bug infecting the trees and if they did not fell the infected ones and burn them now, soon there would be no trees left. It had happened before, the old Indians said their fathers said. The answer was that the trees were alright and would last our time. What money would have been saved by the appointment of an inspector! Though Governor Douglas, who understood the Indian character, made due allowances for John's behaviour the present government looked on him with suspicion. He on one occasion took a prisoner out of Judge Haynes' Court while in session, not through any cowardice on the part of Mr. Haynes, but be it remembered that the white settlers were in the minority in those days and the Indians, who then could be numbered by the hundreds, could have done in a sparsely settled district the same as those across the Line. All honour to those in authority that they knew enough to keep the peace.

Another Indian friend I made was Shla-wha-la-kan, a very old man who brought his father, Tam-tu-sa-list, to visit me. This man had been a great chief and warrior, the father of the tribe. Now he walked on all fours just like a child seated, his elbows on the ground—he could just enjoy the sunshine and smoking tobacco. Joe McKay told me that this man was known to be one hundred and twenty-five years old from Hudson's Bay Company records but really was older.

That summer my sister came out for a short visit and I used to send Hosachtem with her for a guide. One day he stood in front of her on a narrow trail and asked her for her boots—a pair of nice, strong Balmorals, and held her up till she promised to leave them with me for him when she returned to Hope. She was so amused with the little incident that she always remembered it and left substantial tokens for Hosachtem.

My husband had sold some cattle for the Westminster market that had to be delivered about the middle of October and as he thought that a ride behind a drove of cattle would be too tiring for me he said that when he returned from the last drive we could hire two Indians and a small pack train so that I could have a comfortable camp. It was, therefore, the 28th of October when we started for Hope, I carrying the baby in his birchbark basket. We got on nicely and, in fact had an enjoyable time, till we started to leave Powder Camp—then it began to snow. There was already from one foot to two feet on the trail. The snow as we neared the Zig-Zag grew dense and a cold wind sprang up. My husband took a blanket and cutting a hole in the middle made me poke my head through. It made a very splendid covering for both the baby and self but it was as nothing more than a pad on the horse. I could not guide her so had to trust to her horse sense. By this time I could not see the horse ahead for the swirling snow. My husband had a bottle of whiskey from which he made me take a sip now and then, though he would not touch a drop himself. He said it was the worst thing a man could do under the circumstances. We arrived in Hope on the first of November and the Indians returned with packs and animals.

My mother was still keeping her little school at the parsonage, but had lots of room for us. I had taken Lily along to look after the baby so she went to school that winter—my mother had all kinds of pupils. Some of them afterwards made good citizens. We were very cosy at the parsonage and Hope seemed warm after the cold snowy mountains.

We found Hope very quiet—even dull. The Hudson's Bay Company post now consisted of a store run by Mr. Yates, just kept going for the benefit of their pack-trains coming in from the Upper Country. There was not even a preacher once a month, nor was there a constable or doctor. John Wirth was still there in his business, and Wing, the Chinaman, still had a laundry and small store. George Landvoight's store was now in charge of Jim Wardle.

I saw my old friend, Mrs. Landvoight, again. It was not long after this that George Landvoight met his death. One morning he went to the sawmill. Then, as he was coming across a saw-pit on a narrow plank, he slipped and fell about six feet. He picked himself up, walked home, ate lunch, and said he felt sleepy, and lay down and slept and slept, till his wife, alarmed, sent for a doctor from Yale, the nearest to be got, who examined the patient and found that a nail had pierced his skull and entered his brain. He never woke, but he now lies in the little Hope graveyard.

In January '72 my little Wilfrid was born, but in April I caught such a bad cold I had to wean my boy.

As soon as we heard that Mr. Hayes had brought the cattle back from their winter quarters on the Okanagan Lake, my husband crossed the Hope Mountains to meet him and take charge as Mr. Hayes wanted to visit his people in Maine. But first he built a cabin in which he deposited all his belongings and an Indian lady named Augusta [cared for them]. Then he departed to the land of his childhood (if he ever was a child). It was agreed that on his way back he should visit Colonel Younger and purchase one of the thoroughbred Shorthorn Durham bulls.

My cold got much worse and my husband thought that if I could get back to the dry country it would soon get better. So at the end of May, though the snow was still on the road, he brought over a few pack and saddle horses for the journey.

I was anxious to get the children home again before the weather got too hot, so bidding goodbye to my friends at Hope, we started out carrying the baby in front of me. I have lived much in the mountains but I think there is no time so lovely and wonderful as the spring. The snow melts in patches and at the edge of these patches flowers spring up in full bloom—white, yellow, blue, and sweet smelling. I am no botanist so I cannot name them but it is well worth all the discomfort of a snowy trip to see them. We camped in just such a spot on the Summit. The mosquitoes did not mind the snow but seemed to swarm over it. We had picked a spot that was almost dry for our tent, but streams from the melting snow ran all round us. In the morning our shoelaces were all gone, our clothing scattered, stockings in shreds—the bushtail rats had been busy. I lost a gold pencil and a small pearl brooch. Still, the wonder of the flowers compensated for all. It made me think and wonder why those flowers were there. We got home alright and I got rid of my cold and the boys throve.

In July my husband had a letter from his partner to say he would return in a few weeks. In the midst of broiling weather he did return, saying he had got the finest bull he ever saw from Colonel Younger on the condition that he would take it away from California at once, and as it had appeared to give out with the heat he had left it at their camp on Nine Mile Creek—that he had made a record drive. Not long after an Indian came galloping up to say the bull was dead. Mr. Hayes and my husband got their horses and went to see—it was true, the bull was dead, driven to death over a mountain road in the heat. In an hour or so my husband returned, called me, and asked me how much money we had. I counted our all—just fourteen hundred dollars. "Give it to me," he said. "I am going to California for another." And he did at once. That was the spirit of the pioneer.

In due time Red Oak arrived from California and my husband drove him over the Hope Mountain but let him take his own time to travel. Red Oak left his mark on the Princeton and Chilliwack stock for many years. Colonel Younger, who bred him, was a Kentucky gentleman who was trying to retrieve war losses in California. At the time my husband went for Red Oak, the poor old gentleman was in great trouble about his son, Coleman, who was "wanted" by the U.S.A. as he was supposed to have been out with Jesse James. The poor old Colonel, when the civil war was over had, hoping for peace and quiet, gathered up his cattle and horses from the Blue Grass Hills and driven over to the California mountains.

That winter we rented the Hudson's Bay Company house at Keremeos from Mr. Lowe who had rented the Hudson's Bay Company farm and house from the Chief Factor, McLean. Mr. Lowe had a speculation in pigs—there you could not turn your toe without encountering pigs. Tom Cole and Mrs. Cole were to feed them all winter so I had my good neighbour, Mrs. Cole, to help me, and she was lots of amusement too. My first daughter, Beatrice, was born in the Hudson's Bay Company house that February, 1873. The Hudson's Bay Company house at Keremeos was just built and fairly comfortable—a nice large fireplace and big living room, two bedrooms and a kitchen. Mr. Lowe came nearly every weekend to see how his speculation came on and we had occasional calls from Manuel Barcelo and Frank Richter whose smoke we could see every day though trees and brush hid their houses.

The Keremeos Indians were friendly though some of them had a hard name. There was one I found most gentlemanly and kind helping me to bring in a runaway cow. After the cow was secured I asked him in to have a cup of tea. He wiped his feet before he came in, drank his tea, said "Thank you" and left. Just as he was leaving my husband rode up, hurried into the house and asked "Why did you ask that man into the house?" I answered "Why not?" "That was the notorious Palootken." Then he told me that Palootken had been told to bring in the chief's runaway wife, alive, and the man she had eloped with alive or dead. So he killed the man, smeared himself all over with the blood of his victim, tied the woman up, put her on his horse and took her back to the chief, explaining that he could not carry both woman and man on his horse—"See, here is his blood," he said. I asked my husband why he was allowed to go free. He said that it was done across the Line and there was no extradition treaty—the Indian he had killed was considered too bad to bother about.

That summer I again visited my mother at Hope but as I had three small children with me it was no picnic. While in Hope I met the sweetest, most gracious lady that ever lived in the upper country—Mrs. Ellis. She had just come out a bride from Ireland. To me, after seeing no one but Indians, she looked lovely. Mrs. Ellis was so pleased with my little Bea. Shortly after this Mrs. Ellis took her first trip over the Hope Mountains to Penticton which was to be her home for so many years, and where all who knew her soon learned to love and respect her.

When I returned to Similkameen I found little change except that my friend, Dr. Cosotasket, had traded wives with Dr. Scuse and as all parties were agreeable it was alright from their point of view. Cockshist had eloped with a Thompson River woman, very good looking as most Thompson River women were. There were still a few scattered miners. John and William McKillop made rather good stakes up the South Fork of the Similkameen. Mrs. Landvoight had given me a recipe for soap and, as we had a barrel or two of butter we could not use or sell, I turned it into soap which we could use a lot of.

The Indian women used to gather and dry Saskatoons, so I did the same and when they brought me trout which they caught by the hundreds in baskets they set in the One Mile Creek, I paid for them with butter and then dried and smoked the trout, making delicious kippers for winter.

As I had now three children I found travelling with them rather nerve wracking and refused to take any more trips into Hope.

I had lots of fun watching Indian debates and doctors from my log at the fence—if I had known what most of the debates were about I might not have been quite so amused. There was great unrest stirring across the Line and some were kinsmen of Quinisco, the late chief, and his brother, Incowmasket, the present one. Incowmasket had a loving memory of Governor Douglas and a great respect for the powers that be so kept his people from too open sympathy. And indeed the

Indians on our side of the Line had in those days little to complain of for the few whites there were in the country treated them honestly and fairly. Well, I watched the doctors and came to the conclusion that they used a force or power that we know little or nothing of. You may call it animal magnetism, telepathy, or give it any name, but it was something very real.

I am afraid I have been mooning over my memories. I put in a good time one way and another in the early 70's.

In October '73 my husband asked me how I would like to go to the Okanagan and take charge of Red Oak and fifty of our best thoroughbreds. He himself would be there all winter and would cut a very short trail over to the Similkameen so he could continue his fortnightly drives to Hope through the summer. He would, he said, build me a good house and make everything comfortable. I loved adventure, so in spite of my growing family, I agreed to his plan and never have I repented my decision. My husband arranged with Johnny McDougal to build a house for us. Johnny always cut our hay in a natural meadow, also oat hay which he planted for us.

In November we started out on the journey. First went the cattle, Mr. Hayes and his packs and outfit. Then the pack train with winter stores and my belongings, then myself and Marie who carried one of the children. I carried two—one in front, and the other tied on at my back. My husband rode first with one outfit then the other and relieved me when he could of one of the little ones.

We had a jolly time in spite of the bad roads and went rather a roundabout way by Dog Lake. I wanted to call at the Ellis's place but as it was not in the immediate road I could not, but I can't but remember the trail around Dog Lake. It was round a cliff—such a narrow ledge the horses with the packs could barely make it. My husband told me to trust to my horse and not to try to guide him, and this I did. In one place where the cattle had broken down the trail one could see down a dreadful abyss into the lake. I was afraid, but the Indians did not seem to be and the horses took it in their stride. I had learned that even if you are terrified it is best not to show it, then you get the credit for being fearless—I certainly was not.

Our evening camp (at Trout Creek) made up for all—there were two camp fires, one for Hayes and his outfit and ours. Yacumtecum was cook. Yacumtecum told yarns about the Big Men who live in these mountains and the creature now known as Ogopogo. The Indians did not call him that but spoke as if it were some supernatural entity and pointed out where it lived on an island in Okanagan Lake as we passed the spot. My husband always laughed at Indian yarns but I did not, for I thought there must be some foundation for what they said. They told me more than they told most white people. As we passed they showed me pods of the Indian hemp and the red berries of the Rattle Snake weed. They told me rattlesnake yarns galore, and how one time Mr. Lowe was bitten in the heel by one. He pulled off his boot, pulled out his pocket knife and slashed off the bitten portion—he had a nasty cut, no more.

When I first sighted the beautiful Okanagan Lake it was in a dead calm. The distant mountains were reflected in its mysterious depths—a deep silence prevailed. The Indians, unused to vast water stretches, ceased their merry talk and gazed at the blue waters with awe—there was not a cloud in the sky—no sign of life, save a few late swans. There was frost in the air. We rode silently through wild rye grass that was up to our shoulders on horseback, then we came out on our meadow at the harbour. I believe it was the only natural one on the lake.

The cattle seemed to be perfectly at home. Mr. Hayes turned his pack horse up the hill to his cabin, but we continued along the mountain slope till we found McDougal. From him we heard that the hay crop was satisfactory but that our house would not be finished for a month. So my husband and the Indians hunted about for a nice spot to put up tents. They helped me down from my horse, then released the children, made a fire, got water from a long way off and left us to look after ourselves while they hurried getting camp comfortable for the night. I left the children in Lily's charge and had a good wash up and, by the time I had made the children clean and comfortable tents were up and supper ready. We invited McDougal to share our supper but he said that he had terrapin cooked for himself and would not miss the feast.

We had a merry supper and when it was over McDougal joined us, expatiated on the delights of terrapin stew, and gave us the general news, which might have been true or not—it was very amusing. After putting the children to bed I joined the story tellers. Lily played with Cockshist and Yacumtecum. Saul, the Chief, came up for a chat and was properly introduced. They told hunting yarns. One I remember was of Forbes Vernon, for whom the city of Vernon was named, who had joined a party of government hunters, and in the heat of the pursuit had climbed a steep, dangerous cliff from which he fell on his head. When they reached the spot they thought him dead. The chief said not to move him but to bring a tent and blankets and they would try to bring him round. His skull was smashed but it might be healed if they only let him lie, so they put up a tent over him and put hot milk in his mouth. The next day he opened his eyes. They fed him but would not let him move for a month. Then they packed him on a rawhide home to his place and now he was well.

Johnny had some tobacco he had grown from seed the priests had given him and he had grown, cured and fixed it up himself. The talk turned on the Monster (Ogopogo). Johnny wanted to bring a team across the lake to assist haying so he drove them to the Narrows where he often crossed the horses he used hunting, but he had always taken a chicken or little pig and dropped it into the lake when they neared the middle. This time he forgot the chicken and was towing the horses by a long rope. Suddenly something, he couldn't see what, dragged the horses down underwater and the canoe he was in would have gone too had he not severed the rope with his sheath knife and hurried across. He never saw any vestige of his team again. These stories had a strange charm for me. I could have sat up all night and listened to them but the air was getting cold so I turned in and slept the sleep of the just, having first been promised a visit from the Chief's wife and Theresa [Thérèse], both ladies of high standing and near of kin to Chapeau Blanc, the Penticton Chief.

The Indians told that the Indian name for the Mission was Ne-hawk-a-sin and that the priests were good men and had taught them many things besides religion.

When I first went there in '73, the Mission was in charge of Father Pandosy and Father Richard. They had a fine orchard and garden and kept cattle, chickens, ducks and geese. That reminds me of a kindly visit I had in the spring from Brother Surel who brought Edgar the largest goose egg I ever saw. Edgar promptly asked if Brother Surel was called the lay brother because he laid large eggs. The priests were kindly neighbours and I am sure it was to them that I owed the good-will of the Indians. The Mission had been established since 1859 or 1860. These good, kind men were the only connecting link we had with the church (of any kind) except for one visit from Bishop and Mrs. Silletoe [Sillitoe], which I certainly appreciated and enjoyed, but that was some years later.

The Mission was close to Eli Lequime's trading post on the left bank of the lake. Mr. Eli was mother, nurse, and doctor to all sick and afflicted people, and their house was open to all. Mrs. Eli at this time had three children. She worked all day long and never seemed to tire. Her marriage with Eli, I am told, was very romantic. She first met Eli at a dance given by a mutual friend in Sacramento, California. It was a case of love at first sight. They were both from France and he proposed to her at once. Next day they were married and started off for B.C. to seek their fortune. They were well mated and fine people to make good colonists.

Near them Cyprian Lawrence [*sic*] lived with his wife, Thérèse—the niece of Chapeau Blanc. Fred Brent had a flour mill, the first established in the district (in '71). The Christian Bros., one of whom was married at that time and Bushrey [Boucherie]. These were our nearest neighbours, but the lake was between us and [there were] only one or two small boats on the whole lake. The Vernons were at [the] head of [the] lake at Coldstream and the Ellis' at the foot of the lake at Penticton, forty-five miles each way, so we had not many visitors.

In January '74 Louisa was born. I had now four children and had lots of work to keep me busy—I never had a dull moment. We had moved into our new home in December, on Christmas Eve. It was very warm and comfortable. The only drawback was water—the cooking and drinking water my husband packed from a distance. The washing water had to be melted snow and it was hard work to melt enough. My husband said that he would bring down a stream from the mountains which he afterwards did. Eli sent me over a fine dog, half Mastiff and half Bull dog, which he said I really needed. We called her "Guard" and that she really was. Once we were awakened at night by her barking. Mr. Allison looked out but could see nothing, but in the morning he found an unfortunate man clinging to the picket fence. He said it was the only place the dog would allow him to go. Another time I had hired a dumb man (afterwards known as "Dumby") to help me with the cows. I told him to come early in the morning and if he called at the house I would go with him to the corral and help with the cows. Five o'clock came, six o'clock came and still no Dumby. I could hear the cows and calves at the corral, cows outside and calves in the chute. It was time for me to do something. So I took the pails, went toward the corral and found Dumby prone on the ground with Guard sitting on top of him! The poor boy had been there for some time and could not cry out and make himself heard. I called the dog off and made Guard understand he was a friend.

In the spring of '74, which was mild and pleasant, the Indians were all sick. They had an epidemic of very bad grippe, and all were ill at once. There were not more than one or two families on our side of the lake besides Saul, who was only a small chief. I used to make large kettles of soup and send [them] down to the ranch with buckets of milk. At one home there was no one fit to cook, but soon some of them were well enough to do so. Some two or three died and their near relatives asked my husband to get me to make shrouds for them which I did. Then poor young Michelle was dreadfully ill—the Indians expected him to die any time, so we beat a few eggs in a bowl and put some whiskey in it and my husband rode down to the ranch, opened Michelle's mouth and poured a spoonful down his throat every ten minutes or so till finally he opened his eyes. After that the others fed him in the same way till he could eat alone. Some of the women fancied the cakes I made them and soon learned the way to do it themselves. When they all recovered they all moved off on a hunting trip except one man who told them to go. He wanted to die he was so sick. So they laid him on skins, piled blankets over him and left him to die at sunset. As soon as they were gone my husband rode down to see if the Indian needed anything but he was already dead, smothered by the blankets most likely. That was the first case of that kind that I knew of but afterwards I found it was nothing unusual, just a custom.

The Indians did not return for some weeks and then there seemed to be great unrest among them. They talked of a Great Chief across the Line named Joseph—such stories of his strength—and how he drank a cup of blood every morning, no matter what or whose blood it was. This was all nonsense, for Joseph was really a good man, fighting as a chief for his people's rights, but it indicated the starting of the unrest among the Indians. No one really knows what we owe to the influence of the priests and Joe McKay.

Well, my life was pleasant in spite of everything. At hay making I used to leave my children for an hour at noon while I took the haymen their lunch at the meadow. In the bend of the harbour the mites would watch me depart on my pony—little Willie perched on a stump shouting "Trot, Ma, trot." He loved to see Pet trotting. My husband told me to keep off the grass and follow the trail. This seemed to me a decided roundabout way, so one day I thought I would take a short cut through some very green grass. Pet only made two jumps into it and mired up to her girths and I had the humiliation of calling the haymakers to my rescue. Another day going home I saw such a sweet pretty little animal, dark grey with a white stripe down its back. It seemed very tame so I got off the horse to catch it and found myself enveloped in a mist of very unpleasant spray. I had a loaded quirt with me and struck out with it, killing the poor little skunk. Then without pausing to think I picked it up and tied it to my saddle as I would a grouse and rode home, to the joy of the children who always expected me to bring them home something—the something generally was a terrapin.

One day one of the haymakers failed to appear and my husband rode into the Indian ranch after him, entered his cabin and found him sitting in a state of nature, squatting with some bones on the ground. He said he had lost all of his clothes, even his shirt and pants, and could not go to work unless they were redeemed. The bones were his gambling equipment. Of course, my husband lectured the man and redeemed his clothes—we could not afford to lose a haymaker.

When the haying was over my husband went to Hope with his steers. That very night there were wild unearthly whoops and yells and drum beating. I knew Saul was not at home. The noise was blood curdling. Next day some of the women told me that Killestim-nix-quilly had arrived from a battle with the Britons [Americans?]—he had come naked, with a strand of bark for a bridle, bare-back, and his horse nearly dead and he wanted help for his people. The war dances were kept up every night till Saul came back and then the Indians either moved off or he stopped them. When my husband returned he said he had met the naked Indian riding bare-back. He would not stop to speak but he thought that Saul would protect us. I suppose he did as far as he could but I got well scared first. I had read of what was going on in Washington and Oregon in the papers.

And one day when I saw a dozen armed Indians charging down on the house, shouting and yelling, I grabbed a heavy 44 Navy revolver my husband gave me for protection, locked the front door, and putting the children in the back room, stood ready to empty it at them. But for some reason of their own they whirled their horses round, shouted and rode off—leaving me trembling and unnerved when it was over.

That winter the lake froze over and we sent our teams over to the Mission for oats and flour. Kind Mrs. Eli and the good priests sent over lots of little comforts. It got so cold that winter that the mercury froze in the thermometers. We fortunately had lots of sheds and shelter for the cattle. That counted as much as extra feed but Eli who had little or no shelter for his cattle on one or two excessively cold nights had men on horseback armed with whips driving them round and round his corral. We only lost about fifty head of cattle that winter in spite of the cold but we were decidedly short of flour, rice, sugar, salt and many other things.

I think it was the summer of '75 [*sic*] that the McLean boys kept the scattered settlers in a state of unrest. People now will wonder how four or five young men could terrorize a large district but when one considers that people were living twenty to thirty and in some cases fifty miles apart, and all the men were working in the fields, perhaps for a distant neighbour, and the women kept the home fires burning, believe it or not, it is true the McLean boys, with the exception of Hector, kept us in terror. I had heard about them and Nick [*sic*] Hare but scarcely gave them a thought till they came to the lake. Nicola, Kamloops and the vicinity were out after them.

The McLeans were the sons of a Hudson's Bay Company Factor, their mother a chief's daughter nearly related to Kamloops Louie [Louis]. They were always considered fine young men. They had a beautiful sister who was brought up in a convent and most accomplished. She was in Kamloops society and met a man of high standing in the Province and became engaged to him. They were very intimate, too much so—then he went down to the lower country and married the daughter of a man of standing there, leaving the poor girl to bear her disgrace the best way she could. The brothers were furious, if they could have got at that man they would have killed him then and there. They took to drinking and running wild, and took whiskey to the Indians. A summons was issued but they tore it up—then a warrant was taken out and the man who brought it driven out of camp. Johnny Ussher who had known and been friendly to the boys for years said he would take another warrant and tell them that it would be much better for them to give themselves up for trial. He hunted them up, and found Nick Hare had joined them, and began talking to them like a friend. One of them upped his gun and shot him. This was a signal to the others. They all in turn shot at him—then leaving their camp, continued a career of murder until finally they were arrested by John Chappalo at Nicola.

It was after they had killed Ussher that I was expecting my husband to return from one of his drives. I looked out of my window and saw six Indians passing. Frosty Nose was with them so I ran out to the fence with little Edgar following me to ask if they had seen him coming. They stopped, and one put up his gun pointing at an object behind me. Frosty Nose rode up to him, threw up his arms, and said something to him. I turned to see what he had aimed at—it was my son, little Edgar! When I turned again they had all ridden on except Frosty Nose, who, never at a loss for a lying excuse, said that the man had seen one of our pet deer in the distance and would have shot it had he not intervened.

Times were very risky so I did not argue. I was afterwards told that it was one of the McLean boys on his way to the head of the lake and that he thought I had gone out to take off their attention to [from] those who would arrest him. His sister, a fair girl wearing a sunbonnet, passed riding a side saddle and carrying an infant. Poor girl, she was going to her mother's people! The Indians are good to those of kin to them.

My husband returned from his drive next day and looking over the cattle found a three year old steer not long killed, with one hind quarter cut off. The Indians said the McLeans had done it. He hurried to the harbour to give information but our boat was gone. Afterwards an Indian brought it back and said that he had found it across the lake.

After a wild career of death and destruction these misguided boys were taken and hanged, the eldest twenty, the youngest fifteen.

I led a perfectly ideal life at this time. We rose with the sun, when the cows had been attended to put up our lunches, caught a pony, piled the children on and went out for the day, sometimes taking the boat and drifting about in the harbour or pulling it along by hand in the reeds, watching the little fishes and water beetles playing in and out of the water weeds, feeding them bread crumbs, which as they slowly sank the small fry would fight over. It was a great amusement to the children. We did this frequently in hot weather, then between three and four would pull out of the reeds and fish till we had enough for supper and breakfast. If we were a little late our pet deer would swim out to meet us. This was rather dangerous as we had hard work trying to keep them off the boat. They felt that where the children were they should be too. Guard would come down to the boat with the deer but did not attempt to swim. We had four pet deer, all brought up on a bottle. They walked all over the house lying on the children's beds in the nursery whenever they could. We kept these little pets until they were about four years old. Of course, they did not live in the house after the first year but took quite naturally to the cattle sheds and fed with the cattle.

The Indians we employed were always civil but there was a strong undercurrent of unrest.

In 1876, before taking up his duties in the House of Commons, Mr. Dewdney and his wife paid us a nice long visit. The kikenees [kokanees] were running and an Indian brought us any quantity of them for a cent each so I got a lot of them and pressed everyone into service cleaning the fish, splitting them down the back, and rubbing in spice and salt—my husband and Mr. and Mrs. Dewdney tucking up their sleeves and working with a vim. We had a winter supply and it was no light work but when the fish were smoked they were certainly appreciated. I do think my brother-in-law enjoyed the relaxation for he always was on hand at the milking and helped manfully though "Lady Durham" kicked him over more than once. We had a good time that fall.

My husband was made a J.P. that year. He did not want the billet but saw how necessary it was during the McLean's time.

During this period we had several visitors—our neighbour, Tom Ellis and R. L. Cawston, then not long out from "back east," O'Keefe and Greenhow, and Price Ellison—the Mission side of the lake was rapidly getting settled.

Mrs. Postill, too, who had recently come out with [her] sons and daughter, Lucy, visited me. She, with the exception of Mrs. Ellis and the unfortunate McLean girl, was the first [*sic*] white woman I had seen for years. Lucy was good company.

That fall when Mr. Hayes brought the cattle to winter quarters he brought a very sick woman with him. Poor Augusta was fading away—in vain he got patent medicines for her. Then she begged for an Indian doctor so Tamula was brought and he made night hideous with his singing and drumming. One evening my husband and the children were playing—they generally did before they were put to bed—when Hayes came bursting into the house white and trembling. He said he could not stay in his cabin a moment longer as he felt that there was more there than the eye could see. The doctor had begun by chanting a low song and dancing, making gestures as if he were drawing some skin from Augusta who lay on a pile of skins on the floor. Then he hauled with all his strength towards a mat, then clenched with someone or something that alternately threw him and was thrown. Then there was a dreadful climax—a struggle in which the perspiration just poured off the doctor and he breathed hard. Hayes then fled—he had no doubt that the man was wrestling with some unseen enemy. He would not return until the noise and singing ceased. This went on for a week and then the poor woman died.

I think that it was in the spring of 1877 that one morning when we had finished milking that we took our horses and went off to visit a colony of ants that the children took a great interest in. They first took a pickle bottle and put some small red ants in it, also some bread crumbs soaked in whiskey. They were going to try experiments. First they rode up to a nest of large black ants (I lay on the ground watching them), then they selected an equal number of black fellows and put them into the bottle with the red prisoners and watched the battle that ensued. The poor blacks were soon dismembered by their little foes. Then, tiring of that, they put the soaked bread crumbs near the black ants' nest and watched them taste the bait and stiffen out while their friends came and picked up the little drunks and three or four would carry them home—well, we were amused. Then came a chorus of laughter and looking up I saw to my surprise my old friend, Mr. Anderson and Mr. Sproat and a lady with them. The lady was Mrs. Anderson's sister, Mrs. Tarbold, I think her name was. I had never seen her before, but I was so happy to meet my old friend again. The party had come across the lake on business. Mr. Sproat and Mr.

Anderson were the Commissioners to settle Indian affairs and had business with Saul and his tribe, so they only paid me a flying visit, but it was a nice treat for I saw so few people. Little Beatrice and Edgar used to visit the Ellis' but I had to stay at home.

I missed a pleasure by not being at Similkameen that summer. Doctor Dawson passed through and stayed at our home, and my husband went out with him for a day. One cannot be in company with such a man without learning a lot.

The Indians were much quieter and more content after the visit of the Commissioners.

That winter the lake partially froze. Solid ice bridged it at the head and the narrows. The Indians took advantage of the open water [at Sunnyside] to pass over to the Mission every day or two, but as spring advanced ice down at Penticton receded from both banks and a solid cake of ice of several miles in length broke off forming a huge floating island which drifted up and down the lake with the wind and current.

On the morning of which I write there was a large open streak of water between Sunnyside and the Mission, with the ice island becalmed just below our harbor. Everything was so still, mountains and trees reflected in the lake, perfect, unbroken. We had had no mail for nearly two months and my husband wanted outside news so he thought he would take the boat over and return immediately. Edgar, then nearly ten years old, took the tiller and as there was no breeze to sail, my husband rowed across. I watched the boat as long as I could and then went about my work, watching through the window to see the lake. About noon I saw the boat, sail up, coming home. There was quite a strong wind—she was just flying—but to my horror I saw the ice island was flying too—and if she was not quick enough the boat would be crushed between the cakes of ice. I ran to the children, told them I was going to meet their father and that they must stay in the house till my return. Then I ran down to a cliff above the lake which was now in a terrible tumult. The ice [was] closing in on the poor little boat, which seemed on wings. The passage had narrowed to a few yards and, as I watched in horror, to a few feet. Then with a dreadful crash the two cakes came together sending a formation of ice and water up to the sky—but the boat I could not see, only rough lumps of ice piled over the cake that was largest. As I watched two black dots seemed to emerge from the debris and come toward Sunnyside. As they got closer I saw that they were each carrying something long. They came nearer. It was Edgar and his father each carrying an oar. The ice they were on was rapidly breaking up and they jumped from block to block. They got nearer and I saw a more solid mass upon which they could walk, but between it and shore there was a long lane of water which ran dark and deep. Looking above me I saw an Indian riding madly along the road and recognized Sher-man-i-shoot [Chiru-man-choot]. I tried to beckon and called but he took no notice, then when I looked again at the ice I could see neither Edgar nor his father. They might have rounded the bend but it did not seem possible. My courage failed. I tried to retrace my steps—I was on a deer trail—it seemed too narrow and my feet too big. I turned off the trail up a ravine. I hardly knew where I went, then I threw myself on the ground—I don't think for very long. I struggled on to another trail above the lake, which was now seething in tempestuous fury, and was watching the water when I felt a hand on my shoulder. It was my husband. "Edgar?" I asked, "With Chiru-man-choot." The Indian, seeing their danger, had galloped to their rescue, and finding a deep lane of water between the shore and the ice, had pushed a dead tree into the lake, got astride of it, and paddling with his hands, reached the ice and made them come on board his improvised boat which they all paddled back.

That year my husband met with an accident that affected his whole life. He had just taken a drove of cattle to New Westminster. The weather was intensely hot, but he always used a trail he had cut for his own use. He never met anyone on this road. He was rather more than a day late but I thought nothing of that as business often detained him. When he came it was late in the day and he looked very pale. The first thing he asked was what day it was. When I told him, he said he had been three days on the road and must have been insensible for thirty hours or more. He remembered leaving the Similkameen and passing the small lakes, entering the timber—then no more till he felt his horse poking its nose in his face and trying to wake him up. He looked at his watch—it had stopped. He felt stiff and cold but mounted and came home. We never knew what had happened—thrown by the horse or sunstroke. His memory was never the same.

It was the summer of '78 that I met Mrs. Tommy Christian, a dear little girl just out of a convent. Her guardians had made the marriage.

She told me she had never seen Tommy Christian till the day she married him. Fortunately, they got on well together. But when he was working at his mine she liked to stay with me once in awhile. She was with me when John was born.

Penextitza was one of the head men at the Head of the Lake, a chief, and like our own Highland Chiefs, always took a tail of young men (gillies) with him, also an interpreter, whenever he went. He was too dignified to understand English. When he did any trading at Eli's or the Mission he would stand back in state, surrounded by his satellites while the interpreter did his business for him, only nodding assent or shaking his head to the white men.

I was very much surprised one day when he rode up to my door and the interpreter came forward and asked to see my husband. He said that he had business with him. I told them my husband was out but, if they would come in, lunch was on the table. The interpreter talked with Penextitza, who, with a wave of his hand to his little band, rode to the hitching post, dismounted, and came to the door hat in hand, like a gentleman. His followers rode on.

Penextitza was a perfect gentleman and during lunch kept up a pleasant conversation on the weather, the crops, the cattle, the races at the Head of the Lake, and the children. He said he had known Governor Douglas and was a friend of his, also Mr. Anderson and Mr. McKay. Then when lunch was over he said I must excuse his leaving so soon but he wanted to push on to his home, and bowed himself out. And that man was considered uncivilized by our civilized people!

My husband and his partner could not agree so they agreed to divide the cattle next spring. I was not sorry as I did not care for Mr. Hayes.

The winter of '79-'80 was the worst the Okanagan ever knew. I don't think they have ever had one as bad since. Up till January '80 we had no snow and the weather was mild, but on New Year's Day the snow began to fall and lay deep on the ground, deep for Okanagan —three feet. When it ceased snowing it froze, then there was a thaw and rain. It froze hard and formed a crust. We had plenty of hay and did not care, but the deer did. The hard crust cut into their delicate legs and they could not move round to feed. They got thin and weak and the Indians caught them with lassos, killed those fit for food and earmarked the others before letting them go. In March there was another thaw. We all thought the winter at an end and were lavish with the last of our hay. The snow all cleared off. Then it began to snow again—for days it snowed. Our feed was now done. We tried to buy at the Mission. The good priests and Eli and others were in the same fix, some even worse off. Mr. Allison made up his mind to drive fifteen miles down the lake on to the hills below, leaving Red Oak and a few cows. Next day he and Hayes drove the cattle down the lake—it was a long drive but the only thing to do. It was late when the tired cattle got there. Some fed, others lay down content, but the wind veered.

Memoirs of
A Pioneer of the Eighties

As I have told before, the winter of '79 and '80 was one of the worst ever known in the Okanagan. At Christmas the weather was seasonable and pleasant. The children had their usual Christmas tree. I had given them one ever since Edgar was a year old. That year it was an unusually good Christmas for both their Aunt Jeanie and Mrs. O'Reilly had sent them toys in addition to those their father had bought at New Westminster. So they enjoyed their last Christmas at the lake more than any they had yet had. At New Year one of Mr. Ellis' Indians came up from Penticton with a message. He reported the weather as good at Penticton and on the Similkameen. He had just started home when the snow began to fall and it did fall.

My husband had a lawsuit with his partner, Mr. Hayes, over land and as there was only a verbal agreement between them, he lost over three thousand dollars. They then agreed to divide the stock and part company—I was not sorry.

Everyone on the lake lost two-thirds of their cattle that winter except Tom Ellis, who lost none. It was the end of April before we had a division of the cattle and horses. The beasts were still weak—even the wild deer. Our little boys would run after a bunch of deer, lasso one, earmark it and let it go. They were too poor to kill, nor would anyone have killed them had they been fat, for in those days when there was no game warden no one killed out of season. Our losses had been so heavy that my husband came to the conclusion that he could not afford to keep up two places and sold the place to an old cow puncher, John

Phillips. I begged him to keep our little home and argued the long, long winters at the Similkameen and the scarcity of winter feed, but his mind was made up and that was that.

It was with a sad heart I went around to our old haunts, said goodbye to my little mountain garden that Dumby and I had ploughed—I drove the team and he held the plough. We visited the little mountain spring which my husband had led down to the house in an underground ditch. We said farewell to the harbour, the ant-hill, and I stole the little humming-bird's nest in the rose bushes of the mountainside. It was a sad cavalcade that left our dear little home where we had all been so peaceful and happy. It had been a busy life, too; no day was spent in idleness.

My children were good and obedient. I had taught the four older ones to read and write, and as I had few books fitted for children, I had made stories from English history, and Grecian and Roman history, too. I don't think they ever forgot what they learned at Okanagan, though they learned little enough after. I, myself, had learned patience, to fish and cure the fish, and dry venison. Dumby taught me to gather straw and grass and make hats for the children, even my husband did not scorn the hats I made. I now could mend the little boots, make moccasins, cut rawhide into strands and make a braid for lariats to lasso the horses.

When we left the house we had a small band of about a hundred and twenty head of cattle—but they were everyone thoroughbred Shorthorn Durhams. These were driven first by Tom and Catherine. Then seventy-five horses, pack and saddle animals, were driven by Michelle and Marie. The children and I brought up the rear. Carrie and George were in boxes slung on either side of a horse.

We descended to the meadow and when we were abreast of the meadow out came Bill and Min and Mary, our pet deer. The children were delighted for we thought we would never see them again, but there they were and joined the cavalcade. They continued with us for about five miles and then the horses stampeded. I was so concerned about Carrie and George, who could scarcely keep their seats in the boxes but were bumped and bruised with every jump the horses made. I got off my horse and refused to remount till the children were taken out of their boxes and carried—it was done after some argument.

That evening we camped at the Look-look-shuie, or Trout Creek, which was booming and very wild. The men decided it would be impossible to cross the horses with their packs on though the stream would fall a little after midnight, and if they rose early enough it would be easier to cross. So they went to work and felled the largest tree they could find across the stream to form a bridge, cut off a few limbs and crossed all the saddles, packs and rigging, then tied up the Bell mare and a few colts. That kept the horses together. The cattle knew the trail as some of them had been over it before. None of us enjoyed the camp. The children grieved for their pet deer, the Indians were sorry we were leaving and we were very sad to leave the beautiful lake with its psychic atmosphere.

Next day, as we passed through some timber, we found groups of from ten to twenty deer dead, huddled together and not one that had been touched by wolves or panthers. They were just frozen stiff.

When we arrived at Princeton we found the roof of the house had broken down from the weight of the snow and everything in a mess with six inches of snow on the flat. So we camped in the garden while the Indian boys cleaned out the milk house as a temporary abode. We learned from some Indians that the McKillops were up the Similkameen mining near the Roche River, also Boshan at a bench he always worked on and Billy Royal at the Whipsaw where he had a cabin. These were the only whites besides ourselves in the upper Similkameen. At Keremeos Barrington Price was running a new flour mill and doing fairly [well]. When the Indians heard we were back they soon came riding up from Chu-chu-ewa to see us and we found a few of the usual matrimonial changes. My good friend, Tatlehasket, had sent away his old wife and taken one much younger, and Cosotasket had exchanged his and now Sinsenecks was Mrs. Cosotasket. Incowmasket had kept both his and Penquinac (Princess Julia) his daughter, was prettier than ever.

Our Okanagan Indians after visiting a few days with the Similkameens left and went home.

Our first white visitors were Henry Nicholson and Barrington Price, both college men from Oxford, I think, and very nice gentlemen but with a strong taste for brandy. We could only offer them a little Scotch and not much of that. I did hear Mr. Nicholson observe that "This is the driest crib I ever struck." They did not stay long, but we were glad to buy their flour and send our pack train down for a load of their supplies.

It did not take long to put a roof on the house, start the fires and dry the inside. I found that a lot of my books had been "borrowed." We had brought our dear old dog with us from the Okanagan but she did not like the Similkameen any better than I, so we had to keep her on a chain, and when it was dark we gave her a good long run every evening. When the snow went off there was almost a tropical growth, and the river rose rapidly.

As we could not hope to make a living out of the few cattle we had left, my husband hoped to live off this land. He had purchased nearly four thousand acres from the government and a piece near the canyon from Colonel Luard and the Sinnet or Lindsay property, which they both gave over to him, and he also paid Dick Tatlehasket (who also claimed it) the price he asked. As Forbes Vernon had cancelled the townsite of Princeton my husband pre-empted it, that gave us nearly five thousand acres. He undertook to look after Mr. Haynes' and the Greaves' cattle, keeping them herded on good pasture and delivering them to their drivers when wanted. This, with the store, gave us a good income. I was condemned to keep the store. There were several Chinese miners on the banks of the river.

In the fall of '80 there was an earthquake which shook the country for miles, reaching the Okanagan. Our Indians were much disturbed except Cosotasket and Tatlehasket and a few others, hard old nuts. They thought the "Father" was angry and sent for the priests, and many were baptized. They resolved to build a church and to have only one wife and there was a sort of revival among them.

That winter, '80-'81, we sent the cattle over to John Phillips on our old place. I longed to go with them but I had to make the best of it in Princeton. We invited some miners and road men and gave them a good Christmas. The Chinese, Ah Lee, Ah Jack and Sam, lived in the old cabin and helped to build fences and get fire wood.

In the spring of '81 John Phillips brought the cattle back from winter quarters. They were in fine condition, increasing, too, for the yearlings were now two years old and the old calves yearlings.

The Indians were still religiously inclined but Incowmasket sent pretty Chinchin away and kept the mother of his boy and Penquinac.

(I saw a long article in the "Province" about a month ago describing Penquinac under the name of Princess Julia—she was christened Julia by the Priest and her father, Incowmasket, [was] called Moses). The good priests came up the river every month always ready to christen, marry or bury anyone, and they got nothing but abuse. The old priests were good men.

That spring my husband had a letter to say that Professor Dawson, Junior, would pass through our district. I am not sure that I have this date right. I have lost my memorandum but I always remember his short visit. Professor Dawson, who camped near our house, said he liked to camp better than stopping at a house. My husband brought him in to lunch. When I looked into his animated countenance and bright, intelligent eyes, I quite overlooked his physical misfortune. We had a delightful hour dining during which the professor seemed quite at home and talked with great vivacity. My husband went out with him into the mountains and said he was as good at climbing as the most active man in the party.

We saw most of our old friends that spring—Tom Ellis, who said that he was building a house in the mountains to get his family out of the torment of mosquitoes at Penticton during the hot weather. R. L. Cawston, too, came up with his beef steers and always called in to have a game with the children. A constable, too, came up from Osoyoos with a prisoner. He left his prisoner at the cabin with the cowboys and came over and had lunch with us. It was always nice to meet with well-educated men. This constable was an Oxford man and very interesting. After lunch he left with his prisoner. I did not see him again for months and then under very different circumstances.

The river rose rapidly that year. Our old scow had gone with the ice and the only means of crossing was in a dugout canoe owned by Shla-wha-la-kan and he usually put his own price on the accommodation which varied from fifty cents to five dollars. This year his daughter, Sally, had got married for the fifth time. She was quite a young girl but there were skins and blankets exchanged every time and it was profitable to the old man, but this time it had not been very satisfactory and he was irritable. So when a party of miners came out over the Hope Trail and signalled for the canoe, the old man took his time about going and when he did we noticed that he did not land but kept his boat some distance out in the water. We had no means of knowing what was going on but after a long time we saw him land. Then he went back to the canoe with a bundle. Two white men stepped in with him and came across. We noticed that they seemed half clad and when my husband went out to speak to them they unfolded a tale of woe. Shla-wha-la-kan had refused to take them in his boat unless one man gave his coat, the other his shirt and pants, so he had to cross in his underwear. He had to buy overalls of course. Selling an outfit to the old man's customers was profitable for our store. Mr. Allison thought that he would build a scow and cross anybody for the fixed price of fifty cents.

About the end of August that year we were sitting on the veranda when a Chinaman rushed up and told us "He gone, he gone, too muchie devilo come—he go." The man was so excited that it took a long time to get any reasonable statement from him, but the result was that a party of Chinamen leaving Hope had been joined by Mr. Haynes' constable, who had taken a prisoner to New Westminster early in the summer and was on his way home. He camped with them. He had a flask of whiskey with him and as long as it lasted the constable appeared alright and kept up with them travelling. Then when that was finished he began muttering and the Chinamen thought he saw devils and dead men. When they neared the Nine Miles he bolted, screaming. They followed but could not find him. It was now two days that they had hunted. My husband, who was a very kind-hearted man, could not bear to think of the poor man lost in that wild country, so he got up and sending for a horse went with the Chinaman. He said that he would come back when he had found his man, and thought he would stay at Billy Royal's cabin till he did. He sought the constable that night. Next morning they saw tracks of bare feet. Billy Royal followed them up and then came back in a hurry to say he had located the missing man but thought it better to have someone with him when he roused the constable, who was either sleeping or unconscious. He was lying by the river-side clad in his vest with his watch and chain and nothing else. He tried to run when he saw them but Billy Royal roped him; then they took him to Billy's cabin and clothed and fed him. As he appeared better my husband asked Billy to look after him that day and let him rest and the next day to bring him to the house. That night Billy came to say that he was too violent —he had tried to throw himself in the fire. He had left the man securely tied [and] we must take charge of him. So with Billy and an Indian, my husband started with horses to bring him down. On horseback he seemed to recover till they came to the river which was still high, then in the deepest place he threw himself off his horse and tried to drown himself. I was watching them and saw my husband make a dive for him, and the Indian also dismounted. There was a struggle and then they all landed safely. For some hours after that he seemed slightly better—he recited the Church of England Evening Prayer service all through and went to bed quietly enough. But in the night we were awakened by Guard growling. My husband went out and found her circling around her prisoner who besought us to kill the savage beast. He was brought into the house once more, then I made a disturbance for I was ill. My husband ran and brought Incowmasket's wife who stayed with me till Elfreda was born next morning. Mr. Allison tied the constable on to a horse and dispatched him in charge of two Indians to Barrington Price, who was a great friend of his.

I longed more than ever to go back to Okanagan in the fall of '81 when the cattle started back. I hated store-keeping. The poor little children, I felt, were neglected but it had to be.

When the cattle left the cowboys left, too; but we had the Chinamen in the cabin as before, and we made the best we could of the winter of '81 and '82. It was a mild winter and in the month of March '82, the hills were green and the grass in fine condition. So, on the twenty-eighth, my husband and Edgar, now a good-sized useful boy, started off to the Okanagan to bring the cattle home. The children joined me in raking up chips and cleaning up the winter disorder. The Chinamen had gone back to their mining so we were all alone, except Lily was with us, and Tatlehasket, who had brought us two fine yearling deer. I made him put them into the milk house till I had time to cut them up, before he rode down the valley. When the first of April came I rose with the sun and took my salt and spice to the milk house to cure the venison, charging Lily to get breakfast and then call me.

The milk house must have been about seventy-five feet from the house and had a window looking at the kitchen door. After about an hour I went over to hurry Lily with the breakfast. Will and Beatrice were up. Will had put on his oldest clothing he had in anticipation of a hard day's work, so I went back, leaving as I thought everything alright. After another half hour I heard crackling. I looked out and saw nothing so went at the salt and venison. Again I heard loud crackling, so I went to look around.

This time I looked up to the roof where the sound seemed to be coming. It was ablaze near the stove-pipe. I rushed into the house and upstairs. The children had heard nothing; they were laughing. Lily was at my heels going upstairs. Her room door was open and the room on fire. We got the children, who still were in their beds in my room, downstairs and out. I gave the baby, Elfreda, into Beatrice's charge and told her to keep away from the house. Guard watched George who was his favourite. Then we came back to the house. Someone remembered that there was about a hundred pounds of gunpowder in tin cans upstairs and there was a yell from them that the powder might explode, so Lily ran upstairs and threw it out of the window, also ten or eleven saddles. Then I made her come down as the flames were growing on the cloth- and paper-lined rooms below.

We threw chairs and bedding out of the front door. I went into my room but it was all aflame. On my bedroom walls, three of them, I had many treasures—an autographed letter from the Duke of Wellington about India House affairs, and one from Earl Grey regarding the Reform Bill, and many other old relics. In my bookcase was a Church of England Prayer Book and Bible combined, printed in the reign of James the First. There were prayers in it for Charles I as Prince of Wales. And such a lot of good books. It was too hot for me and the flames were too much so I just tried to grab my brother's picture. The fire was too strong so I caught up a bucket of water near at hand and threw it over it, snatched the picture off the wall and retreated choking. Will, in the meantime, took a small piece of bacon off the store room counter and an open sack with about fifteen pounds of flour. Then we left the doomed house.

Looking up at the building it looked red hot, then the melted glass poured from the windows. The store shelves with flour and everything were red hot. Then it crashed. We watched the burning; then I thought of shelter for my children.

The little old cabin was dirty and all the other buildings had now caught fire. No broom! Well, pine brush would do, so we twisted pine boughs together and swept out the cabin, but there was no bucket to pack water to wash it. We had no effects to move into the cabin for all that we had thrown out of the house had burned as the wind veered from south to east. There was the sewing machine that we had carried farthest from the house with only the woodwork burned, and the small portion of flour and bacon Will had saved. Higher up the flat there was a row of Aparajos standing ready for use with a few horse blankets piled over them—there was our bedding ready to hand. The top canvas would do for a tablecloth—but what would we eat off it? There was glowing fire enough but no cooking utensils. I scattered the children over the flat to search for anything useful. They came back with an array of old yeast powder tins and an empty lard pail—treasures to destitute people. Then all hands helped in getting in the Aparajos and getting ready our beds. Will, rummaging in the shelves of the cabin, found a coffee can full of rice and an old Bible. The rice we agreed to keep for Freda and the Bible would be our literature.

Well, the beds were made and a glorious fire started in the big fireplace at the end of the cabin. The sky was overcast and there was a snowstorm. The children were famished not having eaten their breakfast. They said scones would do. I looked at the sack of flour—there was no bread board. Lily said we could bake on stones the way the Indians did, and hauled up a large flat one for a baking board. For a rolling pin they again searched the old camps for a whiskey bottle. This they found in the sack of flour and I proceeded to make the scones without salt, and Lily cooked them in front of the fire. Jack brought spruce twigs for tea, and all had hunger for sauce. We always joked over anything unpleasant so we laughed and joked over the table, at our looks, and at the dishes, chips of wood, and yeast powder can cups! When we were finishing our meal we heard a voice say "Wie, wie, nic" and turning saw a mounted Indian (Squakan). He said he was hunting and saw the flames and smoke from the Big Hill and came to see. We asked him if he had any food with him, but he answered only a little sugar in his cache near his hunting ground. I asked him to sell some of his sugar, just enough for the baby, which he did. A tin cup he carried was his measure and for that I paid him one dollar. I had a few dollars in my pocket and a hundred dollars in gold dust in a buckskin purse that Beatrice had in keeping, but of course that was no use now. Squakan said he was going home in a few days and would then tell Mr. Price of our condition. With that he rode away.

I could fill a small volume with our struggles during those few days but must be brief. On the fifth day we heard a bell and looking down the road saw an Indian with a pack-horse loaded with flour, beans, and bacon from our kind neighbour, Barrington Price. Some of the children were in their nightclothes and the weather was still cold, but we managed and good Ah Lee, who came from his mining to get provisions, made the children wooden sandals or clogs. Then my husband and Edgar came posthaste as they had heard a report of the fire and left the cattle with the Indians and posted on. I was so glad for I knew that he would soon have everything in shape again; as good never comes but it pours, good dear Mr. Cawston got a lot of old clothes from his aunt, Mrs. Lowe, brought calico, needles, thread, scissors and brought up Mrs. Lowe's children's old clothes; they were much appreciated by the children. It was a great experience, and I learned the real value of things by it.

We moved out of the cabin as soon as my husband returned. It was said to be haunted and may have been. At any rate, it was dirty and infested with mice that ate the hair off our heads while asleep. One of the cowboys came along and Mr. Allison hired him to help build a new bridge. The bridge had been swept away at last high water, and the logs lay in the calf-pasture. They were thirty feet long. These my husband built into a temporary shelter for the family, and afterwards we used it for a nursery for the younger children. Bill McKeon hauled the logs and we soon had our buildings up and took possession with cheerful hearts.

Then the usual business began but it was hard work cooking without a stove. I thought that with all small hands helping, I could build a bake oven. This I did on the bank of the river using cobble-stones and clay. All hands gathered the stones, Will and Beatrice mixed mud, Lily packed it to me and I built it. Someone found a half-melted door from the old stove which made a good door for the new oven.

One day near June I had put three ducks, nicely dressed, and a huge custard into the oven, and all was cooked ready to be eaten by hungry people. I had no tea or coffee so browned some dried peas and used them for coffee, which also was ready. Two well dressed men rode up and said they were starving and would I give them something to eat. One was from California, Mr. Sharon, and the other a French artist, Jules Tavernier. I dished up the dinner we were waiting for and told them to sit down. I thought there would be enough left for us hungry ones but, no, they ate all the ducks and pudding. They talked in French, thinking I could not understand them. They said my bread was like cake and the ducks the best they had ever tasted. They also wondered where I had got the coffee but that, I think, may have been the rich cream they had with it. But I felt proud of the oven after that. The next day Sir Thomas Hesketh and his valet rode up and camped near by. He got my boys out with him to show them where the Duck Lakes were. He was in luck for the lakes were black with ducks. When he saw them he said he had never seen such a sight before. He was only passing through—it seems Sharon was his brother-in-law but they agreed better apart.

That year I met for the first time A. E. Howse, who had just been appointed Indian Agent. He was a fine looking young man and a man's looks went a long way with the Indians. I thought he was rather young for the position but I did not appoint him. I was sorry we had nothing on hand when he called for supplies. He had, I knew, a hard task before him settling petty quarrels; no one can satisfy both sides. Mr. Howse has ever shown himself to be a public-spirited man. At the time he came I think we were out of everything but sago.

The winter of '82 and '83 we sent the cattle to winter at Joe Linton's ranch at the Line. Joe was a good man to look after them but his ranch was on both sides of the Line and the Americans objected to the cattle straying over and he had to herd them.

We had our usual good time this Christmas, more guests than ever, but we had turkeys and venison in abundance and had lots of fun. Young people can always enjoy themselves.

Joe Linton drove the cattle back in the spring, a few were missing but that was not his fault. He had done his best. In the spring my boys brought in a young wolf which we raised on the bottle. He was a lovable little creature and quite unlike the snapping, snarling coyotes we had tried to tame before. He flourished with the children and they loved him.

On the fourteenth of June that year, there arrived from San Francisco Captain Nichols and a mining expert, Mr. Ferguson, with an American, George Reynolds, for guide. They were in search of the copper that my husband had discovered in '58 [1860]. Others had been up the river and seen it, carried the news, but they were not sure of its whereabouts. My husband directed them to the place but when they got there, with the river being high, they sat down on the opposite bank and did not try to cross. Captain Nichols, who was a spiritualist, went off by himself and consorted with his unseen friends. Then he declared that the spirits said there was nothing there. They returned to Princeton and Captain Nichols went back to the States, but Mr. Ferguson, who liked the looks of the place, lingered and when the river fell, went over, took samples and staked claims. Then they went to Victoria and interested E. G. Prior, Mr. Leroy[?], Mr. Jones, Mr. Pooley and others. They hired two Vananda Cornishmen, Gill and John Mitchell, to work it that winter. It would take too long to tell of this affair in this article. Coulthards eventually bought my husband's share—that was after his death for he would not sell while he lived.

That winter the cattle again wintered at Joe Linton's place but American ranchers adopted our brand (a), and stole our cattle in a legal way.

When I began these articles I hoped to carry them on to the Nineties, but old age and ill health will not permit me to do so.

In the summer of 1883, some Chinese, mining on what is now known as Asp's place, struck very rich diggings—a hundred dollars per man was what they were said to be making. These men called themselves the Quong Yuen Co. There was another Chinese company, calling themselves the Lee Man Company. These men, when they heard of the other men's good luck, went in a body and drove the Quong Yuen off, pulled up their stakes and held the ground. The Quong Yuen appealed to my husband as magistrate, and as he had no constable, he swore in two cowboys and with them reinstated the Quong Yuen. Then the Lee Mans, in conjunction with some disreputable men (one just out of the Westminster Pen) brought a suit against my husband for damages. He was summonsed to New Westminster, but would not notice the summons as it stated that he was in partnership with the Chinese. I begged him to employ a lawyer and bring a countersuit for perjury but he said he had no time for such nonsense. The result was that he lost fourteen hundred dollars; but John Robson, who was then Premier, said if he had been Gold Commissioner they could not have touched him, so he promptly made Mr. Allison Gold Commissioner for the district, an office which he held for some years till business at Granite Creek necessitated the appointment of Mr. Tunstall who resided there.

The cowboys during a slack time drew their wages and, dressing themselves in the most elaborate cowpuncher style, rode down the valley. There was Bill McKeon, Billy Elwell and Harry Hobbes, three of the best and most cheerful perverters of the truth I ever knew. What they did or told at Oroville, I don't know, but they returned in a week smiling, and said it would not be dull long. Next day, sure enough, several strange men passed with pack horses loaded with miners' equipment; some even stopped to ask about the "new strike." There was one party of eight or ten men with Wild Goose Bill Jenkins at their head that insisted that there had been a very "big strike." He had seen the gold dust the cowboys brought down to Oroville with them. I told them to go and ask the boys, which they did, but they did not get much satisfaction. They lingered around the house prospecting in the river. Finally they worked it ten or twelve miles without finding much; then they struck it rich and named their claim "Rich Bar." Such it proved to be. They worked hard, except for one man, Johnny Chance, who was too lazy to work. They made him cook but as the weather grew hotter that was too much exertion for him, so his partners gave him a gun and told him to get them a few grouse. He departed and strolled about till near sunset he found a nice cool creek that emptied itself into the river. Here he threw himself down hill with his feet paddling the cool water, when a ray of light fell on something yellow. He drew it towards him, picked it up and found it was a nugget of pure gold. He looked into the water again and there was another, then another. He pulled out his buckskin purse and slowly filled it, then picking up his gun he strolled back to camp where he became a hero and the discoverer of Granite Creek.

We had a visit from Canon Cooper and, I think, Father Pat. The Canon recommended a tutor for the children so my husband put up a new building to accommodate the public and cowboys and we cleaned out the old cabin for a schoolroom. We kept up this school for the children for some years and had a variety of teachers. Settle was the first, then J. M. Kinnear, then Miss McLean, a lovely girl, and last a Mr. Robert Lowe. Edgar went to Lauren [Lorne] College, Bishop

Sillitoe's school at Westminster, where he did not learn more than the others at home. That was his own fault for he thought more of hunting and fishing than books. The children at home, I think, taught some of their teachers to ride and range the country. It is hard for up-country children to sit and study in those glorious summer days that we generally have.

It was in 1884 [*sic*] that an Aide-de-camp came riding up the valley from General Sherman to see what provision we could make for a troop of horses. He had obtained leave to pass through B.C. to the coast with an escort. We had plenty of oats that we bought at Keremeos but no hay; but the big bunch-grass field (since sold to Mrs. Lowe) was then flourishing, knee deep in grass. We could not accommodate anyone as the new house was not finished, so when the General came they all camped in the big calf-pasture and turned their horses into the bunch-grass field.

When the General announced he was coming to call I had nowhere to receive him but the nursery or the kitchen, so I had chairs placed outside the door for him and his staff. He made himself at home, took a chair, turned back in [to] front, and bestrode it like a horse. Resting his chin on its back he surveyed us all. Then he asked abruptly how many children we had. I told him nine. "Where are the rest," he said, "parade them all." I told him the little ones were in bed but he insisted that I should "parade them in their night shirts."

General Sherman was a healthy, intelligent man with shrewd piercing eyes that seemed to take in everything and look into your mind. With him was General Nelson Miles, Captain Chas. King and Lieutenant Mallory, who came to the place and played with the children every chance he got. He was a young Southerner and not quite at home with his brother officers. The General was delighted to see my little boy, Jack, just seven, perched on his big horse, riding back and forth with his messages and little Jack was proud to ride the General's horse. They did not stay long for some of the men deserted, so they passed through the country as quickly as they could. [Before leaving he presented Jack with a sword].

I had another visit from my friend, the constable, from Osoyoos, this time "clothed and in his right mind." I asked him to lunch. We had a large cold roast of beef on the table and as the day was hot the house doors stood open. Wolfie who had been neglected came and stood in the doorway sniffing the air, then with a sudden bound was up on the table and off with the beef in a twinkling. The poor constable nearly collapsed and murmured something improper about a savage animal, but we were amused by his terror.

I would like to tell about the building of our new house (a large one) and of the new bridge, the coming of my son-in-law S. D. Sandes and the starting of Princeton by him and many other things, but I am unable to do more at present. I shall leave sundry notes behind me, which may or may not be, of use to my children. My pen is shaking in my hand and I really must stop writing for a time at any rate.

I would have liked to tell of my first meeting with my good old friend F. P. Cook and my dear friends, Mrs. Cawston and Mrs. Daly whose hospitality we so often enjoyed. Also Sam Pierce, Chas. Asp and others, but they came not long after the time I write of, later in 1884.

*When the River Rose**

I think it was in the middle of June, 1894 after a cold and backward spring that there was a sudden change in the weather, the night frosts suddenly ceased and it set in unbearably hot.

Then both the Similkameen and the Tulameen rose at once, and the Similkameen from a small wasted stream became a roaring, raging flood tearing on, gathering all the flotsam and jetsam within its reach—great logs and slender saplings—eating away the banks, and moving huge boulders that we had for years considered landmarks.

Our house was standing on the river's bank, but not on the brink. There was a sugarbeet patch of rich deep soil and a storehouse between us and the river, so at first we had no fear of the flood. Mr. Cawston had come up a few [days] before the one of which I write, and we sat on the kitchen steps which led down to the river where we got our water. We were all as usual enjoying the shade after the burning sunshine of the day, and discussing the cause of Mr. Cawston's visit, the shape of the road over the Mountain, which he wanted to ascertain in order to drive a bunch of beef steers to Hope, when we noticed some very large logs floating down. The bank seemed to be hit by them as they passed. Mr. Cawston made some joking remark about the sugarbeets. He decided to hold his drive for a few days until the river fell.

*PABC Microfilm, Roll 93A, The Allison Manuscripts A.

Our bridge had gone out the year previous. After Mr. Cawston started for Keremeos the river continued to rise. Mr. Allison and I sat and watched the sugarbeets going down the river as it ate away the soil of the bank—we sat and watched as long as we could see; but could not stop the damage. When we did go to bed the river was at least twenty feet from the house, but the whole patch between seemed to be saturated with water. All night long we could hear the roaring of the river, and once or twice there came a shock that seemed like logs bumping against the corner of the house. After a while, tired out, we slept the sleep of the just.

We woke next morning with the daylight. My husband said, "It sounds funny, I will just get up and look." In a few moments he was back. He told me quietly that he thought I ought to get up and dress, adding quite calmly that half my bedroom was undermined and would soon have to be cut adrift from the house.

I got up at once and made the children get out of their beds. Then I went out to take a look round. The river was running under both my room and Louisa's. There were two rooms above these, and it seemed as if that part of the house was doomed. I saw my husband and the boys coming with two long saws. I asked what they were going to do and was answered, "Saw the house in two—and try to save half. Get out the bedding and furniture and store [them] near the side hill."

So to work we went taking all our things out of the doomed part of the house while the boys sawed manfully to split the house in two. We had most fortunately built a new stable to accommodate ten horses and a harness room over near the side hill. The horses had not been occupying it for more than a week, and my husband said rather grimly that if we could not save half the house, we could turn the horses out and live in the stable. The boys did turn the horses out, for they had not time to feed them.

The river was still rising. At noon we moved the cook-stove out to a shed near the stable. When my husband and boys had sawed off four rooms from the house and lowered them into the river, I gave them a lunch under the old shed and went with Grace and Carrie to see what was going on.

We found that the dairy was gone, the calves' shed, the blacksmith's shop and the slaughter-house and numerous other buildings.

There was yet a small chicken-house clinging to the bank and the door was swinging open. Grace cried out, "I am going in there." I begged her not to try, but she ran on and jumped in and as she did so the chicken-house began to float downstream. She jumped quickly back and fortunately landed on solid ground. Next we inspected the garden. It was going quickly. The asparagus bed we had planted twenty-five years before was rapidly disappearing. Some of the asparagus roots were 17 feet long, we measured them afterwards. The young fruit trees had gone and now the currants and gooseberries were going. Rose and Carrie sat on a dry spot and watched the demolition. "The Lord giveth and the Lord taketh, blessed be his name," said Rose. Carrie jumped up, seized a shovel and cried out, "He shan't get away with the currants and gooseberries if I can help it" and set to work digging them up.

By this time some people from the new town of Princeton had come to see what was going on. They offered help, but that was out of their power, for who can curb a torrent. When night came we had most of our effects out of the house except books and papers. We hoped to save the nursery, sitting room and Mr. Allison's office and half the dining room. We thought that it would be safer to sleep in the stable.

The small children had had a glorious day, wading in the puddles and using our wash tubs for boats, and little Alice was paddling a tub for her own canoe when Jack Pioto, an Indian friend, rode up and splashed into about two feet of water, grabbed her by one arm and swinging her up onto his saddle brought her to the stable and said the ground was too rotten near the river for children to play there.

When we were ready to retire for the night, we looked from our stable at the house and thought that though much smaller than in the morning, we still had a pretty good house left. So we went to bed tired out and thankful.

When we arose next morning and looked, the house was gone and the river flowing where it had stood. So for the second time we lost our home and most of our possessions.

Our loss when the river rose was serious. We had altogether lost fourteen buildings including the house, our garden and a lot of good ground. The girls' flower garden alone was left with its bright flowers.

We made the big stable comfortable and even managed to entertain such of our friends as passed our way. Soon we had another garden started, though we missed our well established asparagus bed. But the currants and gooseberries flourished as well as ever.

Appendix 1

Account of the Similkameen Indians of British Columbia*

The tribe at present inhabiting the upper valley of the Similkameen are immediately descended from a small band of the warlike Chilcotins, who established themselves in the upper valley of the river about a hundred and fifty years ago, and intermarried with the Spokanes. They have much deteriorated, both physically and mentally, within the last twenty years, and are rapidly becoming extinct. The average stature of the men is about five feet six inches; their frames are lithe and muscular, and their movements quick and graceful. Their complexion is very light, and they have small hands and feet. The colour of their hair varies from jet-black to red-brown, and in some cases it is almost curly. They are born horsemen and capital shots. The sharp horns of the mountain goat were formerly fixed on shafts of hard wood and used as spears both in hunting and warfare; stone knives and hatchets were also used.

The summer dwellings of the Similkameen Indians were made of mats of cedar bark, manufactured by the Hope Indians, which were thrown over a circular frame of poles. The winter houses were simply pits dug in the ground and roofed with poles and earth. All sickness was supposed to be the work of an evil spirit, who fastened on a victim and hung on, drawing away his life, until charmed away by the doctor, who worked himself into a state of frenzy, singing and dancing while he was trying

*British Association for the Advancement of Science, section 2, *Report* 60 (1891): 815.

to lure the evil spirit from his patient. Many of the medicine-men exercise strong mesmeric power over their patients, and they use several herbs as medicines; their panacea for all ills, however, is the vapour-bath.

When an Indian died he was laid out in state on a couch of skins; everything put on the body was new; his bow and arrows were laid at his side, along with his knife. His friends then assembled round him to feast, and when the feast was over his friends advanced, and taking his hand bade him farewell. Immediately after a funeral takes place the encampment is moved, lest the spirit of the deceased should revisit it.

A widow or widower is forbidden to eat meat and certain vegetables for a month, and must wear quantities of spruce bush inside their shirts, next their skin.

Cannibalism was never known among the Similkameens.

In the mountain is a certain stone which is much venerated by the Indians, and it is said that striking it will produce rain.

Polygamy was allowed, and if the husband and wife tired of each other, the price of the woman, or its equivalent, was returned by her father or guardian, and the parties were then free to contract another matrimonial alliance; but adultery, though it was generally compromised, was sometimes punished by cutting off the woman's nose or slitting her ears.

Occasionally sick persons were buried before they were quite dead, and a good deal of infanticide was practised.

The author has not found these Indians to be thieves, and gives them a general good character in other respects.

Appendix 2

The Big Men of the Mountains

On the shore of the beautiful Okanagan Lake, Torouskin encamped. The summer was well advanced, and with the great heat of the long, long days, a dead calm set in. The lake that had so recently been rough and tempestuous now shone still and placid as a mirror, reflecting the surrounding mountains and groves of vine maple and cottonwood that fringed its margin. The white swan floated majestically on the smooth surface; the loon, uttering her sad wailing cry, dived into the depths of the beautiful lake; in the cloudless sky above circled the osprey.

Near Torouskin's camp the snow-born Look-look-shouie emptied its icy waters into the great bottomless lake. The Look-look-shouie, like the lake into which it flowed, had undergone a remarkable change since the summer set in; the deep dark torrent that had raged so furiously had now dwindled into a small pellucid stream alive with kik-e-ninnies [kokanees]. Torouskin's aged grandsire lay stretched on the upper bank of the Look-look-shouie, smoking Quillshettlemen in a small pipe of dark green stone, and watching the antics of Torouskin's children as they splashed about in the clear, cold stream, endeavouring to catch the bright denizens of the water. As the venerable old man gazed, he recalled the days of his own childhood. So absorbed was he in his dreams that he never noticed the approach of his grandson until he felt the touch of Torouskin's hand on his shoulder. "Wherefore dost thou gaze so earnestly at the stream, father of my father?" "My thoughts," replied the old man, "were back in the days of my childhood when I too was young;

then would my mother take me by the hand and swinging a basket over my shoulder, lead me forth up the stream to my father's fish trap. There we would fill our basket with the shining kokanees. Sometimes we would stray into the silent woods and gather ripe berries until we grew weary, then flinging ourselves down on the soft moss watch a family of skunks frisking about catching large brown beetles. Oft I would stand on my mother's shoulder and thrusting my hand into a hole in a dead tree, draw forth from its nest a young sparrowhawk. Day by day would I watch the downy little balls until their eyes were opened, then would I take one home. Ah! How fondly did I treasure my little pet till it found wings and flew off leaving me mourning. Thus hath it been all the days of my life, all that was loved, all that was treasured, hath gone—even as that much-loved bird. Youth, strength, everything I prized has departed and I remain useless, helpless." "Nay, say not so, my father," said Torouskin tenderly, "for thy wisdom remaineth. Who so esteemed in counsel as thou art? Even now I was about to ask thine aid in weaving osier baskets such as my father used to catch these fish, even as thou and thy father caught them of old."

The old man, soothed with these words, smiled with pleasure. Torouskin, summoning his children, started off to cut willows in a grove near the lakeshore; but bright-eyed Minat-coe lingered and taking her grandfather by the hand led him out to gather bundles of wild hemp, the filaments of which her deft fingers would twist into strong twine to bind the osier baskets.

Happy was the group which sat on the shore of the great Lake weaving the long pliant osiers into a trap or conical basket. The old man sat smoking, or instructing the younger members of his family. "Ke-ke-was" (grandfather), said the lively Minat-coe, "what if it should happen to my father even as it happened unto thee, when thou wert young, when the Big Men came down from their caves, allured by the abundance of fish?" "Jest not, my child," replied the old man fondly stroking Minat-coe's glossy head, "for, once they took him hardly would he escape." "Tell us about the Big Men, Ke-ke-was," cried everyone in a breath. The old man shook his head. "Tell me, Ke-ke-was," persisted Minat-coe, coaxingly, and the old man slowly filling his pipe began thus:

"In the days that are gone I hunted in the mountains alone and fearless. Game of all kinds was plentiful and every night I returned to our camp my horse heavily laden. At last my father and mother grew weary of meat, and longed for the bright trout that frequent these waters. My father went up the stream a day's journey from our encampment, and built a fish trap, similar to the one we are making now. When he had finished, he put me in charge of it. I visited it daily, every morning. I went at sunrise and returned with fish enough for all our tribe. Suddenly the supply of fish ceased. Day after day I went but found nothing in the trap. Thinking it must have been robbed, I resolved to watch, so taking my blanket with me one night, I lay down by the trap. The moon had not risen, and the night was dark and cloudy. All night I watched but no one came near the trap. Towards morning I fell asleep and soon I began to have troubled dreams. I heard a shrill shrieking whistle as of the north wind, and my senses were oppressed by a vile, suffocating odour. Suddenly I woke to a consciousness of being lifted off the ground. Upwards I was lifted until I found myself on a level with a monstrous face.

"I was too frightened to observe much, for a huge pair of jaws opened, and emitted a laugh that sounded like thunder. I expected every moment to be put into that huge mouth and devoured; but the great creature in whose hands I was, stooped down and lifted up my blanket which had fallen to the ground, and wrapping it carefully around me, placed me in the bosom of the goatskin shirt he wore. I struggled until I got my head into the air, for there was a fearful smell of garlic about this huge creature that nearly choked me.

"Soon he began to whistle. It was the same sound I had heard in my sleep and thought was the north wind. The Big Man calmly filled the basket with fish out of my trap, then, slinging it onto his shoulders, began to ascend the mountain still whistling with all his might. Once he stopped and taking me out of his breast he took a fish and tried to cram it down my throat, but seeing me choke he desisted, and putting me once more in his bosom went on his way whistling.

"Peeping out of the bosom of his shirt I saw we were in a huge cave. It was dark save for the red glow of some smouldering embers at the farther end. Throwing a few twigs on the embers, the Big Man blew them until with a sharp crackling sound they began to blaze, then I saw how vast a cave we were in. It was somewhat low for its size, and from the roof hung garlic, meat and herbs. Taking me out of his shirt, the Big Man tied me with a rope by the leg to a log that lay near the fire. There he stood looking at me, and then for the first time I had a good look at him. Thou knowest Torouskin, that I was ever esteemed a large man, but standing by the Big Man my head was scarce level with his knees. His body was covered with garments of goatskin and was white, and he had a long bushy beard that hung down to his waist. After taking a long look at me he went to a dark corner of the cave and presently returned with an armful of soft furs which he threw on the ground at my feet and signed me to lie down. He next began to string fish on a long slender willow which he hung in front of the fire. I watched his movement with fear and curiosity; soon I heard a shrieking whistle outside the cave. At first it seemed distant, then it came nearer and soon it ceased, and with a loud trampling noise another Big Man entered the cave. He had evidently been hunting, for he carried three fine does supported by their necks from his belt as thou, Torouskin, would hang a grouse. Pulling them from his belt he threw them on the ground and advancing squatted down beside the Big Man who had taken me, and they began to converse in voices like thunder. As I watched the two Big Men I was struck with the mild kindly look on their big faces. Presently my captor came to me and loosing the strong rope that held me, took me over to the firelight for his companion to look at. The other Big Man after examining me closely burst into a fit of laughter in which his companion joined. Then he seated me on his knee while his friend took the fish from before the fire and they began to eat their evening meal. They gave me a portion and seemed much amused to see me eat. Suddenly one of the Big Men gave a howl of pain, and moaning, held out his hand for his friend to look at. The other Big Man examined it tenderly and big tears of sympathy streamed down his cheeks. Standing on his knees I could see that a fishbone had run into his thumb and as their fingers were altogether too clumsy to remove it I seized the bone in my teeth and pulled it out. The Big Man smiled, looked grateful and soon dried his tears. I afterwards found that these Big Men were extremely sensitive to pain, the least hurt would make them cry and moan.

"After they had eaten their supper my captor rose and rolling a large stone to the mouth of the cave, blocked the entrance. Then he took me and laid me on my bed of skins, carefully tucking me in.

"The fire died down and the cave grew dark, then I heard the most horrible sounds which I felt could only be the snores of these men. Long, long was I kept by my kindly captor. In vain I tried to escape but they watched me too closely. Every day I went out in the fisherman's shirt until the run of fish was over. Every day the hunter came back laden with game. When they left me alone they always left me securely tied. They treated me with the greatest kindness and were affectionate with each other, but they would never let me go free and my heart grew sad, and I longed to see my own people once more. I watched unceasingly for a chance to escape, and at last one night I observed a ray of light stealing in between the rock and the entrance. I rose softly and found a crack left open through which the moonlight was streaming; it was large enough for me to force my way through. As soon as I was outside the cave I ran with all my might. I cared not whither as long as I was free. For months I wandered living on roots and berries, and at last I struck the headwaters of the Look-look-shouie and following down stream I found my father's camp.

"How my father and mother rejoiced to see me again! But even now as the winter approaches I dread to hear the shrill shrieking whistle of the north wind as it rises in gusts and sweeps over the great Lake, for in it I hear the whistle of the Big Men."

"Ke-ke-was," cried Minat-coe when the old man had finished his story, "are the Big Men spirits? Do they die even as we die?" "Who can tell my child, no one knows. There are strange things in these mountains."

Next morning Torouskin went up the stream and built a dam and set a trap which he visited daily. He always returned with an abundance of fish. One day he returned empty-handed and in terror. At first he refused to tell the cause of his fear but when pressed by the old man, he told the following story:

"I went to the fish trap as usual this morning and after I had gathered the fish into the basket and was about to return I heard a shrieking whistle! Nearer and nearer it came. I hid in the long grass trembling and waited and waited. Then with a heavy tramp that shook the earth, a man of monstrous size came whistling along. His face was turned upwards watching a large white swan. He passed close to me and I quaked lest his huge foot should crush me; he never heeded me, but went on gazing after the swan and so passed my hiding place, whistling. A strong smell of garlic filled the air around. When he had passed my hiding place I crept out and came home as fast as I could run regardless of my fish. Never will I doubt the wisdom and truth of the aged, for, as thou sayest Ke-ke-was, there are many strange things in these mountains."

Appendix 3

The Glittering Hair

Long, long ago, when my Grandfather was a boy, an old man told him the following story of The Glittering Hair.

Before Incowla's time, there lived a very Great Chief named Immanchuten, who lived in a beautiful lodge made of Buffalo hides, tanned and painted with the historic records of his tribe. Immanchuten was young, rich and handsome. He had fields of corn, large pasture lands, herds of cows and horses; besides a great number of robes of Bear, Wolf and Marten skins, Saddle Cloths, Fire Bags and leggings of rich beadwork embroidery. All men feared and honoured him; for his fame had spread throughout the land as a mighty hunter and a brave warrior. At this time there also lived in a small kindred tribe, nearby, a youth, the sole survivor of his family. His parents having died of a fell disease, left him with nothing but one poor pony. "Take him," said his dying father, "be good to him and he'll be good to you."

The poor boy feeling desolate and lonely, resolved to forget his sorrows in work, so he went to the Chief Immanchuten and said, "Give me work for myself and horse." "What can you do with that miserable little scrub?" demanded the Chief. "Give me work and you will see how hard I can work, and as for the horse—he is my only friend." "Can you prepare my field for the corn crop?" "Try me, Great Chief, only try me," replied the boy. "Well take your pony and prepare the ground." Gladly the boy harnessed his horse with the poor rawhide harness and hitched him to the rough wooden plough he had made; then he went to work till evening, when Immanchuten came to inspect his workmen. "Well done," cried the Chief, "You have done better than all the others. Work again tomorrow."

Early the next morning the boy and his horse went at work again and they worked till evening, when the other workmen ceased working—but still he went on, for Immanchuten had forgotten to come. It grew dusk. Glancing round, the boy Katla saw a glimmering light rising from the ground at a spot where his plough had loosened the ground; he stooped and raking in the dirt with his fingers drew forth a long glittering golden hair. It was fine as silk and glowed with the radiance of the sun. Katla looked, fascinated—he passed it through his grimy fingers, and it curled round and round them glowing like a flame. Then he hid it in his shirt bosom. But the bright light streamed from it still.

The boy stopped work—took his horse to shelter—threw a robe over it and gathered its supper, the golden hair glittering and glowing in his shirt the while. Then he buried it in the ground, thinking that after he had eaten his evening meal he would take it up again. As he stood thinking Immanchuten came and called him to supper. Glancing round, he saw the bright light from the hair. Katla put his foot over it to hide it. Still it glowed and shone. "What have you there boy?" cried Immanchuten. "Nothing," answered the boy. Immanchuten, stooping, drew the long glittering hair from its hiding place. Amazed, he stroked it and it glittered and curled around his fingers like a living thing. He too was fascinated. Then he turned to Katla and in anger cried, "You would have hidden this from me. Go, go and never return unless you can bring her upon whose head this grew."

Katla was overwhelmed with grief, for in the short time he had worked for Immanchuten he had learned to love him. "Go," thundered the Chief. Katla ran weeping to his horse; while he clung to the pony's neck weeping, the horse turned his head, and with a look of human intelligence in his eyes said, "What ails you Katla?" The boy had never heard a horse speak before and, still weeping, he told the story of how he had found the sunbright hair. Then the horse said, "Come early tomorrow morning, and I will take you to the woman with the sunlit hair. You shall win back Immanchuten's respect."

The boy patted his horse and hid himself from the Chief's sight till morning, when he rose, and running to his horse said "Are you ready?" The horse only neighed. So he sprang on his back. The horse taking the bit in his teeth started down the valley till he came to a canyon where they lost sight of Immanchuten's beautiful painted lodge, and the encampment of his people, and their fields. Then the horse neighed three times and Lo! Katla's rags changed into a beautiful Buckskin shirt, all overlaid with fringes and embroidered with beads. His leggings also were a mass of beautiful beadwork. He had a long string of large white beads round his neck, also another of Bear's teeth. In his long black locks were Eagle feathers. But the greatest surprise of all was his horse: it was now a lovely charger with glossy skin and arching neck and distended nostrils, and it pranced and danced under a handsome saddle and flowing saddle blanket fringed with Bear-skin.

Proudly it trotted through the canyon to where a large prairie stretched. Here it broke into a mad gallop till it passed quite over the prairie and stood at the edge of a vast lake where without hesitation the horse plunged in and swam for miles and miles till he reached the further shore.

Now on the further side of the Lake the shore was clothed in forest, a dark gloomy forest.

They were in midnight darkness, and still the horse went on. Then as he made an abrupt turn, Katla became aware of a glow of light which increased as they went on till it became a glare. The heat was dreadful, and by the crackling noise the boy knew the forest was burning. As they journeyed on, the glare became greater and the heat more dreadful; flames burst from the dark woods and leapt from tree to tree! tongues of fire licked up the underbrush. The trees began to crash and fall around them. The fire roared, till the boy nearly fainted, when Lo! he heard through the roar of the burning forest the cool splashing sound of water.

Looking through the smoke he saw a vista in the forest through which a wild stream flowed; into this the beautiful horse plunged, and following down it, bore his rider to safety from the burning forest to a lovely spot where a gentle slope stole up from the stream to the Mountain. So gradual was the slope it must have been many miles in length. It was covered with rich grass.

A long trail seemed to run up to the mountain, and on either side of the trail were Lodges. There were men and women, a very great assembly. Now the horse and boy rode proudly up the trail between the Lodges. Men, women and children ran out to see the handsome stranger and his beautiful horse, for none of them had a horse like that, save the Chief's daughter.

Many of them begged for a ride on the beautiful horse. To some he granted their request, but none could long sit on the gay, spirited animal, till one came, a woman with a glory of sunbright hair that flashed and gleamed. As she stood before Katla, begging for a ride on his lovely horse, he affected to be unwilling to allow the girl to mount his noble horse, saying that her small hands could not hold nor control his steed; but when the Chief, her father, assured him that his daughter could ride any horse owned by her tribe and that without saddle, the boy consented. The girl sprang lightly into the saddle; the boy bounded up behind her, muttering a cry. The horse bolted, plunged into the stream, and soon disappeared from the sight of the astonished chief and tribesmen. At first they merely thought the Chief's daughter could not control the animal and waited long, expecting her to return; but when they realized that she had indeed gone, they too mounted and started in pursuit, but they never sighted the horse and its riders. They were gone.

When the horse had dashed into the stream he headed up it for the forest, and when he gained the forest, it was night, and Lo! all the fires had burned out. The darkness was intense. There was no light save the princess's sunbright hair, which glittered and glowed, shining out as a light in the darkness.

Now when they came to the lake, the horse plunged in as before. As they swam through the water the princess's hair was reflected in its depth like a glowing star. "Now," thought Katla, "Now will my Chief be pleased." And he rode on gaily, quite regardless of the girl's entreaties to be allowed to return.

At noon next day they stood before the Lodge of Immanchuten, who seeing the beautiful sunlit hair, thought he had never seen any one as lovely. Her hair hung down her back in long tendrils and light seemed to radiate from it. Her skin was white as milk; her cheeks like roses. He was astonished and delighted. He begged her to dismount and enter his Lodge; everything he had was hers if she would deign to stay with him as his wife.

The girl was much struck with the dignified young Chief and thought that she never before had seen such a handsome man; but, hesitating, she said: "I am a Chief's daughter, and not as other women am I, for my father found me, when he was on a distant warpath. I was sent from the clouds to comfort my mother who mourned the death of her first babe. None of my brothers or sisters are like me. I must be treated as a Chief's daughter and a princess. Bid your boy go bring my glass that I may dress my hair every day; meanwhile give me a lodge to myself among the women, or I will go back to the Clouds if I may not return to my father."

Now Immanchuten, instead of thanking Katla for what he had already done for him, told him roughly "Go, bring the glass—do you expect a Chief's daughter to live without a glass to see how to dress her hair, and such hair."

Poor Katla once more slunk out of sight and went weeping to his horse. "Weep no more Katla," said the Horse kindly, "you were good to me. Now I will be good to you. First you must tell me why you weep." "I have brought the princess, as my Master bade me, thanks to you, dear friend; but now I must get her glass. How can I go back to her father's people; they will know us and kill us." The horse laughed, a kindly laugh, and said, "Come to me tomorrow morning."

Again Katla hid till morning—then he went to his horse, and after greeting him, bounded on his back. Off went the horse as before.

The boy found the horse under him changed from a noble glossy steed, into a poor shaggy, shambling Pinto Pony, and his own clothes changed into those of a Medicine Man: the beads round his neck changed into a string of dried toads, the beautiful Bears' teeth into a wriggling snake. His hair became frowsy and full of feathers.

His horse shambled over the prairie through the lake and forest, then down the stream that led to the encampment of the princess's father. When they arrived at the encampment they found every one bewailing the lost girl. When they saw Katla and his pinto they rejoiced for "Now," they said, "we shall find our princess. This certainly is a very great doctor. He will find out where she is."

The old Chief came out of his Lodge and promised Katla blankets, horses and tobacco if he would find out where his daughter had gone. "Show me her house," said Katla, "I must first look at it, and take something from it that she has held in her hands. Then I will ride out with it, and it will lead me to where she is." Katla was now quite bold for he was sure that he was not recognized.

They took him to her Lodge and on the wall hung the glass. Katla took it—"Now I go to look for the maiden," he said as he left the Lodge and climbed slowly on to his horse. Then when he was out of sight, the horse once more became a beautiful swift animal, and away he went faster and faster, through forest, lake, prairie and canyon, till he stood once more before the Lodge of Immanchuten.

Now as Katla rode up to the door of Immanchuten, he felt sure of a kindly welcome, and indeed the Chief advanced to meet him with a smile and his hand held out in welcome. The princess came running from her Lodge and snatched the mirror. As she admired herself in it she cried, "Now will I gladly stay if you will bring me my own horse."

"Katla," said the Chief, "Go once more. Get the horse and I will make you my head man, and your voice shall be heard when the Chiefs and warriors meet in council." "I will try," replied Katla, "one more visit to Sun-lit Hair's father's encampment, but they will surely kill me this time." Again Katla stood weeping before his horse, and again the horse comforted him.

This time when they reached the stream, the horse bade the boy dismount and wait while he went in search of Glistening Hair's horse, and told him that if he did not come back soon and the water became very troubled and muddy, to return home, for by the muddy water he would know that his true friend, his horse, was dead. Saying this the faithful horse plunged in the stream.

Katla waited all night, and part of the next day. Then Lo! at noon, the sky clouded, the wind rose; the water rose also, and foamed and roared in a turbulent manner. Katla watched and wept for now he felt sure that his friend was dead and he would see him no more.

Just as he was giving way to despair, he heard a splashing and dashing sound. Through the foaming flood he saw two horses' heads appear. Gradually they emerged. Then his own dear horse and another beautiful creature stood side by side on the bank. "Come quickly now," said the horse.

Katla mounted, and away they flew, ever faster and faster in a mad race, on and on till they stood before the princess's Lodge. As soon as she heard the horse neigh the beautiful girl ran out. Her joy knew no bounds. She threw her arms round her horse's neck, "Now, now," she cried, "Am I content to abide with Immanchuten." And cutting off one of her long glittering curls, she hung it around Katla's neck. There it hung glittering like a golden coil.

Immanchuten kept his word with Katla, made him head man and gave him cattle and horses. His voice was ever heard amongst the wise men. And he was esteemed the wisest, for he ever sought courage of his horse.

And both Katla and his horse lived many, many years and prospered.

Notes

Notes to the Introduction

Notes are indicated by page and line number and are introduced by key words in italics; for example, x:36 *Central Province.*

ix:16 *Ceylon Regiment. Ceylon Calendar, 1825,* p. 144.

ix:20 *East India Company. Annual Register, 1798* (London: W. Otridge & Son et al., 1800), p. 111.

ix:24 *Calcutta. Asiatic Journal* 4 (1817) : 627.

ix:27 *married Louise. Asiatic Journal* 19 (1825) : 851.

x: 2 *Colombo in 1824 and 1825. Ceylon Almanac, 1833,* p. 155, states that Lieutenant Deacon was appointed 3 August 1815, staff officer, Galle. In 1824 he was staff officer, 16th Regiment, stationed at Colombo (*Asiatic Journal* 17 [1824], p. 678), and in 1825, staff officer, Ceylon Regiment (*Ceylon Calendar, 1825,* p. 145).

x: 6 *Ratnapura. Ceylon Almanac, 1833,* pp. 111, 142.

x:15 *in 1829. Fasti academiae Mariscallanae Aberdonensis . . . 1593–1860,* ed. P.J. Anderson (Aberdeen: New Spalding Club, 1889–98), 2: 458.

x:16 *James Skinner.* Bishop James Skinner (1818–81) was a son of John Skinner (1769–1841), dean of Dunkeld, who in turn was a son of Bishop John Skinner (1744–1816), bishop of Aberdeen from 1786 to 1816 (*DNB* 18: 343). Bishop John Skinner was the second son of Rev. John Skinner (1721–1807), minister at Longside, Aberdeenshire, who was imprisoned for episcopal preaching in 1753. For further information, see ibid., pp. 344–46.

x:25 *at Hope.* On 2 June 1868 Bishop George Hills recorded in his journal: "I was most comfortably housed by Mrs. Glennie, who occupies the Parsonage. I found that I knew many years ago her husband Mr. Stratton Moir who came to Durham in 1833 with James Skinner. Mrs. Glennie was born in Aberdeen & belonged to an Episcopalian family. Bp. Skinner of Aberdeen was Godfather to her daughter Miss Susan Moir. Her family & the Skinners were intimate. She knew James Skinner & his brothers' four children" (Journal of the Rt. Rev. George Hills, D.D., MS, Archives of the Ecclesiastical Province of British Columbia, Vancouver School of Theology [hereafter cited as Hills' Journal]).

x:36 *Central Province.* During the scramble for plantation lands in Ceylon between 1836 and 1846, all the civil servants bought property in the Ambegamoa Valley (then called Upper Bulatgame). Philip Anstruther bought 1,374 acres there in 1841 (information supplied by Dr. T.J. Barron, Department of History, University of Edinburgh). The prospects for the success of the coffee plantations were not fulfilled, and as the result of the crash between 1846 and 1849, most of these plantations returned to the wilderness.

xi: 1 *sea-captain of Amsterdam.* Baptismal Register, St. Peter's Church, Fort, Colombo. I am indebted to Mr. J.R. Sinnatamby, deputy surveyor general (retired), Colombo, for examining the register.

xi: 6 *Ambegamoa.* I am indebted to Dr. T.J. Barron for supplying the information that, in a list of European residents drawn up by the colonial secretariat in 1843, an S. Moir is stated to be the proprietor of a coffee plantation at Bulatgame and that an A.R. [Alexander Rogers] was a superintendent of a coffee estate at Kundesolle. Dr. Barron also informs me that the Proceedings of the Ceylon Agricultural Society for the half-year ending 1 July 1843, containing a list of lands purchased from the Crown, indicates that in Saffragam, Southern Province, S. Moir purchased 456 acres at Koomarewelle in Medde Korle and 270 acres at Kotembage under Kaduwate Korle on 21 November 1842.

xi:10 *29 September 1845*. Baptismal Register, St. Peter's Church, Colombo.

xi:27 *London School*. For further information on George Ferris Whidborne Mortimer (1805–71), see *DNB* 13: 1022–23.

xii:23 *the Bible*. Bishop Hills described Stratton Moir's book as "a curious prayer Book of James I, date 1615, bound with N. Testament" (Hills' Journal, 2 June 1868).

xiii:35 *Skagit River*. A.C. Anderson, "Journal of an expedition under the command of A.C. Anderson of the Hudson's Bay Company undertaken with the view of ascertaining the practicability of a communication with the interior..." (part of the typescript of "History of the North West Coast," typescript copy of original MS in the Academy of Pacific Coast History [Bancroft Library], University of California, Berkeley, University of British Columbia Library, Special Collections Division).

xiv: 8 *consumed much time*. Eden Colvile to the Governor, Deputy Governor and Committee, Hudson's Bay Company, 21 October 1852, *London Correspondence Inward from Eden Colvile 1849–1852,* ed. E.E. Rich assisted by A.M. Johnson, with an introduction by W.L. Morton (London: Hudson's Bay Record Society, 1956), p. 168.

xiv:17 *domain in England*. Hills' Journal, 5 June 1868.

xiv:19 *20 August 1860*. Pre-emption Record 29, Hope (F.W. Laing, "Colonial Farm Settlers on the Mainland of British Columbia, 1858–1871," typescript, Provincial Archives of British Columbia [hereafter cited as PABC], copy, University of British Columbia Library, Special Collections Division). Since January 1860 it had been possible to file a claim for a pre-emption of unoccupied, unreserved, and unsurveyed crown land on the payment of a registration fee of 8d. Not until after the government survey had been completed did the purchase price of 10s. an acre have to be paid (Governor James Douglas, Proclamation, 4 January 1860).

xv:28 *Panama fever.* Peter O'Reilly's Diary, 1860, 10 October 1860, MS, PABC. Peter O'Reilly's annual diaries are hereafter cited as O'Reilly Diaries.

xvi:10 *moved into their home.* Ibid., 8 December 1860.

xvi:12 *a dance.* Ibid., 8 February 1861.

xvi:18 *champaigne galore.* Ibid., 11 February 1861.

xvi:20 £800 . . . *a writ.* Ibid., 6 March and 22 April 1861.

xvi:25 *crops were destroyed.* Hills' Journal, 6 November 1861.

xvi:29 *offering advice.* O'Reilly Diaries, 17 January 1862.

xvi:32 *fine gentleman.* Ibid., 18 January 1862.

xvi:37 *great disgust.* Ibid., 22 January 1862.

xvii: 2 *Bread &c &c.* Ibid., 23 January 1862.

xvii: 6 *credit at the Fort.* Ibid., 5 March 1862.

xvii:15 *and a half months.* Ibid., 2 February 1862.

xvii:17 *by the Bishop.* Ibid., 29 April 1862.

xvii:20 *Christ Church, Hope.* Edgar Dewdney and Jane Shaw Moir were married by the Rev. A.D. Pringle on 23 March 1864 (British Columbia, Colonial Secretary, Marriage Licences 23 March 1864–14 June 1867, MS, PABC); see also New Westminster *British Columbian*, 30 March 1864, where she is described as "the eldest daughter of Stratton Moir, 'Dhekinde,'

Ambegamoa, Ceylon and step-daughter of Thomas Glennie of Hope."

xviii:21 *Fort Hope.* Hills' Journal, 3 June 1860; see also Governor James Douglas to Colonel R.C. Moody, 20 November 1860, B.C., Governor Douglas, Private Official Letterbook, 27 May 1859–9 January 1864, MS, PABC.

xviii:25 *question him.* Governor Douglas to the Duke of Newcastle, 25 October 1860, Great Britain, Parliament, *Papers Relative to the Affairs of British Columbia*, 1862 (Cmd. 2952, 1st series), 4:28 (hereafter cited as *BCP*).

xviii:30 *passes & buildings.* Hills' Journal, 3 June 1860.

xviii:33 *in the press.* See, for example, *Colonist*, 7 November 1861: "It is a notorious fact that when a road is to be located or a district explored, a magistrate, a constable, a Hudson's Bay servant, or peradventure an Indian, is sent out to explore and report upon the same, and after the location is decided upon, the Chief Commissioner with his staff of Royal Engineers is instructed to make the road."

xix:19 *horses and mules.* Hills' Journal, 6 August 1860; and O'Reilly Diaries, 6 August 1860.

xix:25 *prospects for agriculture.* Douglas informed the Colonial Office that "the peculiar feature of the country is the profusion of grass that covers both woodland and meadow, affording rich pastures for domestic animals, a circumstance which gives to this district an extraordinary value, as every part of the surface, whether hill or valley, may be turned to account and made available either for tillage or stock farming" (Governor Douglas to the Duke of Newcastle, 25 October 1860, *BCP*, 4:28).

xix:28 *just below it.* W.A.G. Young to O'Reilly, 14 August 1860, Colonial Secretary, Correspondence Outward, PABC.

xx: 5 *this important service.* Moody to Douglas, 24 August 1860, R.C. Moody Correspondence, PABC.

xx: 9 *on the Brigade Trail.* Sergeant William McColl to Moody, 23 October 1860, Colonial Correspondence, PABC.

xx: 17 *good military positions.* Douglas to the Colonial Office, 28 January 1861, B.C., Governor Douglas, Despatches to London, 8 June 1859–28 December 1863, PABC.

xx: 18 *surveyed by McColl.* The road was carried over an elevation of 4,000 feet "without a single gradient exceeding 1 foot in 12, a fact very creditable to Serjeant M'Call and the detachment of Royal Engineers employed in marking out the line" (*BCP*, 4:30).

xx: 24 *Similkameen River.* McColl completed the survey of Princeton in November 1860 (O'Reilly to the Colonial Secretary, 29 November 1860, Colonial Correspondence, PABC).

xx: 26 *west of Vermilion Forks. Colonist,* 4 October 1860.

xx: 33 *Marston.* On 20 September 1860 Marston filed at Hope a pre-emption claim for 160 acres lying at the extreme point of the forks of the Similkameen (Laing, "Colonial Farm Settlers," p. 434). He seems to have remained only one winter at Princeton and then abandoned his right. In 1897 Samuel D. Sandes acquired the land, when he pre-empted a total of 331 acres. In 1899, when Sandes sold it, what had been Marston's claim passed into the hands of W.J. Waterman. It formed part of the townsite of the present town of Princeton.

xxi: 14 *Hope community.* Moody's record of the road building is contained in the files of the B.C. Lands and Works Department, 1861, Colonial Correspondence, PABC. At the time the road was discontinued, it extended for twenty-five miles. Beyond that point there was a mule trail, thirty-two miles long.

xxiii: 25 *did not appear.* O'Reilly Diaries, 1 September 1868.

xxiii: 28 *perfect hurricane.* Ibid., 2 September 1868.

xxiii: 30 *quite private.* Ibid., 3 September 1868.

xxiv: 1 *Yorkshire in 1825.* Pioneer Form completed by Susan Louisa Allison, PABC. See also John C. Goodfellow, *The Story of Similkameen* (Penticton: *Penticton Herald*, [1958]), p. 42.

xxiv: 25 *chimeral.* J.F. Allison to his parents, 25 January 1849, John Fall Allison Letters, in the possession of Mrs. Elvie Sisson.

xxiv: 39 *own energy.* Allison to his parents, 16 September 1849.

xxv: 3 *dunning for money.* Allison to his parents, 3 September 1851.

xxv: 6 *Factory store.* Allison to his parents, 31 December 1851.

xxv: 8 *one thousand miles.* Allison to his parents, 31 December 1852.

xxv: 10 *find it.* William Allison to his parents, 31 December 1852, John Fall Allison Letters.

xxv: 12 *family in 1854.* Allison to his parents, 31 March 1853.

xxv: 15 *November.* Allison to his parents, 30 September and 14 November 1857.

xxv: 23 *matters.* Allison to Dr. Robert Allison, 4 December 1857.

xxv: 25 *Fraser River excitement.* Allison to his parents, 15 June 1858.

xxv: 40 *future.* Allison to his parents, 1 September 1858.

xxvi: 1 *posting books.* Allison to his parents, 12 March 1859.

xxvi: 6 *at large.* Allison to his parents, 26 June 1859.

xxvi: 9 *through the Winter.* Allison to his parents, 30 September 1859.

xxvi: 11 *six dollars a day.* Allison to his parents, 23 October 1859.

xxvi: 14 *open the trail.* Allison to his parents, 18 May 1860.

xxvi:16 *Similkameen River.* Allison to his parents, 8 July 1860.

xxvi:22 *ten dollars a day.* Allison to his parents, 11 August 1860.

xxvi:28 *I have seen.* Allison to his parents, 12 November 1860.

xxvi:31 *better road.* Allison to his parents, 6 October 1860.

xxvi:41 *chosen by O'Reilly.* Allison's was the third pre-emption claim at Princeton to be recorded. On 20 September 1860 he filed for 160 acres at the junction of Similkameen River and Red Earth Fork (Laing, "Colonial Farm Settlers," p. 434).

xxvii:11 *anything better.* Allison to his parents, 10 November 1860.

xxvii:20 *30 feet.* Arthur T. Bushby, "Journal of Trip to Kootenay, 31 August–26 October 1864," 4 September 1864, MS, PABC.

xxvii:40 *trust in princes.* Allison to his parents, 12 November 1860.

xxviii: 2 *Mission Creek.* Notation on J.F. Allison's "Rough Sketch of Proposed Route from Princeton to the Okanagan Lake," 18 July 1861 (Colonial Office Correspondence [Map Division], PABC; see also O'Reilly Diaries, 18 July 1861).

xxviii: 4 *Princeton–Kamloops Trail.* Moody to E.H. Sanders, 19 June 1862; and Captain H.R. Luard to Allison, 19 July 1862, B.C. Lands and Works Department, 1862, Correspondence Outward.

xxviii: 7 *Hope–Similkameen Road.* Articles of Agreement between A.N. Birch, colonial secretary in charge of the Land and Works Department, and J.F. Allison, for repairs of the mule trail from Hope to Similkameen, Colonial Office Correspondence (Map Division). See also A.R. Howse to Allison, 22 June 1864; and Joseph W. Trutch to Allison, 27 August 1864, B.C. Lands and Works Department, 1864, Correspondence Outward.

xxviii: 9 *concerning poor mother.* Allison to his parents, 28 September 1863.

xxviii:17 *always is.* Arthur T. Bushby, "Journal of Trip to Kootenay," 22 October 1864.

xxviii:20 *hospital at New Westminster.* Allison to George Allison, 19 May 1866.

xxviii:26 *August 1868. Colonist,* 12 August 1868.

xxviii:30 *photograph of his wife.* Allison to George Allison, 22 November 1868.

xxx:32 *six weeks.* Allison to his parents, 7 January 1874.

xxxi: 2 *familiar language for her children.* Clive Phillipps-Wolley, *A Sportsman's Eden* (London: Richard Bentley & Son, 1888), p. 77.

xxxi:12 *California in 1872.* On 26 September 1872, the *Colonist* reported that the cost of the animal was "upwards of $1000."

xxxi:27 *cattle and produce.* J.F. Allison to his parents, 5 March 1874.

xxxi:31 *not elected. Colonist,* 27 October 1875; and New Westminster *Mainland Guardian,* same date.

xxxii: 7 *Washington for some time.* See J. Orin Oliphant, "Winter Losses of Cattle in the Oregon Country, 1847–1890," *Washington Historical Quarterly* 23 (1932): 3–17 (hereafter cited as *WHQ*). The winters of 1862 and 1880 were disastrous, and heavy losses also resulted from the cold winters of 1874 and 1878. Oliphant attributes the losses principally to the failure to provide sufficient food for the cattle and to lack of water.

xxxii:35 *thousand dollars.* Allison to Mrs. Robert Allison, 12 June 1881.

xxxiii: 19 *idea of Wilfred.* Jane Shaw Dewdney to Mrs. Peter O'Reilly, 29 July 1871, Jane Shaw Dewdney Correspondence, PABC.

xxxiv: 10 *only twice before seen Europeans.* H.H. Gowen, *Church Work in British Columbia . . .* (London: Longmans Green, 1899), p. 23.

xxxiv: 28 *at present.* Allison to Mrs. Robert Allison, 12 June 1881.

xxxv: 16 *she frequently saw.* Angus McDonald, the fur trader, wrote: "This Mrs. Ellis was rather good looking on her first arrival, but she is strong and young and the labor of making four or five children took much of the crimson out of her cheeks and she looks pale and loose of skin. These ladies [Mrs. Haynes and Mrs. Ellis] go down to New Westminster to be delivered of their babies. Would it not be better for them to be delivered of them where they make them? Mine always performed that serious work alone" (Angus McDonald, "A Few Items of the West," ed. F.W. Howay, William S. Lewis, and Jacob A. Meyers, *WHQ* 8 [1917]: 204).

xxxvi: 1 *forget their troubles.* Mrs. J.F. Allison, "Early History of Princeton," *Princeton Star*, 23 February 1923.

xxxvi: 5 *at Hope.* "Beatrice, Louisa and Wilfred have been wintering with their Grandmama at Hope" (Allison to Mrs. Robert Allison, 12 June 1881).

xxxvi: 25 *isolated home.* Hester E. White, "General Sherman at Osoyoos," Okanagan Historical Society, *Fifteenth Report* (Vernon: *Vernon News*, 1951), p. 59. A reprinting of "Report of Journey made by General W.T. Sherman in the Northwest and Middle Parts of the United States in 1883," by J.C. Tidball, colonel, aide-de-camp, brevet brigadier-general, in *Report of the Secretary of War*, no. 1, part 2 (Washington, 1883), 1: 231–42.

xxxvi: 33 *model pioneer home.* Phillipps-Wolley, *A Sportsman's Eden*, p. 76.

xxxvi: 34 *I formerly could.* Allison to George Allison, 2 March 1889.

xxxvii:18 *silver and gold.* Susan Louisa Allison to George Allison, 16 April 1899, Allison Family Papers, in the possession of Mrs. Elvie Sisson. When the minister of mines sent Major William Downie to inspect the Granite Creek district in 1886, Downie visited Allison's copper mine and saw some very fine specimens of peacock (Major William Downie, *Hunting for Gold* [San Francisco: The California Publishing Co., 1893], p. 284).

xxxvii:23 *Friday Creek.* Charles Camsell, *Preliminary Report on a Part of the Similkameen District of British Columbia,* Geological Survey of Canada (Ottawa: Government Printing Office, 1908), pp. 13–14.

xxxvii:35 *gold rush of 1885.* George M. Dawson, *The Mineral Wealth of British Columbia,* Geological and Natural History Survey of Canada (Montreal: Dawson Brothers, 1889), p. 39.

xxxviii:18 *hitherto discovered.* Report of Thomas Elwyn, 23 November 1885, in *Annual Report of the* [British Columbia] *Minister of Mines* (Victoria: Richard Wolfenden, Government Printer, Government Printing Office, 1887), p. 493.

xxxviii:19 *April 1885.* British Columbia, *Government Gazette,* 16 April 1885. Allison was appointed assistant gold commissioner on 9 April 1885. He had been appointed justice of the peace in June 1876 (ibid., 10 June 1876).

xxxix:17 *on her pack-train.* "Notes of an interview with Rev. Edward Ernest Hardwick, at his home, One-Mile Creek, Princeton, 15 July 1930," typescript, PABC, p. 10.

xl: 1 *early Sixties.* O'Reilly to John Trutch, 1 July 1896, Trutch Papers, University of British Columbia Library, Special Collections Division.

xl:37 *many headed monster.* Jane Shaw Dewdney to Mrs. Peter O'Reilly, 1 March 1886, Jane Shaw Dewdney Correspondence.

xli:13 *wonderfully well.* O'Reilly to John Trutch, 7 December 1892, Trutch Papers.

xli: 20 *no Ball.* O'Reilly to John Trutch, 29 December 1893, Trutch Papers.

xli: 25 *to the utmost.* Mrs. Peter O'Reilly to John and Sir Joseph Trutch, 5 September 1893, Trutch Papers.

xli: 32 *good pay.* Susan Louisa Allison to George Allison, 16 April 1899, Allison Family Papers.

xlii: 4 *die of it this time.* O'Reilly to John Trutch, 6 May 1895, Trutch Papers.

xlii: 12 *biting it.* O'Reilly to John Trutch, 9 October 1897, Trutch Papers.

xlii: 21 *thorough housekeeper.* MS of a short story written by Mrs. Allison, in the possession of Mrs. Elvie Sisson.

xlii: 30 *Canadian laws.* An Act to Amend Certain Laws Respecting Indians and to Extend Certain Laws Relating to Matters Connected with Indians in the Provinces of Manitoba and B.C., Canada, *Statutes*, 1874, 37 Vict., c.21.

xliii: 27 *utter destitution.* "Sketches of Indian Life," MS in the possession of Mrs. Elvie Sisson.

xliii: 29 *In-Cow-Mas-Ket.* Stratton Moir, *In-Cow-Mas-Ket* (Chicago: Scroll Publishing Co., 1900).

xliii: 39 *demands of the Indians. Mainland Guardian*, 10 September 1875.

xliv: 16 *mind.* Introduction to "Tales of Tamtusalist," MS, Allison Family Papers.

xlv: 31 *Advancement of Science.* British Association for the Advancement of Science, Section 2, *Report*, 60 (1891), p. 815. See Appendix 1, pp. 73-74.

xlvi: 7 *with the collection.* "Notes of an Interview with Rev. E.E. Hardwick," p. 4.

xlvi:16 *regular succession.* Ibid., p. 15.

xlvi:18 *hues of the rainbow.* Ibid., p. 17.

xlvi:21 *London papers.* Ibid., p. 18.

xlvi:37 *Cassiar.* S.D. Sandes to Hon. E. Dewdney, 5 December 1904, Allison Family Papers.

xlvii: 5 *in 1893.* O'Reilly to John Trutch, 23 May 1893, Trutch Papers.

xlvii: 7 *for her friend.* Mrs. Peter O'Reilly to John and Sir Joseph Trutch, 27 February 1893, Trutch Papers.

xlvii:11 *Drill Hall.* For Lady Aberdeen's account of this affair, see *The Canadian Journal of Lady Aberdeen 1893–1898,* ed. John T. Saywell (Toronto: The Champlain Society, 1960), p. 146.

xlvii:17 *served with dinner.* Mrs. O'Reilly to John Trutch, 25 February 1898, Trutch Papers.

xlvii:24 *that year.* O'Reilly to John Trutch, 26 January 1897, Trutch Papers.

xlvii:28 *84 years.* O'Reilly to John Trutch, 25 March 1897, Trutch Papers.

xlvii:37 *than for him.* O'Reilly to John Trutch, 12 May 1905, Trutch Papers.

xlviii: 4 *deeply sorry for her.* O'Reilly to John Trutch, 22 May 1905, Trutch Papers.

xlviii:10 *Edgehill.* Victoria *Times*, 20 January 1906.

xlix:21 *Princeton.* The material in this paragraph is based on Harry D. Barnes, "The Early History of Hedley Camp," *British*

Columbia Historical Quarterly 12 (1948): 103–25 (hereafter cited as *BCHQ*).

xlix:24 *a small town.* "Notes of an Interview with Rev. E.E. Hardwick," p. 26. Hardwick described the social life as follows: "The people always were a friendly lot, and there were picnics in the summer and parties and dances in the winter evenings. The young people skated and had sleighing parties, and in the summers the boys had their games. . . . We have had generally an especially good football team, having quite a few men in the district who have played on big teams in the old country. The bars, of course, drew large patronage in their day, and there was a lot of gambling went on in the open space in front of the bars until the provincial law forbade it, or I suppose I should say until the laws against it began to be enforced strictly. After that whatever gambling took place was done in rooms behind the bar or in the hotels."

l:16 *The Lake. CBC Times*, week of 28 February–6 March 1954 (Toronto, 1954).

li:30 *than creed.* John C. Goodfellow, "Mrs. S.L. Allison," *BCHQ* 1 (1937): 131.

1: 2 *gold bearing sands.* Donald Fraser, correspondent in Victoria of the London *Times* and a member of the Executive Council of the colony of Vancouver Island, sent lengthy reports to his paper on mining operations in British Columbia throughout 1859 and 1860. His despatch sent from Victoria on 9 December 1859 reported that the vast extent of the auriferous area was now "established by undeniable evidence" (London *Times*, 30 January 1860). A further despatch, published in the *Times* on 17 February 1860, stated that "the productiveness of the mines is now quite settled in the affirmative."

1: 8 *my stepfather . . . my mother.* For further details on Thomas Glennie and his wife, Susan Louisa (Mildern), the widow of Stratton Moir, see the Introduction, pp. x-xvii.

1:10 *my brother.* Stratton Moir (1841–66) was the only son of Stratton and Susan Louisa Moir. According to the Rt. Rev. George Hills, bishop of Columbia, young Moir, who had entered the employ of the West Indies Trail Service, died of yellow fever at Santa Cruz, "just before the destructive tornado in the W. Indies" in October 1866 (Journal of the Rt. Rev. George Hills, 3 June 1868, MS, Archives of the Ecclesiastical Province of British Columbia, Vancouver School of Theology [hereafter cited as Hills' Journal]).

1:11 *Matheson and Company.* Matheson and Company, merchant bankers, founded in 1848 and still doing business on Lombard Street.

1:17 *Royal Mail route.* The Royal Mail Steamship Packet Vessels left Southampton on the 2nd and 17th of each month for St. Thomas in the Virgin Islands to make connection with the West Indies Royal Steamship Company's vessels travelling to Mexico and Colon (Aspinwall).

1:18 *Atrato.* A paddle steamer launched in May 1853 and commanded in 1860 by Captain Frederick Woolley. The second party of Royal Engineers, comprising Captain J.M. Grant and twelve men, was despatched by her to British Columbia on 17 September 1858. In May 1860, on her return run from St. Thomas, the *Atrato* carried 242 passengers and completed the voyage in 12½ days (London *Times*, 28 May 1860). When the Glennies sailed on 18 June from Southampton, her passengers numbered only fifty-four, but she carried £10,320 in specie, jewellery valued at £5,230, 370 bottles of quicksilver worth £2,500, and a full cargo of merchandise. Probably most of her cargo was destined for California and British Columbia (ibid., 19 June 1860).

2: 5 *Tugwell.* Rev. Lewer Street Tugwell, an ordained missionary, was sent out to British Columbia by the Church Missionary Society to assist William Duncan, a missionary catechist who had been working among the Indians at Fort Simpson since 1857. Tugwell, described by Bishop Hills as "a promising young clergyman of a right spirit and ready to devote himself to the work of the Lord" (Hills' Journal, 10 August 1860), left for Fort Simpson immediately after his arrival at Victoria, taking six months' provisions, two goats for milk, and two canaries belonging to his bride. He baptized the first Tsimshian converts on 26 July 1861. Soon after, his health broken, he and his wife left the colony.

2:17 *Bishop of Demerara.* The *Times* lists the Bishop of Antigua, Rt. Rev. William Walrond Jackson, D.D., as passenger on the *Atrato* (19 June 1860).

2:18 *St. Vincent . . . St. Pierre.* Two of the Windward Islands.

2:20 *St. Thomas.* Passengers from Southampton changed at St. Thomas, at this time a Danish possession, to the intercolonial boats. "The town has a Continental appearance, with red roofs and variously-painted walls, interspersed with green trees," Bishop Hills wrote. "On a nearer approach, an Oriental character mixed in with Danish neatness and taste" (Extract from Bishop Hills' Journal, in *Report of the Columbia Mission 1864* [London: Rivington's, 1865], p. 5).

2:25 *voyage to Colon.* The voyage from Southampton via St. Thomas to Colon took from sixteen to twenty days.

2:27 *Aspinwall.* Colon, a port on Limon Bay, was renamed Aspinwall in 1852 in honour of William H. Aspinwall, one of the promoters of the Panama Railway. Arthur T. Bushby, who travelled to British Columbia by this route in 1858, found the entrance to Aspinwall harbour to be beautiful: "Mountains & magnificent verdure to the very waters edge.—The whole scene on nearing the wharf is was [*sic*] something wonderful what with the fine trees large leaf palms &c black half naked Indians & niggers strange dresses &c" ("The Journal of Arthur Thomas Bushby, 1858–1859," ed. Dorothy Blakey Smith, *British Columbia Historical Quarterly* 21 [1957–58]: 105 [hereafter cited as *BCHQ*]).

2:38 *the dense forest.* Cf. Hills' Journal, 9 February 1865: "The route of the Panama Railway lay through the heart of a primeval forest—of the utmost tropical luxuriance—interspersed with the wildest & most picturesque scenery & along beautiful rivers."

The description of the railway route given by J.D. Pemberton also corresponds with that given by Mrs. Allison: "the railway passes through a deep marsh which quits it at Gatun on the Chagres: thence traversing a dense tropical forest, with occasional clearances and haciendas, and arriving at Barbacoas, it crosses the river, and the summit from which Balboa discovered the Pacific is seen. As the traveller advances, he obtains views of the river, reflecting from its bright surface the deep rich greens of the tropical jungle or forest, or the blossoming parasites which hang in festoons above the banks. Having passed the summit level savannahs and the spires of Panama are descried" (J. Despard Pemberton, *Facts and Figures relating to Vancouver Island and British Columbia* [London: Longman, Green, Longman and Roberts, 1860], p. 86). In 1865, when Bishop Hills journeyed by the Panama Railway, he recorded that "there was but one carriage, containing about 60 passengers. There are no glass windows but shutters only" (Hills' Journal, 9 February 1865).

3: 3 *onward to the Pacific.* Mrs. Allison's memory has failed her here. The Chagres flows into the Caribbean Sea, and the first part of her railway journey was along its course. Bishop Hills described this portion of the route as follows: "The first thirteen miles was through a deep morass, covered with the densest jungle, reeking with malaria and abounding with almost every species of wild beasts, noxious reptiles & venemous insects" (ibid.).

3:15 *hotel in Panama.* Panama, rebuilt in 1673 after its destruction in 1671 by Henry Morgan, the English buccaneer, had in 1860 a population of ten thousand. Its fortified walls were crumbling, but its Renaissance cathedral was still in good condition (Hills' Journal, 27 May 1863). Fine examples of Moorish architecture were in a dilapidated condition, and many bridges were broken down. About six miles to its southeast, and inland, were the ruins of the old city founded by the Spanish in 1519.

4: 5 *John L. Stevens.* The *John L. Stephens*, a steamship built in New York in 1852 for the Pacific Mail Steamship Company, an American company which in March 1860 gained control of the Panama–San Francisco run (John Haskell Kemble, *The Panama Route 1848–1869* [Berkeley and Los Angeles: University of California Press, 1943], p. 96). A side-wheeler with three decks, the *John L. Stephens* was 275′ long with a 45′ beam and 1,836 tons burden (*Lewis & Dryden's Marine History of the Pacific Northwest,* ed. E.W. Wright [Portland, Ore.: Lewis & Dryden Printing Co., 1895], p. 159). Like the other ships of this line, her company habitually permitted her to be overloaded and overcrowded with immigrants. Her captain was William F. Lapidge.

4:10 *quick-silver.* Quicksilver (mercury) was chiefly used in the rockers in placer mining (see F.G. Claudet, "*Gold,*" *Its Properties, Modes of Extraction, Value &c, &c.* [New Westminster: Office of the "Mainland Guardian," 1871]). In 1862, when Bishop Hills visited Williams Creek, Cariboo, he noted that "no Quicksilver is used as on the Fraser where the gold is in dust. Quicksilver diggings are disliked by the miners, the relating process being injurious to the health" (Hills' Journal, 28 July 1862).

4:12 *Panama Fever.* Yellow Fever.

4:34 *Acapulco.* Half-way between Panama and San Francisco, Acapulco, with its fine harbour, served as the coaling station for the Pacific Mail steamers. "The city, beautifully situated among groves of cocoa and palm, at the base of mountains which rise from the edge of the harbour, one of the most perfect in the world, is still a relic of the former times of Spain," wrote Pemberton. "The colouring is exquisite: the Mexicans in the market-place, selling fruits, shells, and pearls, which seem to be the staple commodities; the old Spanish churches and wells; divers swimming round the steamers; and coaling by torch-light, are studies of peculiar interest" (*Facts and Figures,* p. 88).

5: 1 *Parrot fish.* Highly coloured fish with a strong bill (of the *Scaridae* family) which are found in tropical seas.

5:12 "*Sombrero.*" Sombrero, a British possession, is in the Virgin Islands. Mrs. Allison must have passed it on her approach to St. Thomas. Possibly the people who signalled her ship were the residents of Taboga, an island which she would pass after leaving Panama.

5:15 ***had seceded from the Union yet.*** The secession of the first southern state, South Carolina, did not take place until 20 December 1860.

5:15 *Lincoln.* The election of Lincoln had not yet taken place. He was elected president on 6 November 1860.

5:22 *"floating coffin."* Cf. Bushby's account of his journey on the *Sonora*, another of the Pacific Mail steamers: "it is a dangerous thing to get fever in this country—they told me today that in some of the trips of this very vessel 'the Sonora' they had thrown as many as 200 bodies overboard in one day—no wonder for they pack them so close there are some 1000 on board now—& they have carried 1700" ("Bushby Journal," 2 and 3 December, 1858). See also Bishop Hills' experience when he returned to England in 1863: "In these American ships, the dollar is all that is thought of. In this case several hundred passengers were taken beyond the number consistent with safety and decency" (*Report of the Columbia Mission 1864*, p. 23). The Pacific Mail Company steamers took between eighteen and twenty-one days to reach San Francisco from Panama.

5:25 *the Mission.* The Spanish Mission of San Francisco de Asis a la Laguna de los Dolores, established in 1776.

5:27 *Otter.* The Tugwells, fellow passengers of the Glennies, reached Victoria on the *Oregon*, not the *Otter* (Hills' Journal, 9 August 1860). The *Oregon*, a wooden side-wheel steamer with two decks and three masts, 208′ long, 33′ 10″ beam, and 1,503 tons burden, was built in 1848 in New York for the Pacific Mail Company. After her arrival in San Francisco in March 1849, she was used on the San Francisco–Panama run until 1855. In 1856 she was put in service on the San Francisco–Columbia River run. She normally carried between five and seven hundred passengers (*Lewis & Dryden's Marine History*, pp. 239–40; and Kemble, *The Panama Route*, p. 60).

5:31 *orchards were to be admired.* Cf. the description of Portland in 1860 given by Lieutenant Charles Wilson in his diary of the survey of the 49th Parallel, 1858–62, while secretary of the British Section of the North American Boundary Commission: "The other day I paid Portland a visit, the capital of Oregon, it is built principally of wood & is a regular western city with its drinking & gambling houses, composing nearly half the place; the only redeeming quality the place has is that they have excellent baths & you can obtain the luxury of ice. The valley of the Willamette (a tributary of the Columbia) in which Portland is situated is exceedingly pretty & as it contains rich & fertile land is becoming rapidly settled by squatters" (*Mapping the Frontier*, ed. George F.G. Stanley [Toronto: Macmillan of Canada, 1970], p. 92).

5:34 *Victoria.* The Glennies' voyage from England had occupied fifty-two days as compared with the forty-nine day voyage of Bishop Hills, who arrived at the beginning of the year.

5:35 *did not look very much like a city.* Victoria, which was still a scattered settlement, was not incorporated as a city until 1862. Fort Victoria, founded in 1843, and after 1849 the Hudson's Bay Company Pacific depot, was the centre of all activity until the inrush of gold miners to the Fraser River took place in the spring of 1858. When, in their train, merchants and professional men arrived, some substantial business buildings were erected near the waterfront. Not until the year of Mrs. Allison's arrival was the fort's northeast bastion, on Government Street, demolished. "Victoria is situated upon rising ground," Bishop Hills recorded on his arrival. "It is much more spread out than I expected & bears every mark of substantial progress. The Houses & Stores are almost all of wood. . . . The way up to the House provided for me by Mr. Dundas was deep in mud. Yet there was progress making in improvement & everybody said this is nothing to what things were a year ago. Fort Street however now 1860 Jan. 6 is up to the knees nearly in mud. There are no pavements even of wood. . . . This is pretty much the character of all the streets excepting perhaps Government St. which is a trifle better" (Hills' Journal, 6 January 1860). J.D. Pemberton's 1861 map of the town shows the main streets laid out, the new Government Buildings ("The Birdcages") constructed, and Government Street connected with them by an 800-foot bridge across James Bay. Though town and country lots had been surveyed by 1861, many of the fort buildings were still standing (Map of the Town of Victoria, 1861, Map Collection, Provincial Archives of British Columbia [hereafter cited as PABC]).

5:36 *Oriental or Occidental Hotel.* It was the Oriental Hotel on Yates Street, of which W. McKeon was the proprietor. The Occidental Hotel at Johnson and Wharf Street was built about 1876.

6: 1 *Beacon Hill.* A large public park, not far from the new Government Buildings, had been set aside. Beacon Hill took its name from the fact that the Hudson's Bay Company had erected two beacons to illuminate Brotchie Ledge, a shipping hazard (John T. Walbran, *British Columbia Coast Names 1592–1906,* reprint ed. [Vancouver: The Library's Press, 1971], pp. 38–39).

6: 4 *Douglas.* James Douglas (1803–77), governor of Vancouver Island, 1851–64, and of the Crown Colony of British Columbia, 1858–64. For Douglas's career as a fur trader and a colonial governor, see Walter N. Sage, *Sir James Douglas and British Columbia,* University of Toronto Studies in History and Economics (Toronto: University of Toronto Press, 1930); Margaret A. Ormsby, "Sir James Douglas," *Dictionary of Canadian Biography* 10 (Toronto: University of Toronto Press, 1972), pp. 238–49 (hereafter cited as *DCB*); and Dorothy Blakey Smith, *James Douglas, Father of British Columbia* (Toronto: Oxford University Press, 1971).

6: 6 *head of navigation.* After the Oregon Treaty in 1846, James Douglas, as chief factor of the Hudson's Bay Company, took steps to have the brigade routes from Fort St. James and Fort Colvile converge on the Fraser River north of the 49th Parallel. Fort Hope was established near the confluence of the Fraser and Coquihalla rivers in 1848, and in 1849, when the Brigade Trail was opened across the Cascade Mountains to the Similkameen Valley, Hope was made the head of navigation on the Fraser River. After the 1858 gold rush, a townsite near the fort was laid out and lots were leased, and in November, J.D. Pemberton completed an official survey of the townsite. Hope had a population of five hundred at that time (Governor James Douglas to Sir Edward Bulwer Lytton, 9 November 1858, *Papers Relative to the Affairs of British Columbia,* Great Britain, Parliament, 1859 [Cmd. 2578, 1st series], 2:28 [hereafter cited as *BCP*]). See also F.W. Howay, "The Raison d'Etre of Forts Yale and Hope," Royal Society of Canada, *Proceedings and Transactions*, 3rd series, 16 (1922), section 2, pp. 49–64.

6: 7 *Otter*. Built in 1852 in England for the Hudson's Bay Company's service, the *Otter*, a screw steamer of 220 tons burden, arrived in Victoria on 4 August 1853 after a five-months' journey round the Horn. Soon after her arrival she was sent to San Francisco to be enlarged. She was used to relieve the *Beaver* on the coast. She sank at Bella Coola in 1880, but was later raised and refitted. After her sale to the Canadian Pacific Navigation Company, she was dismantled and used to haul coal until 1890 (*Lewis & Dryden's Marine History*, p. 46). See also note on Captain Mouat, p. 110.

6: 9 *Captain John Irving*. Mrs. Allison has confused Captain John Irving, who was born in 1854 and who did not commence steamboating until 1870, with his father, Captain William Irving (1816–72). William Irving, a deep-sea captain, was born in Annan, Dumfriesshire, Scotland, in 1816 and came to Oregon in 1849 as master and part-owner of the bark *Success*. In 1858 he came to British Columbia to join Captain Alexander S. Murray. In the same year Irving built the stern-wheeler *Governor Douglas*, the first steamer built in the colony, and then the *Colonel Moody*. In 1862 he sold his interests in these vessels and built the *Reliance*; and in 1865, the *Onward*. All his steamers were known for their fine appointments, good service, and excellent meals; Bishop Hills, for one, considered the *Moody* superior to the ships on the West Indies Mail line (Hills' Journal, 1 June 1860). The most famous of the Fraser River steamboat captains, Irving, who was also prominent in municipal politics in New Westminster, had the Royal Engineers construct him a fine residence on Royal Avenue. Irving House, built between 1862 and 1864, today is an historical museum. For further information on Irving's career, see Norman R. Hacking, "Steamboating on the Fraser in the 'Sixties,'" *BCHQ* 10 (1946): 1–41; and W. Kaye Lamb, "William Irving," *DCB* 10, pp. 377–78.

6:15 *Cridge*. Rev. Edward Cridge (1817–1913), chaplain at North Walsham, Norfolk, in 1848 and at West Ham in 1851, replaced Rev.

Robert J. Staines as chaplain to the Hudson's Bay Company at Fort Victoria in 1855. In 1865, five years after the arrival of Bishop Hills and the organization of the see of Columbia, he became dean of Victoria diocese. Later, differences developed between the two men, and in 1874 Cridge joined the Reformed Episcopal Church and was elected bishop in 1875. He served as rector of the Church of Our Lord in Victoria from 1876 until 1902. For further details see Biographical Appendix, "Bushby Journal," pp. 171–72.

6:18 *Good.* Charles Good, son of Rev. Henry Good of Wimborne Minster, Dorset, arrived in Victoria in 1859 and was appointed chief clerk in the Colonial Secretary's Office. He accompanied Governor Douglas as private secretary on his visit to Similkameen in 1860, and undoubtedly he is the person referred to as "the attaché of the Colonial Secretary's Office" who pre-empted land opposite the settlement at Vermilion Forks and commenced improving it (*Colonist*, 23 October 1860). Good already had a farm on Pitt River (Hills' Journal, 24 May 1860), and he also pre-empted one hundred acres on the Hope Flat (F.W. Laing, "Colonial Farm Settlers on the Mainland of British Columbia, 1858–1871" typescript, PABC, copy, University of British Columbia Library, Special Collections Division, p. 220).

In August 1861 Good eloped to Port Townsend with the governor's daughter Alice, who was then only seventeen. They were married aboard a British schooner, the *Explorer*, by an American justice of the peace, but on their return to Victoria, on Douglas's orders, they were married again on 31 August 1861 at Christ Church Cathedral. The marriage proved unhappy, and after Douglas's death there was a divorce.

6:19 *a genuine Douglas.* Governor Douglas was reputed to be a lineal descendant of "Black Douglas," William Douglas, Lord of Nithsdale, who died in 1390 (Angus McDonald, "A Few Items of the West," ed. F.W. Howay, William S. Lewis, and Jacob A. Meyers, *Washington Historical Quarterly* 8 [1917]: 224 [hereafter cited as *WHQ*]).

6:21 *Helmcken.* Dr. John Sebastian Helmcken, M.R.C.S. (1824–1920), the pioneer doctor of British Columbia, who married Cecilia Douglas, daughter of the governor, in 1852. Born in London of

German parentage, Helmcken trained at Guy's Hospital. On 18 October 1849, as clerk and surgeon in the Hudson's Bay Company's service, he sailed on the *Norman Morison* for Vancouver Island. In addition to his service as a physician at Victoria, Dr. Helmcken had a long and distinguished political career. The first Speaker of the Legislative Assembly of Vancouver Island, he served in this capacity from 1856 to 1866. As a member of the Executive Council of the united colony of British Columbia, he took part in the Confederation Debate. Governor Anthony Musgrave chose him to be one of three delegates to confer with Canada concerning the Terms of Union. See *The Reminiscences of Doctor John Sebastian Helmcken*, ed. Dorothy Blakey Smith (Vancouver: University of British Columbia Press, 1975).

6:32 *her father.* Presumably a reference to Alice, daughter of Governor Douglas, and Charles Good.

6:36 *Mowat.* Captain William Alexander Mouat (1821–71), master mariner. Captain Mouat, who was born in London, came to Fort Vancouver in 1845 as second mate on the Hudson's Bay Company's bark *Vancouver.* After 1855, he was at various times in charge of the Hudson's Bay Company's steamers *Otter*, *Enterprise*, and *Labouchere*. In 1866 he was captain of the steamer *Marten* on Kamloops Lake. Later, as chief trader, he was placed in charge of Fort Rupert (see *Lewis & Dryden's Marine History,* p. 21 n5; and Dorothy Blakey Smith, "William Alexander Mouat," *DCB* 10, p. 535).

6:37 *Reliance.* The *Reliance* had not yet been launched. The Glennies probably took passage on either the *Governor Douglas* or the *Colonel Moody*, which were sold on 22 May 1862 to Captain John T. Wright, Jr.

7: 1 *Westminster.* New Westminster, the capital of the colony of British Columbia, whose site on the north bank of the Fraser River was chosen in 1859 by Colonel Moody (see below, p. 116), (see Dorothy Blakey Smith, "The First Capital of British Columbia . . . ," *BCHQ* 21 [1957–58]: 15–50). New Westminster was the first (1860) city to be incorporated in British Columbia.

7: 3 *Sapperton.* The village north of the Royal Engineers' camp, named by Colonel Moody in honour of the Sappers, many of whom purchased land there and erected buildings.

7: 3 *the Camp.* The encampment of the Royal Engineers, about a mile from New Westminster.

7: 6 *Dewdney.* Mrs. Allison's brother-in-law. Edgar Dewdney (1835–1916) was born at Tibberton, Biddesford, Devon, trained as a civil engineer, and was recommended to Sir Edward Bulwer Lytton by C. Kemeys Tynte, M.P., in 1858. Armed with a letter of introduction to Douglas, Dewdney arrived in Victoria early in 1859. On his journey from England, he had "blown in" his capital of £150 before leaving New York for Panama, and he reached his destination penniless. But having "a strong constitution, lots of confidence in myself and . . . the belief that if the country was as good as then represented I could in a short time return to the Old Country and settle down with the girl I left behind me," he was optimistic about his prospects (Edgar Dewdney, "Biographical Sketch," Dewdney Papers, vol. 2, 1861–1916, Glenbow–Alberta Institute). On 22 March 1859 Colonel Moody appointed him to the Lands Department. Then, at the suggestion of Moody, Dewdney settled on Sea Island with the intention of cutting hay for the Royal Engineers, who expected to winter a large number of horses on the Douglas Portage. This occupation he gave up in 1860 to tender with Walter Moberly for the construction of a seventy-mile pack trail from Hope to the Similkameen River. His resources at this time consisted of "a small capital of a $20 gold piece and two guides" ("Biographical Sketch"). In May 1860 Moody appointed him city surveyor for New Westminster and district. (Moody to Douglas, 19 May 1860, R.C. Moody Correspondence, PABC). After completing his section of the Hope–Similkameen Road in September 1861, Dewdney started out on foot from Yale to Cariboo (O'Reilly Diaries, 8 September 1861). Joseph Trutch gave him employment on the Cariboo Road in 1862, and at the time of his marriage in 1864 to Jane Shaw Moir (see above, p. 90), he was surveyor at Richfield. The following year Governor Frederick Seymour sent him to explore a route from Princeton to the Kootenay, the scene of a gold rush at Wild Horse Creek in 1864. Dewdney carried out extensive explorations, including that of the Kootenay River from its source. By September 1865 the

Dewdney Trail, 220 miles from Princeton to Wild Horse Creek, had been completed at a cost of $74,000 (R.E. Gosnell, "Building the Dewdney Trail as Told by the Builder," Victoria *Daily Times*, 21 November 1908). In 1866 Dewdney returned to Cariboo to continue his profession as surveyor. During these early years in the colony, he had obtained much information concerning the agricultural and mineral resources of the country and had acquired land, mining interests, and capital.

Dewdney's political career commenced in 1868 when he was elected to the Legislative Council of British Columbia to represent Kootenay District. He claimed that he was nominated and elected without his knowledge, and he refused to attend the 1868–69 session. He was again elected to the council to represent Kootenay in 1870 and participated in the Confederation Debate. After British Columbia became a province in 1871, he obtained a contract from Sandford Fleming as a surveyor for the Pacific Railway. In 1872, however, he was elected to represent Yale constituency in the House of Commons. This seat he retained in the elections of 1872 and 1874. He was a strong supporter of Sir John A. Macdonald during the Pacific Scandal and later when the Conservatives were in opposition. On the party's return to power, he was appointed Indian commissioner for Manitoba and the North-West Territories in 1879 and also served as lieutenant-governor of the North-West Territories from 1881 to 1888. During the North-West Rebellion, he played an important role in pacifying the Indians. In 1888, and again in 1891, he was elected to the House of Commons for Assiniboia East, N.W.T., and from August 1888 until October 1892, he held the portfolio of minister of the interior and superintendent of Indian affairs.

Dewdney then returned to British Columbia to serve as the province's lieutenant-governor from 1 November 1892 until 30 November 1897. He retired to attend to his varied business interests (J.K. Johnson, *The Canadian Directory of Parliament, 1867–1967* [Ottawa: Queen's Printer, 1968], p. 166).

Dewdney's wife, Jane, died in 1906. Three years later he visited England and while there married Blanche, youngest daughter of Col. Charles Kemeys Tynte of Halswell, Somersetshire, who was probably the girl he left behind him in 1858. On his death in 1916, his second wife inherited his whole estate, including 160 acres at Princeton (Last Will and Testament of

Edgar Dewdney, copy, PABC). For further information on Dewdney, see Sue Baptie, "Edgar Dewdney," *Alberta Historical Review* 16 (1968): 1–10.

7: 7 *Newton.* William Henry Newton (1833–75), a native of Bromley, Kent, arrived in Victoria in 1851 to be an assistant to E.E. Langford, bailiff of the Puget's Sound Company's farm at Colwood. He soon entered the employ of the Hudson's Bay Company at Fort Victoria. In 1857 he was transferred to Fort Langley as clerk, and he took charge there in 1860. He retired in 1864 to farm at Port Hammond, but in 1874 he was recalled to Fort Langley where he died in 1875.

7: 8 *Begbie.* Matthew Baillie Begbie (1819–94) was appointed in September 1858 judge of the Crown Colony of British Columbia. The eldest son of Colonel T.S. Begbie, R.E., Begbie was educated at Peterhouse, Cambridge University, and the Inns of Court. In British Columbia he became famous for his circuits, for his uncompromising principles, and for his success in helping to establish peace and order in the goldfields. He became chief justice of the Mainland of British Columbia in 1869 and chief justice of British Columbia, including Vancouver Island, in 1870. In 1874 he was knighted for his services. Angus McDonald, who knew him well, described him as "six feet four and a half inches in his socks and as straight as a needle. He has a fine education and speaks well in French and German, Italian and Spanish with a good store of Greek and some Hebrew, but no Gaelic" ("A Few Items," p. 223). For further details on Begbie's career, see "Memoirs and Documents Relating to Judge Begbie," *BCHQ* 5 (1941): 125–41; and the four articles by Sydney G. Pettit, *BCHQ* 11 (1947).

7: 8 *Bushby.* Arthur Thomas Bushby (1835–75), son of a successful merchant in London and the owner of two estates in the West Indies. Bushby was attracted to British Columbia by the reports of the gold discoveries which appeared in the London *Times.* Provided with a letter of introduction to Governor Douglas from the Governor and Committee of the Hudson's Bay Company, he left Southampton on 3 November 1858. He, and his fellow passengers from Panama on the *Sonora,* including Colonel Moody, Captain W. Driscoll Gosset, treasurer of British Columbia, Rev.

W. Burton Crickmer, chaplain for the goldfields, Thomas Elwyn, and John Carmichael Haynes, arrived at Esquimalt on Christmas Day 1858. In February 1859 Douglas appointed Bushby private secretary to Judge Begbie; this appointment Begbie soon changed to that of clerk of the court, assize clerk, and registrar. Bushby retained the office of registrar of the Supreme Court of British Columbia until 1870 when he became postmaster general. He also served as resident magistrate at New Westminster and as county court judge both on the Coast and in the Interior.

In 1862, by his marriage to Agnes Douglas, Bushby became son-in-law to the governor. For further details, see Dorothy Blakey Smith, "Arthur Thomas Bushby," *DCB* 10, pp. 112–14.

7:11 *charming . . . place.* All visitors to Hope were struck by the beauty of its setting. Bishop Hills was impressed by the scenery, when, only two months before the Glennies reached there, he visited it for the first time: "No spot can be more beautifully situated than Hope. The River Fraser flows past it. The site is on the River Bank—on either side all noble mountains opposite an Island. To the back, mountain scenery, trees from the foot to the summit & deep valleys between through which flow the rapid & beautiful Coquialla & its Tributaries & in which are situated several lakes. This Evening we walked up the Coquialla, crossed its picturesque Bridge & proceeded along the Brigade trail, a walk winding through trees & flowers & where at times you might fancy yourself in the wilder parts of some cultivated domain in England. The scenery is a combination of Swiss & Scotch. It had been raining & all nature was fresh & lovely & fragrant. About 3 miles brought us to Dallas Lake, a sweet spot where one felt one could live for ages. O Lord how manifold are thy works" (Hills' Journal, 5 June 1860).

7:12 *Ogilvie's Peak.* According to William Yates, this peak was named in honour of J.D.B. Ogilvy, who was the Hudson's Bay Company's agent at Fort Hope in 1859: "There is a peak on the other side of the Coquahalla called Ogilvies Peak. Ogilvie climbed it on a wager of five dollars and a champaigne supper. He went up and placed a white flag on top" ("Reminiscences of William Yates," typescript, PABC, p. 11).

7:14 *Charles.* William Charles (1831–1903), son of John Charles, a Hudson's Bay Company factor, was born in Edinburgh and educated at the University of Edinburgh. In 1852 he travelled via Panama to Portland and two years later joined the Hudson's Bay Company. After serving at Fort Vancouver, Fort Hall, and Boise, he was transferred to Victoria in 1858. In 1860 he was put in charge at Fort Hope. Later he was in charge at Fort Yale and Fort Kamloops, which in 1868 he said he found "about the dullest place" he ever was in. In 1870 he was transferred to Victoria to be cashier in the Company's office, and in 1874 he was promoted to chief factor in charge of all the Company's posts in the Western Department. His wife, Mary Ann, born at Fort George (Astoria), was the daughter of James Birnie, a Hudson's Bay Company official in Oregon (E.O.S. Scholefield and F.W. Howay, *British Columbia from the Earliest Times to the Present* [Vancouver: The S.J. Clarke Publishing Company, 1914], 3: 18–22; obituary, *Colonist*, 22 May 1903).

7:16 *Yates.* William Yates, an Orkneyman, entered the service of the Hudson's Bay Company when he was seventeen. He travelled to Norway House via York Factory and in 1851 crossed the Rocky Mountains to serve at Fort St. James under Donald Manson. He was then stationed at Fort McLeod and in 1856 moved to Fort Hope. Hope, as the transfer point to water transport of the furs brought overland by the brigades from New Caledonia, Fort Kamloops, and Fort Colvile, was the scene of much activity. It was even busier during the early days of the Fraser River gold rush. Then, and later, Yates, whose knowledge of the Indian languages was said to be unequalled, was credited with keeping peace between the miners and the Indians. "Had a conversation with a man named Yates," recorded Bishop Hills in his journal on 4 June 1860, "a servant of the Hudsons Bay Cy. 11 years in their employment. Speaks the native language. Lives with an Indian woman & has a child. Is not married. Defends the unmarried state as happier. Has known instances where men have been married & of unhappiness resulting.... I asked if he would be comfortable to live in an unmarried state in his own country. He said there was a great difference. There were Churches in Orkney & white women. I shewed him that the sin was the same here as in Britain."

7:17 *O'Reilly.* Peter O'Reilly (1828–1905) was one of the Anglo-Irish-men who served as gold commissioners in the colony of British Columbia. Born at Ballybeg House, Kell, County Meath, he was the son of Patrick O'Reilly and Mary, the daughter of Major Blundell of Ince Hall, Lancashire. After serving seven years in the Irish Revenue Police, Peter O'Reilly came to British Columbia in 1859, carrying a letter of introduction to Governor Douglas from General J.G. Portlock. On 19 April 1859 Douglas appointed him stipendiary magistrate for the District of Langley. On 12 September O'Reilly took over the District of Fort Hope from R.T. Smith and remained in charge there, with responsibility for Similkameen and Rock Creek, until 31 May 1862 when he was succeeded by Edward Sanders, who had been at Yale since 1859. Subsequently O'Reilly served as magistrate and gold commissioner in Cariboo, Kootenay–Columbia, and Omineca. In 1863 Douglas appointed him a member of the Legislative Council of British Columbia, and he remained a member of this council and of the council of the united colony until he was sent to Omineca in 1871. In 1881 he became Indian Reserve Commissioner for British Columbia. His wife Caroline Agnes, whom he married in 1863, was the youngest sister of Joseph and John Trutch (Margaret A. Ormsby, "Some Irish Figures in Colonial Days," *BCHQ* 14 (1950) : 61–82).

7:18 *Moody.* Lieutenant-Colonel Richard Clement Moody (1813–87), second son of Colonel Thomas Moody, R.E., was born at St. Ann's garrison, Barbados, and educated at Royal Military Academy, Woolwich. He was gazetted second lieutenant in the Royal Engineers on 5 November 1830 and promoted to lieutenant in 1835, captain in 1847, lieutenant-colonel in 1855, colonel in December 1863, and major-general on 25 January 1866, when he retired on full pay. In 1841 he went to the Falkland Islands to be the first governor.

In August 1858, Sir Edward Bulwer Lytton appointed Moody chief commissioner of lands and works and lieutenant-governor, with a dormant commission, of the colony of British Columbia (Lytton to Douglas, 16 October 1858, *BCP*, 2:70). Accompanied by his wife and children, he reached Victoria on 25 December 1858. He was sworn in as lieutenant-governor in May 1859.

Moody had command of the detachment of the Royal Engineers sent to the gold colony. One of his first undertakings was a journey in January 1859 to Fort Yale where some miners were defying the law. Shortly afterwards he chose the site of the capital city, New Westminster, and began to draw up elaborate plans for it (see above, p. 110).

When Mrs. Allison first saw Colonel Moody, he was visiting his wife, who had been sent to Hope with her baby and four other small children to escape the mosquitos at New Westminster and wait for their new house to be painted. Moody himself intended to remain there until the end of September, but on 25 August, Captain Parsons, probably aware of the governor's displeasure at this absence from the capital, sent Mrs. Moody a hasty note: "Please send the Colonel here by *this boat*, or we shall be in a pickle. I do not recommend your coming as the Painting is not quite finished" (Capt. R.M. Parsons to Mrs. Moody, 25 August 1860, Mary Susanna(h) (Hawks) Moody Correspondence, PABC).

After the disbandment of the corps, the Moodys left the colony on 11 November 1863. For further details, see *DNB* 38: 332–33; and Lillian Cope, "Colonel Moody and the Royal Engineers in British Columbia" (M.A. thesis, University of British Columbia, 1940).

7:19 *Luard*. Captain Henry Reynolds Luard (1829–70), brought the main body (121 men) of the Columbia detachment of Royal Engineers round the Horn on the *Thames City*, arriving in Victoria 12 April 1859. At New Westminster he was executive officer of the Department of Lands and Works. For further details, see F.W. Howay, *The Work of the Royal Engineers in British Columbia, 1858–1863* (Victoria: King's Printer, 1910).

On 28 October 1860 Luard recorded a claim for a preemption of 178 acres in the Similkameen about one and one-half miles below the junction of Vermilion Forks. John Fall Allison later settled on this property and finally purchased it. After her husband's death, Mrs. Allison gave the land to Edgar Dewdney, who laid out a townsite. It was this townsite that Forbes George Vernon, as chief commissioner of lands and works, cancelled (see p. 57).

Just before leaving the colony, Luard on 8 October 1863 married Caroline Mary Leggatt, step-daughter of Thomas Lett Wood. "We have been very gay lately," Mrs. Moody wrote to her mother on 12 May 1863, "Capn. Luard & Dr. Seddall are engaged to two Sisters, Miss Leggatts, and the young ladies have just paid us a visit, nearly 3 weeks—You can fancy that 2 such visitors have made the place quite gay—a dinner party here & at the Mess, Concerts, Theatricals, riding parties, & a ball in the Mess Room —Picnic &c &c &c. The Ball was quite a success. . . . The Ladies were very nicely dressed—The Miss Legatts wore white silk *plain*, with cherry coloured sashes, broard [*sic*], rushings [*sic*] of the same at the top of the lace berthe [*sic*], & one rose in their hair—they looked so nice, we all felt quite proud of them, for now of course we feel that they belong to *us* (The Camp Family)" (Mary S. Moody Correspondence).

7:19 *Parsons.* Captain Robert Mann Parsons (d. 1897), a survey superintendent for the Royal Engineers, left Southampton on 17 September 1858 on the *La Platta* with the first party of twenty men, mainly surveyors, and arrived in Victoria on 29 October 1858 (Douglas to Lytton, 8 November 1858, *BCP*, 2:25). In 1860 Parsons was engaged from the middle of June until the end of the summer in making a reconnaissance of the country adjacent to the Sumas and Chilliwack rivers (Howay, *Work of the Royal Engineers*, p. 7).

7:19 *Seddle.* Dr. John Vernon Seddall, the first resident doctor to practise on the Mainland. He was staff assistant-surgeon to the Royal Engineers and travelled with the main party on the *Thames City*. "Our dear little doctor" was a favourite of Mrs. Moody, for, as she wrote her mother, "The Dr is so kind & good, an example to us all in every way—You never hear anyone who does not speak most affectely & kindly of him" (Mrs. Moody to "My dearest Mamma," 23 September 1862, Mary S. Moody Correspondence).

On leaving the colony in 1863, Dr. Seddall gave his equipment to the Royal Columbian Hospital, recently founded by the citizens of New Westminster on his advice and with the help of Colonel Moody (Moody to Douglas, 26 September 1863, R.C. Moody Correspondence).

7:19 *Oliver.* Dr. Noble R. Oliver, a surgeon who had been trained in the United States. Douglas appointed him on 11 August 1859 to assist the Lands and Works Department and to be employed in the field. Dr. Oliver was in Cariboo from 1863 to 1865 when he went to the Big Bend.

7:20 *Lindsay.* Sergeant James Lindsay (d. 1890). After twenty-one years' service in the Royal Artillery, Lindsay was honourably discharged with the rank of quartermaster sergeant. Between 1861 and 1863 the Royal Engineers used him to inspect the work of civilian contractors on the Cariboo Road. On 3 May 1861 Lindsay pre-empted ninety-eight acres on the Similkameen, and in 1867 he took up a military grant on Pitt Meadows. He was appointed constable in Cariboo on 20 June 1868 and promoted to chief constable there in 1871. After Confederation he was a provincial constable at Barkerville (F.J. Hatch, "The British Columbia Police, 1858–1871" [M.A. thesis, University of British Columbia, 1955], appendix A, p. viii).

7:20 *Corp. Howes.* Corporal Alfred Richard Howse pre-empted land at Hope, but the record was disallowed because the pre-emption fell within a reserve. Later he received a military grant at Langley (Laing, "Colonial Farm Settlers," p. 224). For a full list of Howse's properties, see Frances M. Woodward, "The Influence of the Royal Engineers on the Development of British Columbia," *BC Studies* 24 (1974–75) : 43.

7:21 *Landvoight.* George Landvoight, a native of Hanover, came to British Columbia in 1858 and later became a merchant at Hope. On 10 December 1868 he was appointed postmaster (British Columbia, *Government Gazette*, 16 January 1869) and on 10 June 1876 a justice of the peace. He died in February 1878 after an accident at the sawmill at Hope, when a platform on which he was standing collapsed and threw him to the ground.

7:21 *Wirth.* John G. Wirth (d. 1881) was a native of Bavaria who arrived at Victoria in 1858. He had a hotel at the corner of Humboldt and Government streets, but on his failure to get the liquor licence renewed in 1860, he moved to Hope and opened a hotel there. He became justice of the peace for the electoral district of Yale in 1880.

7:21 *Sutton.* William H. Sutton resided at Hope in 1860, probably as saloonkeeper, since this was his occupation at Yale in 1868.

7:22 *Teague.* William Teague (1835–1916), a native of Cornwall, who came to British Columbia in July 1858 after mining in California, arriving on the *Oregon*. In April 1859 he was appointed constable at Hope and the following year was promoted to chief constable (Hatch, "British Columbia Police," appendix A, p. xii). Cariboo attracted him in 1864, and he mined there for several years. In 1873 he was appointed government agent at Yale, but after fourteen years in this position he resumed mining (Scholefield and Howay, *British Columbia from the Earliest Times*, 4: 220–21).

7:25 *sister-in-law*. Amelia Birnie, daughter of James Birnie and later wife of John McAdoo Wark (1819?–1904), the nephew of John Work.

7:26 *Joe M'Kay*. Joseph W. McKay (1829–1900), the son of a Hudson's Bay Company clerk, was born at Rupert House and educated at Red River. He came to Fort Vancouver in 1844, entered the Company's service, and two years later was sent by Chief Factor Douglas to Fort Simpson to take charge of the north coast trading establishments. In 1849 he moved to Nanaimo, and while there he discovered coal. On Douglas's orders he opened coal mines in 1852 and built the bastion. After E.E. Langford was disqualified for membership in the first House of Assembly of Vancouver Island, McKay replaced him. In 1860 he succeeded Donald McLean at Kamloops and remained there until 1865 when he moved to Yale. In 1876 he was promoted to chief factor. Three years later he left the Company's service to become Indian agent at Kamloops.

7:28 *Portman*. The Hon. Edward N. Barclay Portman (1837–61), a native of Dorsetshire, who had served in the Royal Navy as a lieutenant during the Crimean War. After obtaining a surveyor's commission for British Columbia, Portman surveyed land in 1860 at Fort Hope and in the Similkameen district "at which places he acquired many warm friends" (*Colonist*, 4 February 1861). Presumably it was Moody who sent him to the Similkameen to survey some pre-emption claims. On his arrival Portman seems to have met Charles Good and learned from him that Douglas had ordered the surveying of a townsite. He thereupon asked both Good and Moody to use their influence to obtain for him the position of crown surveyor for the Upper Districts, "including Similkameen, Alexandria, Lytton and Quesnelle River until an officer be appointed to those places" (E.N.B. Portman to Moody, 18 October 1860, Colonial Correspondence, PABC). He also sent Moody a sketch map showing the location of two claims (320 acres) held by Walter Moberly, a claim in his own name, and another in the name of J.F. Allison. Later, on 8 December, he sent a plan of the lands he had surveyed: these included a claim by Sergeant William McColl on the Tulameen River, an Indian reserve at Vermilion Forks, a town reserve, and Lot 1 (94.30 acres) claimed by Captain Luard. Many years later, Mrs. Allison said that she had seen a plan by Portman of a proposed town "which, if it had materialized would have been a beautiful city with a race course, parks, terraces and fountains" (Mrs. S.L. Allison, "Early History of Princeton," *Princeton Star*, 5 January 1923).

Portman wintered in Victoria, and there on 3 February 1861 he died suddenly at a saloon on Yates Street. An inquest into his death found that he had died of apoplexy, "not a too free use of intoxicating liquors" (*Colonist*, 4 February 1861). The rumours that still persisted apparently reached Bishop Hills: "This day was committed to the ground the remains of a young man belonging to a noble family in England of the name of Portman—a grandson of Lord Portman. He had been in the Navy—in Australia—had not done well—had come out here. Seemed to improve—was at Hope where I met him & where he regularly attended Church—came down here—fell into bad company—was frequently intoxicated & died of Delirium Tremens. Alas without a season of repentance" (Hills' Journal, 6 February 1861). For another account see "Lord Portman's Nephew," in D.W. Higgins, *The Mystic Spring* (Toronto: William Briggs, 1904), pp. 164–70.

7:29 *Moberly.* Walter Moberly (1832–1915), second son of Captain John Moberly, R.N., was born at Steeple Ashton, Oxfordshire, and brought to Canada as a young child. He trained as a civil engineer in Toronto. His interest in the West was aroused by the explorations of Captain John Palliser, by Paul Kane, the artist, and by news of the discovery of gold on the Fraser River. He decided to go to British Columbia to investigate the possibility of opening overland communication. After a journey round the Horn, he reached Victoria on 15 December 1858 and presented Governor

Douglas with a letter of introduction supplied by Sir George Simpson. He declined the offer of a government appointment and left for the Fraser Valley to commence exploration for a railway route. On his return to Victoria to report to Douglas, he met Moody, who offered him work at New Westminster. In August 1859, with Robert Burnaby, he explored for coal on Burrard Inlet. In 1860 he formed a partnership with Dewdney to build a trail from Hope to Similkameen River. As a government engineer, he supervised in 1863 the completion of the Cariboo Road from Lytton to Spence's Bridge. Two years later he discovered Eagle Pass through the Gold Range. He was chosen to represent Cariboo West in the Legislative Council in 1864, but he resigned his seat to become assistant to Surveyor General J.W. Trutch. During 1866 he explored the Big Bend of the Columbia and visited the Howse, Kicking Horse, and Crow's Nest passes. His position as assistant surveyor general was abolished on 1 January 1867, and in February he left for the United States to engage in exploration and railway building. After Confederation he returned to take charge of the railway surveys from Shuswap Lake to the Rocky Mountains (see Walter Moberly, *The Rocks and Rivers of British Columbia* [London: H. Blacklock and Company, 1885]; Noel Robinson, *Blazing the Trail through the Rockies* [Vancouver: *News-Advertiser*, n.d.]; and "Walter Moberly's Report on the Roads of British Columbia, 1863," ed. W.N. Sage, *BCHQ* 9 [1945]: 37–47).

7:31 *Wagon Road.* On 24 September 1860 Governor Douglas visited the diggings at Rock Creek and decided to have a wagon road built from Hope to offset the competition at the mines from imports from Oregon: "the contest for the Trade must necessarily be determined in favour of that country which supplies goods at the cheapest rate," he informed Moody (Douglas to Moody, 20 November 1860, B.C., Governor Douglas, Private Official Letter-book, 27 May 1859–9 January 1864, PABC). Moberly and Dewdney had already opened a trail from Hope to the Similkameen which followed closely the Anderson Trail used by the Hudson's Bay Company. In 1861 they constructed the first seven miles of a wagon road, and the work was then taken over by Captain Grant with eighty Sappers and ninety civilians. "This new road leads to Similkameen Rock Creek & the country bordering the boundary line," Bishop Hills recorded in his journal on 3 July

1861. "From there is a continuous range of both gold mining & agricultural land. In this direction will be in all probability the course of the water-oceanic communication. The first seven miles are being constructed by Messrs. Dewdney & Moberly at 300£ a mile. The remainder is in the hands of the Royal Engineers. The line follows the Nicolome [Nicolum] to Beaver Lake the summit of the first range. Then down the Simalaon [Sumallo] to its junction with the Skaget to the Punch bowl pass."

7:32 *Court House.* According to William Yates, the court house, built in the autumn of 1858, was "a very small old place, just big enough for the judge to sit down at the table" ("Reminiscences of William Yates"). There must have been rooms in addition to the courtroom, however, since the diaries of Peter O'Reilly contain references to persons finding accommodation there (see, for example, 22 January 1862: "old G[lennie] took a bed at the court house" [Peter O'Reilly's Diary, 1862, PABC]). Peter O'Reilly's annual diaries are hereafter cited as O'Reilly Diaries.

7:33 *Nagle.* Jessie Melville Nagle, one of the seven daughters of Captain Jeremiah Nagle, a native of Cork, who, after commanding merchant ships to Australia and New Zealand, went to California and from there to Victoria, where he was appointed harbour master in 1859. In October 1861 Douglas suspended him for defalcations in his department, and in December Nagle opened a shipping agency and general commission business on Wharf Street. Nagle moved to New Westminster to open a similar business in 1865 but returned with his family to Victoria the following year. In August 1869 he became port warden for Victoria and Esquimalt.

Jessie Nagle was employed in 1860 as governess by Mrs. Moody, who found her "quite invaluable, not only at lessons but in sundry other ways, she is so quiet & the children are all so fond of her" (Mrs. Moody to "My dearest Mamma," 3 January 1862, Mary S. Moody Correspondence).

7:34 *Mrs. Landvoight.* Mary, a Frenchwoman, married to George Landvoight.

7:35 *Mrs. Sutton.* The wife of William Sutton.

7:36 *Mrs. Pemberthy.* Probably the wife of Edward Pemberthy, who was granted a pre-emption record at Princeton on 20 June 1861 (Laing, "Colonial Farm Settlers," p. 431). In 1868 a Mrs. J. Pemberthy kept the London and Paris Hotel at Richfield. In 1887, a man with the name of Pemberthy, a civil engineer from Portage Lake, Michigan, died at 150 Mile House (*Colonist*, 7 October 1887).

7:37 *Grey.* Probably the daughter of William Grey (Gray), who on 31 December 1866 pre-empted 160 acres on the west bank of the Fraser River at Hudson's Flat, seven miles below Hope (Laing, "Colonial Farm Settlers," p. 216).

8: 7 *per slice.* Possibly it was Mrs. Landvoight's baking that was so much enjoyed by the party of American gold-seekers who travelled through the Okanagan Valley to the Fraser diggings and from there to Hope and Victoria in the summer of 1858. "Here at a bakery we bought the first and best pumpkin pie we had eaten for over ten years, about ¾ inches thick, in square pans—it was good, and you got a big pie for 25 cents" (*The Golden Frontier: The Recollections of Herman Francis Reinhart 1851–1869,* ed. Doyce B. Nunis [Austin: University of Texas Press, 1962], p. 138).

8:14 *pretty little church.* Christ Church, Hope, designed by Captain J.M. Grant, was not built until 1861. The cornerstone was laid on 9 July, and the consecration took place on 1 November. "The little church was quite full," wrote Bishop Hills. "It happened there were in town on their way to Westminster a number of Royal Engineers. They attended the Service & gave a true and hearty character to the proceedings" (Hills' Journal, 1 November 1861). Peter O'Reilly was the first warden. Christ Church, Hope, is the oldest Protestant church on mainland British Columbia on its original site.

8:15 *saloon.* William Yates states that there were fifteen saloons in Hope in 1858. Mrs. Allison is probably referring to the hotel run by Maxime Michaud, who subsequently was the proprietor of a hotel at New Westminster, then at Brighton (Hastings), and later at Langley. Michaud pre-empted sixty acres near Hope on 1 October 1859 (Laing, "Colonial Farm Settlers," p. 220).

8:17 *sawmill.* To supply John Coe's sawmill a wide ditch had been dug to convey water from the Coquihalla River.

8:24 *stockade.* Fort Hope, but not Fort Yale, was stockaded. "The fort here had a gallery all around with block houses in each corner," William Yates remembered. "We had two canon. Mr. Angus McDonald had one and took it to Colville. The other one—I have a portion of it here.... On the 4th of July six years ago there was an Irishman that tried to mine up here and he wanted to celebrate the fourth of July, and he could not get any canon or anything. So he bothered the life out of me to lend him the canon. And do you know what they did? They put in a charge of giant powder. Me and Bill Bristol were standing on Wardell's stoop talking and when it went off the canon flew in bits. One bit flew between me and Bill Bristol. So I got the canon back, or a piece of it, and I have it yet. It was a fine little canon—one of the old King George the Fourth I think" ("Reminiscences of William Yates," p. 7).

Florence Goodfellow describes the Hudson's Bay Company's house and store as being very large and built of logs. "The employees' houses were also built of logs but were much smaller. They formed a large square and had at one time been surrounded by a palisade, very tall and strong. Most of it had been used for firewood before our arrival in 1865 but there was enough left at the back to look imposing.... There must have been a battle with the Indians there at some time as the palisades were full of small bullets which we used to pick out with a knife, but even old Yates, the oldest of the Hudson's Bay employees... declared he had never heard of one" (Florence Goodfellow, *Memories of a Pioneer Life in British Columbia* [Wenatchee, Wash.: privately printed, 1945], p. 18).

8:27 *noise enough.* When Governor Douglas visited Hope on 1 June 1860, "the echoes were startling and long and kindly responded to the guns of the fort and the whistle of the Steamer which greeted the Governor" (Hills' Journal, 1 June 1860).

8:28 *Aparajos.* "My own convictions, deduced from long and extensive experience, is, that the aparejo comes nearer to what I conceive to be perfection in a pack-saddle, than any other form of pack-saddle yet invented," wrote John Keast Lord. "As neither wood nor iron enters into its composition, wherever there are animals from which hides can be obtained, there a person can find all the materials he needs for making an aparejo, tools required for sewing of course excepted. . . . An aparejo may be defined to be two bags made either of dressed, or undressed hides, stuffed with dry grass, and fastened together at the top" (John Keast Lord, *At Home in the Wilderness*, 3rd ed. [London: Hardwicke and Bogue, 1876], pp. 68–69).

9:22 *other places.* The fur brigades from the districts of New Caledonia in the north, Thompson River, and Fort Colvile in the south, comprising four hundred or more horses, converged on Fort Hope. While the furs were being discharged from the horse brigades and loaded onto boats to be taken to Fort Langley, the chief factors of these three districts held their annual meeting. Meanwhile the outfits for the interior posts were being made up into bundles of food, clothing, and trade goods. When all was ready, bundles weighing from eighty to one hundred pounds each were slung on the sides of the horses. According to Edgar Dewdney, "It took a week or two to put things into shape, and all the employees and the packers had a very strenuous time of it. When all the packs were made up and things were in shape for the return journey, the fun commenced, and the Indians and voyageurs put on their best clothes, the half-breeds and some of the officials in their leather dresses and beads with streamers of all colors from the hats. Hope looked gay in those days. Dancing and horse racing were the principal amusements. Everything was very orderly, and I have rarely seen any trouble on those occasions. It was a happy annual meeting of the Hudson's Bay Company officials and their dependents" (R.E. Gosnell, "Building the Dewdney Trail as told by the Builder").

9:28 "*cayooses.*" Cayuses, or mustangs, wild horses which roamed Texas, Mexico, California, Oregon, and British Columbia; "as a rule," wrote Lord, "they are small horses, rarely exceeding fourteen hands high. They are descended from Spanish stock, which must have been originally brought into Mexico by the original conquerors" (*At Home in the Wilderness*, p. 205).

10: 2 *Mansen's Mountain.* The tall and forbidding Manson ridge east of Hope was named after Chief Trader Donald Manson (1798–

1880), who was superintendent of New Caledonia from 1844 to 1856 and who took part in exploring the Hope–Similkameen area for a brigade route in 1846–49. In September 1859 Lieutenant H. Spencer Palmer, R.E., sent to explore this area, accompanied Chief Factor Angus McDonald, who was returning to Fort Colvile, and was himself accompanied for part of the way by Judge Begbie, Arthur Bushby, and Peter O'Reilly. The party made the laborious ascent of Manson's Mountain by a zigzag trail, "very steep and rocky," to the summit of a pass, from which the view of mountain scenery could "scarcely be surpassed.... As far as the eye could reach, an endless sea of mountains rolled away into the blue distance, their sides clothed almost to the summits with an impenetrable forest of every species of pine.... Between me and the main ridge was a deep glen or forest bottom, not free from mountains, it is true, but nevertheless a valley, down which pours a considerable stream [Peers] one of the head tributaries of the Coquahalla."

Since the snowfall at the summit was between twenty-five and thirty feet, this route was very dangerous from the first of October until the end of May. "Mr. Donald McLean of the Hudson Bay Company who crossed in 1857 or 1858, on the 16th October had a very disastrous trip and lost 60 or 70 horses," wrote Palmer. "Traces of their deaths are still visible, and in riding over the mountain, and more particularly on its eastern slope, my horse frequently shied at the whitened bones of some of the poor animals, who had broken down in the sharp struggle with fatigue and hunger, and been left to perish" (Lieutenant H. Spencer Palmer, R.E., "Report on the Country between Fort Hope on the Fraser and Fort Colville on the Columbia River," *BCP*, 1860 [Cmd. 2724, 1st series], 3: 81–82). For further information on the Brigade Trail, see H.R. Hatfield, "On the Brigade Trail," *The Beaver* (Summer 1974): 38–43.

10:12 *the Nicalome and Silver Creek.* Nicolum Creek, some twenty miles southeast of Hope, whose valley was filled with debris by a great mountain slide in January 1965. Silver Creek flows into the Fraser River a few miles south of the Coquihalla River. It was the site of an early silver mine, whose company, the Hope Silver Mining Company, had its head office in Victoria in 1867 (Henry G. Langley, *The Pacific Coast Business Directory for 1867* [San Francisco: Henry G. Langley, 1867], p. 380).

10:30 *except Indians.* The solitary horseman was Angus McDonald (1816–89), a native of Rosshire, who had entered the service of the Hudson's Bay Company as an apprentice clerk in 1838 and who had been in charge of Fort Colvile for many years. Charles Wilson described him in 1860 as "a great curiosity; now about 43 years old, he has spent 20 years of his life in the woods with hardly any communication with whites, in his youth the strongest man & best rifle shot on the continent & still a fine figure & wonderful activity for his age. Some of his hunting tales are very good; he has polished off a large number of grizzlys single handed, deer & buffalo innumerable" (Stanley, *Mapping the Frontier*, p. 113).

10:31 *Pringle's wife and children.* Rev. Alexander David Pringle, M.A. (1828–1908), assistant curate at Christ Church, Paddington, who was chosen by the Society for the Propagation of the Gospel, as a missionary, to be sent to British Columbia. Pringle arrived in Hope in August 1859 and immediately started to preach to the miners on the river bars. Bishop Hills on first meeting Pringle in January 1860 was impressed with his efforts: "He has truly borne the burden & heat of the day in ministering to the gold diggers. He has lived in a cabin of wood—one room—has cooked & done everything for himself. The weather has been excessively cold—some days thermometer down to 20. He has established a Reading Room & Library. The miners looked upon him as their friend & invited him to hold services upon their bars of the River. All luxuries—such as butter & milk he has not known" (Hills' Journal, 20 January 1860). After the bishop's arrival services were held in Pringle's room; there on Trinity Sunday (3 June 1860) some forty-five persons, including Governor Douglas, Colonel Moody, and Chief Justice Begbie, were present.

Mrs. Pringle, with her two small daughters, arrived in Victoria on 24 August 1860, travelling from England with "the Mission party," comprising the Rev. C.T. Woods, the Rev. Octavius Glover, and the Misses Agnes and Catherine Penrice. After her arrival, "the Parsonage . . . a tolerable house with two stories" (*Lady Franklin Visits the Pacific Northwest*, ed. Dorothy Blakey Smith, Archives Memoir no. 11 [Victoria: Queen's Printer, 1974], p. 50) was built. Early in 1861 Pringle pre-empted three parcels of land for his daughters, but he did not complete the requirements. Relations between Pringle and the bishop became strained in

1862 when Hope was in decline, and the bishop ordered the S.P.G. missionary to undertake work among the itinerant road workers without extra remuneration. In 1864 the Pringles left for England where he became P.C. of St. James with Pockthorpe, Norwich.

10:37 *Burdette-Coutts.* Miss (later Baroness) Angela Burdett-Coutts, the benefactor of the Anglican Church in British Columbia, who endowed the see of Columbia with £15,000 (Archbishop of Canterbury to Sir Edward Bulwer Lytton, 27 September 1858, *BCP*, 2:72) and also provided endowments for two archbishoprics, as well as for a peal of bells for a cathedral in the colony. The bells, which were hung in Holy Trinity Church, New Westminster, were destroyed in 1898 in the New Westminster fire.

11: 4 *Indian Village.* When Yates came to Hope in 1856, there were over 250 Indians on the Flat. "Now (c. 1900) there is only one family living there and of the whole Hope tribe there are only about 28 left." Of the 72 Indians at the mouth of the Coquihalla River, there was only one remaining—the widow of Chief Captain John—in the whole rancherie. She was the last of the Coquihalla tribe ("Reminiscences of William Yates," p. 21). In 1963 the Hope band consisted of 116 persons (Wilson Duff, *The Indian History of British Columbia, I, The Impact of the White Man,* Anthropology in British Columbia, Memoir no. 5 [Victoria: Queen's Printer, 1964], p. 28).

11: 8 *amulets and rings.* The Stalo tribes of the Coast Salish occupied the region along the Fraser River to five miles above Yale, each local group occupying a stretch of riverbank. These Indians dried salmon on rocks over which they built roofs to afford protection for the drying fish from rain and sun. The Stalo made coiled and imbricated baskets of cedar roots and wove blankets and rugs of the wool of mountain goats and dogs. For further information, see Wilson Duff, *The Upper Stalo Indians,* Anthropology in British Columbia, Memoir no. 1 (Victoria: Queen's Printer, 1952). There is no reference in this work to silverwork as one of the art forms of the Stalo.

11:18 *Hope Indians.* Wilson Duff states that flattening was achieved in the cradle "by means of a padded wooden board about three feet long, six inches wide, and two inches thick, decorated with painting" (*The Upper Stalo Indians*, p. 90). Lieutenant Charles Wilson, when he first saw the process at Victoria, found it "very disgusting. . . . Whilst we were looking on the poor little thing got so bad they had to loosen the bandage & finally I got them to take it off, the sutures of the skull were quite open & you could actually see the brain beating through them & the head flattened skew ways instead of straight off the forehead" (Stanley, *Mapping the Frontier*, pp. 24–25). Rev. John Sheepshanks (later bishop of Norwich) described the process as follows: "The little baby is carried about in a wicker basket shaped like an open coffin, and slung on the mother's back. As the child lies in this basket a pad, perhaps of bark, is placed upon his forehead, and strong sinews are so placed and fastened with screws into each side of the basket that they press upon the pad, and by turning the screws every now and then additional pressure is put upon the infant's forehead before his skull has grown quite hard. Thus the fore part of the skull is pressed down, and as a consequence the top and back part is bulged out. Thus the normal shape of the skull is changed, and it takes a comparatively oval form. It might be thought that the power of the brain would be injuriously affected by this strange custom. But I am not aware that it is so. I think the 'Flatheads' are to the full as intelligent as any other of these tribes" (Rev. D. Wallace Duthie, *A Bishop in the Rough*, 3rd impression [London: Smith, Elder, 1909], pp. 38–39).

11:31 *Hope–Similkameen Road.* The "Engineers' Road," built by Captain J.M. Grant and the Sappers. "The road lay through the recesses of the Forest by the picturesque Valley of the Nicoleme," wrote Bishop Hills. "Before you the vista is that of an English country road. You seem to be nearby some friendly mansion. Around as you pass along new sights of interest have been opened. Magnificent waterfalls, sublime rocks in every garden, glimpses of light & foaming streams hasting on through winding placid lakes as such as in Europe civilized men would give much and go far to see" (Hills' Journal, 20 and 22 July 1861).

11:32 *called it.* The spelling of "Coquihalla" varies greatly in the early accounts. The river, which bears an Indian name meaning "greedy or hungry waters," rises in the Cascades and flows southwest to enter the Fraser River two and one-half miles above Hope.

11:33 *spent salmon.* Salmon dying after spawning.

11:38 *ugly tear.* According to one of her daughters, Mrs. Allison "rode side-saddle, wearing her long riding habit which looped up to a button on the side" (Alice Allison Wright, "Mrs. John Fall Allison," Okanagan Historical Society, *Fourteenth Report* [Kelowna: *Kelowna Courier*, 1950], p. 124).

12: 1 *small piece of land.* On 20 August 1860 Glennie pre-empted 160 acres two miles from Hope on the banks of the Coquihalla. He obtained his certificate of improvement on 3 January 1862 (Laing, "Colonial Farm Settlers," p. 223). The Glennies moved to "Hopelands" on 8 December 1860: "The Glennies went out to their new house walked with them, 'a gloomy lookout,' " recorded Peter O'Reilly (O'Reilly Diaries, 8 December 1860). The builders of their house have not been identified, though Van Horn may be the Van Doan who was fined by O'Reilly for whiskey-selling on 8 October (ibid., 8 October, 1860).

12:16 *Mabel.* The eldest daughter of William Charles, Mabel (1860–1913), after whom Mabel Lake was named. Her husband, D.M. Eberts, served in the Legislative Assembly from 1890 until 1913, and as attorney general from 1895 to 1898 and from 1900 to 1913.

12:24 *little piano.* The Glennies' household furnishings, shipped round the Horn, arrived in Victoria in December 1860 and at Hope the following January. They included the little piano that had been purchased in London for Jane on her sixteenth birthday from William Evestaff of Sloane Street. "The Piano is a very good one & in perfect tune," wrote O'Reilly (O'Reilly Diaries, 22 January 1861). It was taken to Hopelands by oxcart and carried back to Hope for Edward Sanders's wedding in December 1862 and for Jane's wedding in March 1864. Jane gave it to her sister at the time of her marriage, but it remained with Mrs. Glennie at Hope until she went to live with the Dewdneys (Vancouver *Daily Province*, 21 February 1932). It did not reach Princeton until after the completion of the Kettle Valley Railway in 1914. The second piano brought to the Mainland (Captain Grant had brought one to Fort Langley), it is now preserved in the Provincial Museum, Victoria.

12:31 *silver candelabra.* Bishop Hills coveted these candlesticks when he saw them in 1868: "Mrs. Glennie is full of reminiscences of Scotch Episcopacy. She was intimate with an old lady named Shepherd, a daughter of the Sir John Irving Troup who in 1745 was imprisoned. At that time the Episcopalians in Scotland could only meet in private & Mrs. Shepherd used to send the candlesticks to light the room—a pair of these candlesticks Mrs. Glennie has—which I saw & certainly they ought to be preserved. They are of chaste pattern & would serve for the Altar of some country church. . . . The place of meeting where the candles were sent in the days of persecution was in the Gallow gate of Aberdeen" (Hills' Journal, 2 June 1868).

12:38 *ate them.* Bears were not the only predators: "I called upon the Glennies who have a comfortable house," Bishop Hills recorded. "They lost all their crops by cattle breaking in" (Hills' Journal, 6 November 1861).

13: 1 *Hawkins.* Captain (later General Sir) John Summerfield Hawkins, R.E. (1812–95), chief commissioner of the British Land Commission surveying to locate the 49th Parallel boundary as laid down by the Oregon Treaty of 1846. Hawkins held the rank of captain at the time of his appointment, but he was promoted on 12 August 1858 to lieutenant-colonel. He became colonel on 1 March 1868, lieutenant-general, 1 October 1877, and general, 1 July 1881. On his retirement that year, he was knighted. Hawkins visited Hope in September 1861 (not in the spring of the year) on his way to inspect the silver-lead mine on Silver Creek. He was accompanied by Dr. Hilary Bauerman, geologist, and John Keast Lord, naturalist, both members of the British Boundary Commission (O'Reilly Diaries, 25 and 28 September 1861).

13: 8 *Queen's birthday.* Governor Douglas was present at the celebration in 1861, which O'Reilly thus described: "Salute of 21 guns fired at 12 in honour of Queen's 42nd Birthday—feeding at 2—horse & foot races. . . . The Yankees not at all approving of the proceedings" (O'Reilly Diaries, 24 May 1861). On the Fourth of July, Bishop Hills noted: "Today is great with the Americans.

Guns were fired & shops were closed. In the afternoon all were busy carousing & rejoicing. Not easy however to rejoice as was their wont—a rejoicing which swelled itself to considerable boasting usually. Now the Flag did not wave so haughtily, since no longer are the States United. In firing the guns at 12 the attempt was made to raise a cheer but no hearts or voices were in Tune" (Hills' Journal, 4 July 1861).

13: 9 *Oppenheimer.* Charles Oppenheimer (1832?–90), born at Frankfurt-on-Rhine, emigrated with his brothers Godfried, David, and Isaac to California in 1851. Removing to British Columbia in 1858, Charles went to Yale, which he perceived would become the centre of the outfitting business for the miners. He took pack trains to Cariboo and at Yale constructed a warehouse and store on the main street near the riverbank. In 1862 he left the firm to join Moberly and T.B. Lewis in a contract to build part of the Cariboo Road north from Lytton. It was in connection with this contract that the Hudson's Bay Company launched a suit in 1863 against Oppenheimer and Company. The jury discharged the case. For further details, see Robinson, *Blazing the Trail Through the Rockies.* Later, Charles set up David and Isaac in business in Victoria. In 1873 he himself retired from the firm and went to San Francisco. David Oppenheimer (1834–97) was mayor of Vancouver from 1888 until 1892. Isaac served as alderman during part of this period.

13:10 *Saunders.* Edward Howard Sanders (1832–1902), born at Bridge House, Christ Church, Hampshire, was educated in England, Belgium, and Germany. Sanders held a commission in the Imperial Austrian army from 1849 to 1855 and served in the Crimean War. He arrived in Victoria in the spring of 1859 and on 19 April was appointed justice of the peace. On 13 May he was appointed stipendiary magistrate at Yale. In 1864 he represented Yale and Hope in the first Legislative Council of British Columbia. In 1866 he was placed in charge of the amalgamated district of Hope–Yale–Lytton, and from 1867 to 1870 he was magistrate of Lillooet District.

13:10 *Bouies.* John and James Buie, with their brother Thomas Russell Buie, came to British Columbia in 1858. They engaged in various enterprises. Thomas Russell Buie built the Cariboo Telegraph line in 1868, and in 1872 he was made justice of the peace at Lytton. His wife Agnes, whom he married in 1866, was the daughter of Frank Laumeister, who imported camels to be used as pack animals on the Cariboo trail. Buie Brothers were general merchants and wholesale and retail dealers in liquor in Cariboo from 1865 to 1868.

13:11 *Lawrence.* James Lawrence, who later married Mrs. Fanny Lethbridge, one of Edgar Dewdney's sisters (Dewdney Miscellaneous Material, PABC).

13:12 *Similkameen Indians.* The Similkameen Indians, who numbered around three hundred in the 1860's, were Interior Salish, an admixture of Okanagans and Thompsons, with an infusion of Chilcotins. They occupied the country between Okanagan Lake and Hope from about the 49th Parallel to a distance of forty-five miles north. They were first encountered by Europeans in 1813 when Alexander Ross, a clerk in the Pacific Fur Company, returned from Kamloops to Okanagan Valley by way of Nicola and Douglas lakes, passing over a high plateau to Osprey Lake and Keremeos (John C. Goodfellow, "Fur and Gold in Similkameen," *BCHQ* 2 [1938]: 67–88).

Lieutenant H. Spencer Palmer was impressed with the Similkameens when he met them in 1859:

> These were the first mounted Indians I had met with, and I was particularly struck with their vast superiority in point of intelligence and energy to the Fish Indians on the Fraser river and in its neighbourhood.
>
> "Agriculture, however, is but little known amongst them, and a few potato patches form the extent of their progress in this direction. They appear to live chiefly on fish, viz., trout and salmon, on game such as wild fowl, prairie chicken, and mountain sheep, and on wild berries, several kinds of which, including black and red cherries, abound in the neighbouring valleys.
>
> The greater portion of the tribe were absent when we passed, but those who visited the camp were fine men, and superb riders, and, though poorly clad, evinced a neatness, and an effort to improve their personal appearance, which contrasts favourably with the dirty, slovenly habits of the Fraser Indians.

The Romish religion is universal amongst them, propagated, I imagine, by the members of the Jesuit missions on the borders of Washington territory, and I was not a little surprised to see that, on entering camp, they invariably crossed themselves before making the sign of respect or salutation. Unlike the gaudy but picturesque native burial grounds which dot the banks of the rivers in the interior of British Columbia, the graves of these Indians were scattered about singly over the country, their wandering habits assigning no fixed place of abode, and a small earthern mound or pile of stones, surmounted by a wooden cross, were the only objects that marked the few solitary graves I happened to come across on the trip. I should mention that the "Similkameen" Indians are a portion of the Okanagan tribe, and speak the same language—one so guttural and unpronounceable as to render it almost hopeless for any white man to attempt to acquire proficiency in it (Palmer, "Report on the Country between Fort Hope . . . and Fort Colville," *BCP*, 3: 84–85).

13:14 *Thompson woman.* Rev. John Booth Good wrote that "the Thompsons as a whole were comely to look at and many of the younger women possessed something of a Spanish complexion. But there was amongst them a swarthy almost Negro type or look, very distinguishable from the rest" (John Booth Good, "The Utmost Bounds of the West," typescript, PABC).

13:30 *inspected the road.* Douglas visited Hope from 19 to 25 May 1861 and undoubtedly inspected the Similkameen Road at that time. His impressions of Similkameen Valley, however, were probably drawn from his 1860 visit to Rock Creek.

13:36 *Nefolium lily.* Possibly Mrs. Allison is referring to the white fawn lily, *Erythronium oreganum Applegate* (T.M.C. Taylor, *The Lily Family* (*Lilaceae*) *of British Columbia,* Provincial Museum, Handbook 25 [Victoria: Queen's Printer, 1966], p. 45).

13:37 *Linnear Borealis.* Twin-flower, *Linneae Borealis.* "This dainty plant spreads long runners, creeping over the moss, or trailing from rotting logs or stumps, from which at frequent intervals rise two to four inch stems. These fork at the top, each branch supporting a single trumpet—a demure, pink, rose-flushed and slender bell" (Lewis J. Clark, *Wildflowers of British Columbia* [Sidney, B.C.: Gray's Publishing Company, 1973], p. 478).

13:37 *Tiger Lilies. Lilium Columbianum.* Orange tiger lilies, having maroon spots, are widely distributed in the southern half of British Columbia (see Taylor, *The Lily Family*, pp. 53–54; and Clark, *Wildflowers of British Columbia*, p. 28).

13:38 *Dogwood.* The flowering Pacific Dogwood, *Cornus Nuttallii*, the provincial flower of British Columbia (see E.H. Garman, *The Trees and Shrubs of British Columbia*, Provincial Museum, Handbook 31, 5th rev. ed. [Victoria: Queen's Printer, 1973], p. 90).

14: 1 *Partridge berry.* Probably Mrs. Allison is referring to the Dwarf Dogwood (bunchberry), *Cornus Canadensis.*

14: 4 *Trutch brothers.* (Sir) Joseph William Trutch (1826–1904) and John Trutch (1828–1927), sons of William Trutch of Ashcot, Somerset, a solicitor who moved to St. Thomas, Jamaica, where he became clerk of the peace. Joseph Trutch, like H.P.P. Crease, was educated at Mount Radford School, Exeter. He was then apprenticed as a civil engineer to Sir John Rennie and served his apprenticeship on the Great Northern Railway. In 1849 he sailed round the Horn to San Francisco and there worked for a firm constructing iron warehouses. From San Francisco he went to Oregon and obtained employment with John Brown Preston, the surveyor general of the Territory. On 8 January 1855 he married Preston's sister-in-law, Julia Hyde, the daughter of a prominent New York mining engineer. Joseph Trutch was in England when he heard of the Fraser River gold rush. He applied to Lytton and to Moody for an appointment. Lytton give him a letter to Douglas, and Moody offered encouragement. When he arrived in Victoria in June 1859, Trutch was bitterly disappointed to find Moody unwilling to offer him work since Douglas was curtailing expenditure. Between 1860 and 1863, however, Trutch obtained contracts on the Harrison–Lillooet Road and on the Cariboo Road between Chapman's Bar and Boston Bar in the Fraser Canyon. His greatest achievement was the building of the Alexandra Suspension Bridge in 1863. Since the contract for this bridge permitted him to collect tolls for seven years, there was criticism of his accepting in 1864 the appointment of chief commissioner of lands and works in succession to Moody.

As a council member, Trutch was in the forefront of political developments during the late colonial period. His share in drafting the Terms of Union with Canada was large, and he served not only as one of the three negotiators with Canada but also as the sole negotiator in London. On Confederation Day, 20 July 1871, he was named the province's first lieutenant-governor. In this office he initiated responsible government in the province. In July 1876, on completion of his term, he returned to England. In 1880 he became dominion agent in British Columbia with responsibility for supervising the construction of the Canadian Pacific Railway and administering the railway lands. On his retirement in 1889 he was knighted for his services. Joseph Trutch's career is summarized in Hollis R. Lynch, "Sir Joseph William Trutch, a British-American Pioneer on the Pacific Coast," *Pacific Historical Review* 30 (1961): 243–55; his work as an engineer in C.F. Forbes, "Trutch—Dynamic Road-Builder and Shrewd Operator," *B.C. Historical News* 4, no. 1 (1970): 11–19; and G. Smedley Andrews, *Sir Joseph William Trutch, K.C.M.G.* (Victoria: British Columbia Lands Service, 1972); and his lieutenant-governorship in John T. Saywell, *The Office of Lieutenant Governor*... (Toronto: University of Toronto Press, 1957), pp. 80–87, 176–78. For a critical view of his land policy, see Robin Fisher, "Joseph Trutch and Indian Land Policy," *BC Studies* 12 (1971–72): 3–33.

John Trutch, who was associated with his brother's activities in Oregon, became assistant surveyor general in Washington Territory in 1857. He later became his brother's partner in the Harrison–Lillooet Road, the Cariboo Road, and the Alexandra Bridge contracts. During the construction of the Canadian Pacific Railway, he was on the staff of Andrew Onderdonk, and in 1889 he was land commissioner for the Esquimalt and Nanaimo Railway. John Trutch married Sarah (Zoë) Musgrave, sister of Governor Anthony Musgrave, on 8 December 1870.

The brothers brought from England their mother, Charlotte Hannah Trutch (1810?–76), and their sister, Caroline Agnes, (1831–98), who married Peter O'Reilly on 15 December 1863.

14: 7 *Stevenson.* Robert Stevenson (1838–1922), born in Glengarry, Upper Canada, arrived in British Columbia in March 1859 after crossing the Isthmus of Panama on foot and then went to Washington Territory to mine gold on the Similkameen River. In April 1860 he joined an expedition of thirty-four men led by a Captain Collins of Seattle, an Indian fighter, to mine at Rock Creek. According to Stevenson, on the occasion of Douglas's visit to the mining camp in September, the governor offered him a position in the customs house at Osoyoos, but in 1861 he left with a pack train for Antler Creek, Cariboo. In 1862 he recorded a claim on Williams Creek to be worked in conjunction with the famous claim of John A. Cameron. After Mrs. Cameron's death at Richfield on 23 October 1862, Stevenson helped Cameron take her body to Victoria via the Douglas–Lillooet route, a journey that lasted from 31 January to 7 March 1863. He then returned to Cariboo to mine but in October 1863 left with Cameron to take Mrs. Cameron's body by way of Panama to Cornwall, Upper Canada, for burial. In 1864 he returned to Cariboo and remained there until 1876 when he visited the Cassiar goldfields. In 1877 Stevenson went to Similkameen to investigate a gold-quartz ledge on Blackeye Portage after being told of its existence by O'Reilly. Though he married the same year and bought four hundred acres at Sardis with the intention of settling down, mining still attracted him. He staked twenty-seven square miles of coal lands in the Princeton area, but he was unable to interest James Dunsmuir in developing them. In 1895 he discovered coal on Granite Creek. And with James Jameson, he staked the "Sunset" mine, one of the best copper claims on Copper Mountain. For further details, see W. Wymond Walkem, *Stories of Early British Columbia* (Vancouver: *News-Advertiser,* 1914), pp. 243–87; and the articles in Vancouver *Daily Province* by W.W. Walkem, 10 May, and 7, 14, and 28 June 1913.

14:15 *foolishly refused.* In the autumn of 1859 Douglas first considered placing a tax on pack trains leaving Hope for Similkameen in order to raise funds to improve the trail. Receiving a protest forwarded from Hope by Rev. A.D. Pringle, he stated in January 1860 that he had "expected that packers would not object to pay a percentage on their goods in return for the greater facilities of locomotion afforded them" (Philip Nind to Rev. A.D. Pringle, 26 January 1860, B.C., Governor Douglas, Private Official Letterbook, 1859–1864). The "mule tax" proclaimed on 31 January 1860 levied a tax of £1 on every pack horse leaving Douglas or Yale for the Cariboo mines and was so unpopular that Douglas had to suspend it in March. When the packers at Hope petitioned to have the Engineers' Road completed by the end of 1861, Douglas told them that this could only be done if they would pay a higher toll. "Deputation waited on H E at 11," O'Reilly recorded in his diary on 20 May 1861. "No end of talk, but very little done, Pringle as usual very loquatious." A meeting held at Hope in July to consider paying high tolls coincided with Douglas's receiving a delegation from Yale led by Charles Oppenheimer to press for a Yale–Cariboo Road. When Douglas again visited Hope on 20 September, O'Reilly noted that "deputation waited on H E with reference to the construction of a road direct to Kamloops, also a road to Yale improvements of the streets &c &c to all of which he gave a negative [answer] much to the disappointment of all" (O'Reilly Diaries, 20 September 1861). Encouraged by the gold discoveries in Cariboo and by reports from the Royal Engineers concerning the practicability of building a road from Yale, Douglas had already set in train his plan for a Yale–Cariboo Road. Consequently he discontinued the Similkameen Wagon Road in September 1861 when twenty-five miles were completed. The next year Bishop Hills noted that "from Hope have departed nearly all its inhabitants. Though a stopping place for Steamers yet Yale being higher on the River to which boats can come and from which actual travel begins traders find that at present it is a better place for their houses of business. Then Cariboo mines have thinned all places & many have migrated directly thither" (Hills' Journal, 18 June 1862).

14:23 *Hot Springs*. The hot springs at the southern end of Harrison Lake, thought to have been discovered by some miners returning from Cariboo in December 1858. "St. Alice's Well" was named by Judge Begbie in 1859 (Matthew B. Begbie, "Journey into the Interior of British Columbia," *Journal of the Royal Geographical Society* 38 [1861]: p. 247). It is believed that Begbie was honouring Alice Douglas, afterwards Mrs. Charles Good, and that he named the spring northwest of Harrison Lake, "St. Agnes' Well," in honour of Agnes Douglas, later Mrs. Arthur Bushby.

14:28 *Irving's boat*. The *Reliance*.

14:29 *Douglas on the Harrison Lake.* Port Douglas, named in honour of Governor Douglas, the southern terminus of the Harrison–Lillooet route to Cariboo via Seton, Anderson, and Lillooet lakes. Its situation, according to Judge Begbie, "though romantic and beautiful, and offering to vessels lying in its little lake a secure harbour during seven or eight months in the year, has such natural defects, that nothing but necessity can justify its adoption or retention for a moment. For four or five months in the year, if not for a longer period, it may be said to be inaccessible either by land or water, except on foot" (Begbie, "Journey into the Interior," p. 245). By 1862 Yale had superseded Douglas as the starting point for the Cariboo mines.

When Bishop Hills visited Port Douglas, he found there Italians, Germans, Norwegians, French, Africans, Americans, Scotch, English, Irish, and Canadians. "Amongst curiosities in this way I was taken to the house of a China man, to see his wife & infant a great rarity in this part of the world. The Chinese lady was a sensible woman & stood upon her feet as nature taught her" (Hills' Journal, 2 June 1861).

14:32 *magistrate and constable.* The magistrate was John Boles Gaggin, formerly a lieutenant in the Royal Cork Artillery. He served as constable at Yale until October 1859 and was then appointed magistrate and assistant gold commissioner at Port Douglas, where he remained until 1863. Bishop Hills recorded the following incident involving Gaggin:

> Almost every man in Douglas lives with an Indian woman. The magistrate Mr. Gaggin is not an exception from the immorality. Recently the constable Humphrey was ordered to a distance by the Magistrate. The Indian he lived with was named Lucy, by whom he had a child. He proposed to take her with him. The magistrate opposed some reason to the contrary. "May I depend upon your honour that she shall be safe during my absence." The magistrate promised such should be the case. He violated the promise & induced the woman to come to him. The Constable was highly incensed on his return & unburdened his mind to Mr. Gammage & at length quitted the situation.
>
> What can we expect when the representatives of England thus deport themselves? (Hills' Journal, 19 May 1862).

14:32 *one hotel.* Four-Mile House, the residence of a Mrs. Hanna and her brother (Hills' Journal, 19 May 1862).

15: 6 *Morey.* Frances Morey (1843–1928), the eldest daughter of Sergeant Jonathan Morey, R.E., whose wife and children accompanied him on the *Thames City* to Victoria, arriving in 1859. Fanny was fourteen years of age when they sailed, and her sister Martha (1856–1944) was two. Jonathan Morey (d. 1884) remained in the colony, where he served as chief of police in New Westminster. Shortly after Fanny's marriage to William Stein on 12 November 1861, the Steins moved to California. Martha Morey married James Wardle of Hope on 24 October 1877.

15:22 *Fountain Indians.* Indians from The Fountain, twelve miles below Pavilion, the farthest north of mining operations in 1858. A flat at a sharp turn in the upper Fraser River, The Fountain derived its name from a small natural formation which spouted water (R.C. Mayne, *Four Years in British Columbia and Vancouver Island* [London: J. Murray, 1862], p. 131).

16: 7 *Moresby.* The eldest daughter of William Moresby, a barrister of the Inner Temple, who was the younger brother of Admiral Sir Fairfax Moresby, commander-in-chief on the Pacific Station (1850–53) and later (1870) Admiral of the Fleet, and the uncle of Admiral John Moresby. After practising law in Hong Kong, William Moresby arrived in Victoria in 1861 and opened a law office. He died shortly afterwards, leaving his family in poor circumstances. His wife obtained an appointment as teacher at the school built by the Royal Engineers for their children, but after a public school was opened at New Westminster, Jessie Nagle in August 1862 took over her duties. Young William Moresby went to Cariboo and in 1868 entered the police force. He became assistant jailer in New Westminster in 1878, then governor of the New Westminster prison, and in 1895 warden of the New Westminster penitentiary. Annie Moresby (1844–77) married E. H. Sanders in 1862. Her sister Charlotte married J.C. Haynes at Hope on 26 September 1868, only three weeks after the marriage of Susan Louisa Moir and John Fall Allison. For further information on the Moresby family, see "Notes and Comments," *BCHQ* 2 (1940): 217–18; and John Moresby, *Two Admirals: Admiral of the Fleet Sir Fairfax Moresby and His Son, John Moresby* (London: J. Murray, 1909).

16:13 *parson from Yale.* The Rev. W. Burton Crickmer (1830–1905), curate of St. Marylebone, who was appointed in 1858 as "a missionary chaplain for the goldfields of British Columbia" (Vancouver Island, *Government Gazette*, 16 December 1858). He was sent out to British Columbia by the Colonial Church and School Society. At Derby (Langley) Crickmer opened the church of St. John the Divine for worship on 8 May 1859. When New Westminster became the capital, Langley declined and Crickmer was transferred to Yale. Bishop Hills praised Crickmer, who returned to England in 1862, as "one of my most zealous & useful clergy" (Hills' Journal, 8 August 1860). For further details, see Cyril Stackhouse, *The Churches of St. John the Divine, Derby (1859)—Yale (1860)* ... [Vancouver: Archives Society of Vancouver, 1960].

16:16 *moved to Yale.* The Charleses moved to Yale in June 1864. "Charles & the Wife Kind as ever," reported O'Reilly, "but in trouble at the thoughts of breaking up their establishment at Hope & Moving to Yale" (O'Reilly Diaries, 5 May 1864).

16:17 *Alexandra Bridge.* The first suspension bridge in British Columbia, the Alexandra Bridge was begun by Joseph Trutch on 16 June 1862 and completed 1 September 1863. Its site between Spuzzum and Chapman's Bar was surveyed by Sergeant McColl in October 1861, and the iron bridge was constructed by A.S. Hallide of San Francisco. Its span was 268 feet, the vertical clearance 90 feet and the load capacity three tons. Despite its height above the Fraser River, the bridge was damaged in the 1894 flood. Later replacements of the bridge, one built in 1926 and another in 1962, also bore the name Alexandra.

16:30 *Tingley.* Stephen ("Steve") Tingley (1839–1915), born at Fort Cumberland, New Brunswick, travelled to San Francisco via Panama in 1858 and arrived at Yale in 1861. From there he walked to Cariboo where he mined for two seasons "without any material success," and then he returned to Yale to run a harness shop. In 1864 F.J. Barnard made him a partner in the British Columbia Express Company, and in 1868 Tingley went to Mexico to purchase four hundred horses to stock their ranches at Vernon and Ashcroft (see below, p. 149). Tingley, the most famous whip on the Cariboo Road, was described by Rev. George M. Grant as "a steady New Brunswicker, who had been on the road since it was built, in summer and winter, daylight and dark, storm and shine, and who had never missed time or come to grief in any way" (George M. Grant, *Ocean to Ocean: Sandford Fleming's Expedition through Canada in 1872* [Toronto: The Radisson Society of Canada, 1925], p. 349). Tingley was involved in a tragedy, however. In September 1873 he was returning with his wife and children to Yale from a buggy ride to Alexandra Bridge when his horses took fright at a wheelbarrow, bolted, and went over the bank. Mrs. Tingley was badly hurt in the accident and later died (*Colonist*, 23 September 1873). In 1877 Tingley married Pauline Laumeister, sister of Agnes Buie. Tingley drove the stage coach for twenty-eight years and then sold his interests to Barnard and to Bailey and Company. For further details see Scholefield and Howay, *British Columbia from the Earliest Times*, 4: 40–41.

16:37 *Surveyor General of Oregon.* Julia (Hyde) Trutch was sister-in-law to J.B. Preston, surveyor general of Oregon. Angus McDonald wrote of her: "she once in her sister's house in Oregon played for me on the piano, while she sang the Irish Mother's Wail for her [sister's?] children, and I thought it very affecting. She has no children, which is a pity, she being when young very handsome and kind" ("A Few Items," pp. 220–21).

17: 2 *New Westminster.* It is not known when the Trutches lived at Government House, New Westminster. Possibly they resided there during the interval between the departure of the Moodys in November 1863 and the arrival of Governor Frederick Seymour in April 1864.

17: 9 *health failed.* Probably Mrs. Glennie's poor health was related to a state of depression following Glennie's desertion. Just when he left is not known; according to O'Reilly he was still at Hopelands in May 1864 (O'Reilly Diaries, 6 May 1864).

17:13 *Crease.* (Sir) Henry Pering Pellew Crease (1823–1905), eldest son of Captain Henry Crease, R.N., born at Ince Castle, near

Plymouth, Cornwall, and educated at Mount Radford School, Clare College, Cambridge University, and the Middle Temple. Shortly after being called to the bar, Crease moved to Toronto with his family, but failing to prosper in Canada, he returned to England in 1852 to practise law at Lincoln's Inn. He reached Victoria via the Isthmus of Panama on 18 December 1858, and in 1860 he was joined by his wife and three small children who had travelled via Cape Horn. On 15 December 1859 Crease was called to the bar of British Columbia by Judge Begbie and to the bar of Vancouver Island by Chief Justice Cameron; on 14 October 1861 he became attorney general of British Columbia, a position he retained after the union of the colonies in 1866. In 1870 he was made a puisne judge (British Columbia, *Government Gazette,* 14 May 1870). From 1862 until 1868 the Creases resided at "Ince Cottage," New Westminster; after 1868 they lived at Victoria, where Crease built "Pentrelew" on Fort Street. It was as a member of the Executive Council and as attorney general that Crease drafted the Terms of Union with Canada in 1870, and it was he who opened the debate on the subject of Confederation on 9 March 1870. After Confederation he was in charge of the revision of the statutes in 1871 and in 1877. In 1896 he was knighted for his services. For further details, see H.P.P. Crease to James Crease, 19 April 1900, Crease Papers PABC; and Gordon R. Elliott, "Henry P. Pellew Crease: Confederation or No Confederation," *BC Studies* 12 (1971–72): 63–74.

17:15 *Pooley.* Charles Edward Pooley (1845–1912), born at Upwood, Huntingdonshire, the son of Thomas Pooley, and educated at Huntingdon and Bedford Grammar schools. Pooley obtained a letter of introduction to Judge Begbie and then left Cambridge University to sail round the Horn. He arrived in Victoria on 9 June 1862, went to Cariboo for a few months, and returned to New Westminster. He obtained an appointment as clerk in the attorney general's department and married Elizabeth Wilhelmina Fisher, who had arrived at Esquimalt in the clipper *Strathallan* with her parents and four brothers on 12 January 1863. On 31 January 1866 Pooley became acting registrar of British Columbia; from 1867 until 1870 he was registrar of the Mainland of British Columbia; in 1870 deputy registrar of the Supreme Court; and in 1873 registrar of the Supreme Court of British Columbia. Judge Begbie, who had put him to work chopping wood for kindling when he first arrived, agreed to train him in law, and in 1877 Pooley was admitted to the bar. He also entered politics and served in the legislature from 1882 until 1906. He was Speaker from 1887 to 1889 and again from 1902 to 1906. Later, his son, Robert Henry Pooley, represented Esquimalt in the legislature from 1912 to 1937 and was attorney general from 1928 to 1933.

Pooley's second daughter, Annie, married Harold Victor (later Rear-Admiral) Stanley in 1896. "You will have heard of the grand wedding that is to take place here on the 25th Inst. when Pooley's second daughter, Annie, is to be married to Harold Victor Stanley, second son of Lord Derby," O'Reilly wrote to John Trutch. " 'Pooley Hall' has been enlarged & furnished up, & preparations are being made for a very grand celebration. Both Ld. & Lady Derby have given their consent, & have promised to receive their son's wife as a daughter, & make a provision for them; very nice, is it not?" (O'Reilly to John Trutch, 16 November 1896, Trutch Papers, University of British Columbia Library, Special Collections Division).

17:15 *Fisher.* J. Birch Fisher, at this time a clerk in the Bank of British Columbia at New Westminster. The bank was organized in London in 1862 by a group of bankers and merchants. In 1900 it amalgamated with the Canadian Bank of Commerce.

17:16 *Prichard.* Captain C.J. Prichard, who presented a letter of introduction from Lytton to Douglas on 20 November 1858, was appointed on 16 August 1860 warden of the New Westminster jail on the recommendation of Chartres Brew. "I visited Capt. & Mrs. Pritchard. The former is Governor of the Jail," Bishop Hills noted. "With the latter I had an interesting conversation as to her desire to change from the Church of Rome to that of England. She is a Spaniard, born at Cadiz. She has for some time ceased to attend the Roman worship. I had observed her yesterday at the Service & her husband attentively guiding her in the use of the Prayer Book. They had a Spanish version of the N. Testament & wanted other books. There is no doubt of her intellectual deliverance from the errors of Rome" (Hills' Journal, 3 December 1860). Prichard died suddenly on 13 July 1870 of "congestion of the brain" (Arthur T. Bushby to Colonial Secretary, 13 July 1870, Colonial Correspondence, PABC).

17:17 *old Sappers.* A number of the Sappers of the Royal Engineers had exercised their option in 1863 to retire in the colony and obtain a military grant. The Royal Sappers and Miners had been amalgamated with the Royal Engineers in 1856.

17:20 *Chameleon.* H.M.S. *Cameleon,* a screw sloop, seventeen guns, built in 1860 and commissioned in 1861, stationed at Esquimalt 1863–65, Captain Edward Hardinge; 1867–69, Captain William H. Annesley; 1870–71, Captain Josiah Henry Hatchard; 1871–73, Captain Karl Heinrick Augustus Mainwaring; and 1873–74, Captain Andrew James Kennedy (Walbran, *British Columbia Coast Names,* p. 79).

17:21 *Sparrowhawk.* H.M.S. *Sparrowhawk,* screw gun vessel, four guns, was built in 1856 and stationed at Esquimalt, 1865–68, Captain Edwin Augustus Porcher, and 1868–72, Captain Henry Wentworth Mist. It was Captain Mist who brought to Victoria the body of Governor Frederick Seymour who died on board the *Sparrowhawk* at Bella Coola on 10 June 1869. When the *Sparrowhawk* was sold out of service in 1872, her engines were acquired by S.P. Moody for his sawmill at Moodyville. The gunboat, converted to a sailing vessel and used in the lumber trade, was lost in a typhoon in the China Sea (ibid., pp. 466–67).

17:22 *Alert.* H.M.S. *Alert,* screw sloop, seventeen guns, built in 1856, stationed at Esquimalt 1858–61, Captain W.A.R. Pearse, and again 1865–69, Captain Arthur John Innes (ibid., p. 17).

17:26 *Mrs. Trutch.* Mrs. John Trutch, formerly Sarah (Zoë) Musgrave.

17:26 *Mrs. O'Reilly.* Mrs. Peter O'Reilly, formerly Caroline Agnes Trutch (see above, pp. 115–16).

17:26 *Mrs. Crease.* Mrs. H.P.P. Crease, formerly Sarah Lindley, eldest daughter of Dr. John Lindley, professor of Botany, University College, London.

17:26 *Mrs. Black.* The youngest daughter of Thomas P. Kemp of Cork, Ireland, Elizabeth Kathleen married Dr. Arthur Walter Shaw

Black, M.R.C.S., L.S.A., of London in 1864. Dr. Black, born in Scotland, served in the Crimean War and came to British Columbia after being in Australia for some time. He went to Cariboo in 1862 to mine and practise medicine and was eventually named the first surgeon at the Williams Creek (later Royal Cariboo) Hospital. He was chosen to represent Cariboo West in 1863 in the first Legislative Council of the colony but soon settled in New Westminster, where he became medical officer to the jail and to the Royal Columbian Hospital. As a delegate to the Yale Convention in 1868, he strongly supported Confederation. His sudden death in March 1871 after being thrown from his horse was a great shock to the community. He was accorded full military honours at his funeral as a second lieutenant in the Seymour Artillery Corps and a Hyack volunteer, and a handsome monument was erected in his memory. "Dr. Black (perhaps you have heard for bad news travels fastest)," Zoë Trutch wrote to "My own precious, dearest husband" on 30 March 1871, "died in a fall off his horse two days ago, his wife is expecting a baby shortly poor creature" (Trutch Papers). For further details on Dr. Black, see *Colonist*, 30 March 1871.

17:26 *Mrs. Dickinson.* Caroline Matilda Rogers, who came with her brother Frederick from Liverpool by sailing vessel round the Horn and was married in Christ Church Cathedral, Victoria, in August 1861 to Robert Dickenson, a butcher at New Westminster (*Colonist*, 21 August 1861). Dickenson served as mayor of New Westminster for the following years: 1863–64; 1874–75; 1880–81; and 1884–88. He died in 1888.

17:27 *Mrs. Webster.* Martha Wilhelmina, second daughter of Thomas P. Kemp and sister of Mrs. Black, who in January 1863 was married at Christ Church Cathedral, Victoria, to John Alfred Webster, a prominent merchant of New Westminster who was very active in municipal affairs (*Colonist*, 9 January 1863).

17:30 *Government House.* Colonel Moody's residence at Sapperton, built in 1859–60, served as Government House of the mainland colony during Governor Douglas's visits to New Westminster. A wing containing a ballroom and supper rooms was added in 1863. This was the official residence of Governor Frederick Seymour from

April 1864 until May 1868, though he was not in residence between September 1865 and November 1866, when he was in England.

17:34 *all into disorder.* An Act for the Union of the Colony of Vancouver Island with the Colony of British Columbia, 29 & 30 Vict. c. 67, was proclaimed by Governor Seymour on 19 November 1866. The decision to unite the colonies, which was made while Seymour was in London, was highly unpopular in both colonies (see below, p. 150).

17:35 *Robson.* John Robson (1824–92) did not become premier until 1889. Robson was born at Perth, Upper Canada, the son of John Robson, who had recently emigrated from Scotland with his wife. The family soon moved to Sarnia. John Robson obtained some merchandising experience in Montreal and Upper Canada before moving to British Columbia in June 1859. His wife and daughter, as well as his brother-in-law, Charles G. Major, accompanied him to the mainland colony. He worked as a prospector at Yale, then in the forests, and on the roads at New Westminster, and finally became a journalist. On 13 February 1861, with the help of some members of the business community, he founded at New Westminster the *British Columbian* to agitate for "responsible government, liberal institutions, [and] the redress of all our grievances" (*British Columbian*, 13 June 1868). A "Reformer" in the Clear Grit tradition, Robson waged a relentless war against Governor Douglas, whom he accused of being a "one-man system of irresponsible despotism" (cited in Olive Fairholm, "John Robson and Confederation," in *British Columbia & Confederation*, ed. W. George Shelton [Victoria: University of Victoria, 1967], p. 101). Though Robson welcomed the arrival of Governor Seymour, he lost faith in him when Seymour failed to exercise executive authority to select New Westminster as the capital of the united colony. After the union, Robson was forced to move his paper to Victoria in March 1869, and on 25 July, because of lack of subscriptions, he sold it to D.W. Higgins, proprietor of the *Colonist*, and accepted the position of political editor. From his editorial post, he pressed for confederation with Canada.

After Confederation, the Liberal government in Ottawa appointed Robson paymaster and purveyor for the C.P.R. surveys in British

Columbia. He lost this position in 1879 following Macdonald's return to power. In October 1880 Robson purchased the *Dominion Pacific Herald* in New Westminster, and in January 1882 he changed the title to the *British Columbian*. Elected to the Legislative Assembly in 1882, he became in 1883 minister of finance and of agriculture in the Smithe government. In August 1889, following the death of A.E.B. Davie, he became premier. As premier, Robson was a reformer who tried to check speculation in lands. His death in London on 29 June 1892, following an accident, caused genuine sorrow in British Columbia, though former members of the official class who had once felt the lash of his anger could not quite forget his early days in the colony. "Mr. Robson's death was sudden, what fuss they are making about him," O'Reilly wrote to John Trutch, "he has, I think been a useful man of late—but we remember him in early days! ! !" (O'Reilly to John Trutch, 9 July 1892, Trutch Papers). For further details, see the Fairholm article mentioned above; "John Robson versus J.K. Suter," ed. W.K. Lamb, *BCHQ* 4 (1940): 203–15; and Ivan E.M. Antak, "John Robson: British Columbian" (M.A. thesis, University of Victoria, 1972).

17:35 *Barnard.* Francis Jones Barnard (1829-89), born in Quebec City, married Ellen Stillman in 1853 and moved to Toronto in 1855. After coming to British Columbia in 1859, Barnard worked as a purser on the steamer *Fort Yale* and then packed mail and parcels on foot to Cariboo. In December 1861 he acquired Jeffray & Co.'s Fraser River Express, and in June 1862 he made an arrangement with Dietz and Nelson. The following month he obtained from Governor Douglas the contract to carry the mail from Yale to Cariboo. At first he had a pony express, but by May 1864 he had four-horse coaches running from Yale to Soda Creek. With Stephen Tingley, his own son, and two others, he organized the British Columbia Express Company and bought 6,300 acres for a horse ranch near Vernon in 1864. Barnard represented Yale–Lytton in the British Columbia Legislative Council in 1867–68 and Yale in 1870. He strongly supported the choice of New Westminster for the capital of the united colony and later supported just as strongly the entry of the colony into Confederation. In 1879 he was elected in a by-election to the House of Commons. Re-elected in 1882, he remained in the House until 1886. After his death, his business was carried on by his son (Sir) Francis

Stillman Barnard, who was lieutenant-governor of the province from 1914 to 1919. For further details, see J.B. Kerr, *Biographical Dictionary of Well-Known British Columbians* (Vancouver: Kerr and Begg, 1890), pp. 91–94; and Willis J. West, "Staging and Stage Hold-Ups in the Cariboo," *BCHQ* 12 (1948): 108–209.

17:36 *struggle for the capital.* When, after the union of the colonies, the location of the seat of government was debated in the Legislative Council on 29 March 1867, Victoria was chosen by a 13–8 vote. But Governor Seymour, who preferred New Westminster and had been promised in London that the capital would be located there, now consulted the Colonial Office. After pressure was exerted on the new colonial secretary, the Duke of Buckingham and Chandos, by an influential group of investors, bankers, and Hudson's Bay Company men in London who favoured Victoria, Seymour was informed that the selection of Victoria would not be displeasing to the Home authorities. In the 1868 session of the Legislative Council the matter was again debated. A resolution to fix the capital at Victoria was amended by Robson and Barnard to the effect that it would be inexpedient to move the capital "at this time." This amendment was lost by a vote 5–14, and the motion passed by a vote of 14–5. The date of the removal of the government offices from New Westminster to Victoria was fixed at 25 May. For further details, see Margaret A. Ormsby, "Frederick Seymour, the Forgotten Governor," *BC Studies* 22 (1974): 3–25.

18: 1 *church bells.* See note, p. 129. The bells were designed for "St. Stephen's Cathedral" and engraved "N. Westminster." Rather than not use them, Bishop Hills decided to "place them temporarily at the disposal of the Ch. in N. Westminster on condition (1) That a suitable edifice for their reception upon a scale worthy of the donor or their costly character [be built] (2) That it be understood that they be given up for a Cathedral whenever one was designated, wherever it shall be, when the Bishop requires it" (Hills' Journal, 22 May 1862).

18: 1 *Nagle.* H.H. Nagle was in business with his father as a general agent.

18: 6 *Woods.* Rev. Charles Thomas Woods (1826–95) M.A., Trinity

College, Dublin, came to Victoria in 1860 to be headmaster of the Boys' Collegiate School. His wife was in charge of the Girls' Collegiate School, opened in Victoria on 3 September 1860 and renamed Angela College in 1866 in honour of Baroness Burdett-Coutts. "For a long time people have been crying out for a school for girls of the middle & upper sort," wrote Bishop Hills. "There was certainly a necessity, for the Romanists were in the field & young persons whose parents attend [our] church were duly in attendance upon the Sisters of St. Ann" (Hills' Journal, 3 September 1860). In 1861 when Sophia Cracroft and Lady Franklin visited the Boys' Collegiate, they found there "a very nice looking set of boys—in rank from the Governor's son, downwards," and at the Girls' Collegiate, they found two of Governor Douglas's daughters in attendance, "tho' the eldest is nearly 20 and has been engaged for 2 years" (*Lady Franklin Visits the Pacific Northwest*, pp. 34, 76). The Woodses continued in charge of the schools until 1868. On 20 September 1868 Woods was inducted into the archdeaconry of Columbia by Rev. W.E. Hayman (*British Columbian*, 23 September 1868). He served as rector of St. Mary's Church, Sapperton, and Holy Trinity Church, New Westminster, as well as as chaplain to the penitentiary and the asylum.

18: 7 *Robson.* A younger brother of John Robson, Ebenezer Robson (1835–1911) was born at Perth, Upper Canada, and educated at Sarnia and at Victoria College, Coburg. One of the first four Methodist missionaries to come to British Columbia, he reached Victoria on 10 February 1859 after sailing round the Horn. Immediately after his arrival, Robson went to Cornish Bar, six miles below Hope, and then to Boston Bar. Hope was his headquarters until 1860 when he went to Nanaimo. In 1863 he returned to the Mainland to conduct a mission to the Indians and the road-builders. Because of the poor health of his wife, the former Ellen Hart of Brockville, who had joined him in 1859, the couple returned to Ontario in 1866. Robson came back to British Columbia in 1880, and for the next twenty years he was active in the Methodist ministry at New Westminster, Nanaimo, Vancouver, Victoria, and Vernon. In 1900 he was appointed bursar of Columbian Methodist College, New Westminster.

18: 8 *Holbrook.* Henry Holbrook (1818–1902) was born at Liverpool. He served in the commissariat in the Crimean War, settling in

Odessa after the war as a merchant (Hills' Journal, 28 February 1860). After his arrival in Victoria in 1858, he purchased a lot on Columbia Street at the auction of the New Westminster town lots. There he built a large block in which he conducted a wholesale liquor, grocery, and drygoods business. When his large wharf, known as Liverpool Wharf, burned down, he built a still larger one on what was later the site of the City Market. In 1872 he acquired the deserted barracks, offices, and storerooms of the Royal Engineers at Sapperton. He also operated a salmon cannery.

Holbrook was prominent in political affairs: he was a member of the Legislative Council from 1864 to 1866 and a delegate to the Yale Convention in 1868. As a member of the Legislative Council, 1868–71, he supported Confederation. He served briefly as minister of lands and works in the McCreight ministry after Confederation. In 1881 he retired to England to reside at Chester. For further details, see the *Colonist*, 15 May 1902.

18: 8 *Clute . . . Major.* John Stilwell Clute (1840–1929), born in Kingston, Upper Canada, travelled via New York and Panama to British Columbia in 1862. After a short spell in Cariboo, he joined T.A. Webster as a merchant in New Westminster. Later he formed a partnership with his brother-in-law, Charles G. Major. In June 1866, Clute married Sarah Jane Clarkson, and in 1870 they went to live in Missouri. After his return to British Columbia, Clute became in 1880 collector of customs for the port of New Westminster. He served as mayor of New Westminster in 1887, and in 1898 he was appointed inspector of customs for British Columbia and Yukon. For further details, see the obituary, *Colonist,* 5 March 1929.

Charles George Major (1839–1929) was the son of an English blacksmith who settled at Sarnia about 1830. As a young man Major was apprenticed to John Robson in the drygoods business. He accompanied Robson to British Columbia in 1859, and after working at clearing the townsite of New Westminster and as bookkeeper for J.A.R. Homer, he became a stage driver for Barnard in 1864. Later that year, he and Clute opened a store at New Westminster. He became sole proprietor in 1870. In 1887 Major sold his business and invested heavily in real estate in the new city of Vancouver. His marriage to Mary Elizabeth Clarkson, a sister of Mrs. Clute, was performed in 1866 by the pioneer Methodist missionary, Rev. Edward White (British Columbia,

Colonial Secretary, Marriage Licences 23 March 1864–14 June 1867, MS, PABC). For further details, see Scholefield and Howay, *British Columbia from the Earliest Times,* 3: 156–57.

18:17 *Chilcotin Indians.* The "Bute Inlet Massacre" of May 1864, when a ferry man and a road party employed by Alfred Waddington, who was planning to build a wagon road from Bute Inlet to the Cariboo mines, were massacred by Indians. On learning that the trouble had spread and that eighteen men had been killed, Governor Seymour sent a volunteer force under Gold Commissioner W.G. Cox overland from Cariboo to the Chilcotin country and himself accompanied another expedition under Chartres Brew, chief constable at New Westminster, which sailed from New Westminster to Bentinck Arm. The two forces effected a junction, and eight of the murderers were taken into custody. For further details, see E.S. Hewlett, "The Chilcotin Uprising of 1864," *BC Studies* 19 (1973): 50–72.

18:24 *Shortly after.* Mrs. Allison's residence in Victoria seems to have been in 1865. The Charleses probably resided there briefly before going to Kamloops.

18:29 *Tewso.* Dr. Henry Atkinson Tuzo (1832–90), born in Quebec, was in the employ of the Hudson's Bay Company. In 1870 he resigned to become manager of the Bank of British North America in Victoria, and in 1874 he was transferred to New York to be manager-in-chief of the bank.

18:32 *Gaudin.* Agnes Anderson (1849–1929), the niece of Mrs. Charles and Mrs. Wark, was the second daughter of Alexander Caulfield Anderson and Elizabeth, the eldest daughter of James Birnie. Captain James Gaudin (1838–1913) was born in the Channel Islands. He sailed on vessels engaged in the East Indian and Australian trade and then entered the marine service of the Hudson's Bay Company. Gaudin came to Victoria in 1865 as officer of the Hudson's Bay Company's ship *Prince of Wales.* In 1869 he was master of the *Lady Lampson.* In 1884, he became a B.C. coastal pilot, and in 1888 he was given the command of the dominion lighthouse tender *Sir James Douglas.* Subsequently, he was agent of the Department of Marine and Fisheries and wreck commissioner at Victoria. For further details, see the obituary of Captain Gaudin, *Colonist*, 12 July 1913, and of Mrs. Gaudin, *Colonist*, 21 May 1929.

19: 2 *Clarkson.* William Clarkson (1819?–93) was born in Yorkshire and accompanied his parents to Bowmanville, Upper Canada. He came to British Columbia in the autumn of 1858 and in 1859 was employed by S.P. Moody. Like many of the other members of the New Westminster "Reform League," he was a Wesleyan Methodist. In 1864–65 he was president of the municipal council. His ties with the Reformers were strengthened by the marriage of his daughter "Jenny" to J.S. Clute and of his daughter Mary to C. G. Major.

19: 3 *two sisters.* Four of Dewdney's sisters came to British Columbia. Presumably the reference is to Fanny [later Lawrence], married at this time to C.A.W. Lethbridge, and to Charlotte, who married Rev. J. Cave-Brown-Cave.

19: 3 *Walter.* Walter Dewdney (d. 1892) was appointed government agent at Yale in 1881 in succession to William Teague. He was moved to Spallumcheen (Enderby) in 1884 and to Priests' Valley (Vernon) in 1885. Depressed and in poor health, he committed suicide at Vernon on 24 January 1892. For further details, see *Colonist*, 27, 28, and 29 January 1892.

19: 7 *Homers.* Joshua Attwood Reynolds Homer (1827–86), born at Barrington, Nova Scotia, arrived in Victoria in 1859 and went to New Westminster, where he was a commission merchant. He returned to Nova Scotia in 1860 to marry Sophia Killam Wilson and then came back to New Westminster to build a sawmill. He was soon engaged in exporting lumber to Australia. He was an early member of the municipal council, and in 1863 he was appointed to the first Legislative Council of the colony. He became high sheriff of British Columbia in 1866, and with the removal of the capital to Victoria, he went there to reside in 1868. In 1872, however, he returned to the Mainland. Homer prospered in his lumbering business and soon had extensive mining investments in the Interior. He was elected to the House of Commons in 1882. For further details, see the obituary, *British Columbian*, 21 September 1886.

19:12 *Grandidier*. Rev. Charles Grandidier (1832–84), born at Bains, Department of Vosges, France, was ordained a priest on 27 June 1855 by Bishop Charles Joseph Eugene de Mazenod, founder of the Oblates of Mary Immaculate (O.M.I.). He was sent to England before joining the Oregon Missions. In 1860 he served as a missionary at Olympia and then at New Westminster. Between 1860 and 1863, he visited St. Mary's Mission (Mission City), as well as Yale, Lytton, Douglas, Fort Alexandria, and Esquimalt. When his health failed in 1868, he was sent to England. He returned to British Columbia in 1871 to be superior at Williams Lake, and the following year he was sent to the Okanagan, where he served from 1872 to 1880. He opened the Mission of St. Louis at Kamloops in 1876. In 1880 he was moved to Mission City and in 1881 to Williams Lake. He applied to enter the Carthusian Order in 1880 and in 1883 was dispensed from his vows as an Oblate to enable him to do so. (Information supplied by Rev. Gaston Carrière, Archivist, Oblate Historical Archives, Ottawa.)

19:12 *Pandosie*. Rev. Charles Jean-Baptiste Felix Pandosy (1824–91) was born near Marseilles and entered the novitiate of Notre Dame de l'Osier in Grenoble in 1844. He left for the Oregon Missions in 1847, and on 21 April 1848 he was ordained a priest at Walla Walla by Bishop F.N. Blanchet. An Oblate, he served with the Jesuits at Colvile during the Yakima War. In 1858 he went to Esquimalt and then in 1859 to L'Anse au Sable on the eastern side of Okanagan Lake, where he founded the Mission of the Immaculate Conception. In 1860 he moved the mission to Mission Creek. Though most of his life was spent in the Okanagan Valley, he was posted to Esquimalt in 1861–62, Fort Rupert, 1862–64, and New Westminster, 1864–67. He was sent as superior to Okanagan Mission in 1868. There he planted the first grape vines and the first apple trees. In 1882 he was made superior at Stuart Lake, but in 1887 he returned to the Okanagan. A revered missionary, he was also in Father Carrière's words "at one and the same time a doctor, a teacher, a lawyer, an orator, a botanist, an agriculturist, a musician and a peacemaker."

Lieutenant Charles Wilson, who met Father Pandosy at Fort Colvile in 1860, found him "a very pleasant, well-informed man & has not forgotten the pureness of his native tongue. He has a fine voice & does not despise the cup that cheers & occasionally inebriates, over which it is his delight (when he can meet a person who can appreciate them) to pour forth the fondly remembered songs of *La Belle France*; a long black gown, the skirts of which are pinned up to his waist when on horseback, a pair of corduroy trousers & boots ignorant of blacking, form his attire, a blanket & a piece of bacon behind his saddle & he is ready for travel anywhere" (Stanley, *Mapping the Frontier*, p. 131). For further details, see Denys Nelson, "Father Pandosy, O.M.I.," Okanagan Historical Society, *Seventeenth Report* (Kelowna: *Kelowna Courier*, 1953), pp. 57–66.

19:18 *Soda Creek.* Dewdney established a stock farm at Soda Creek in 1867–68 (*Colonist*, 10 October 1868) but did not stay long with farming, "which," he said, "was too slow in those days" ("Biographical Sketch").

19:21 *Agassiz.* Captain Lewis Nunn Agassiz (1827–80), born at Bradfield, Essex, and educated in Germany, served in the Royal Welsh Fusiliers and was stationed both in the West Indies and Upper Canada. He sold his captaincy to purchase a farm in Prince Edward Island, but not succeeding at this occupation, sailed round the Horn to California in 1858. After mining there, he came to British Columbia in 1861 to mine at Quesnel and Williams Creek. His wife, the former Mary Caroline Shram of London, Ontario, joined him in Victoria that winter. In 1862, on Sanders's recommendation, he was appointed constable at Hope. There and at Yale he served in various capacities until 1866 when he resigned and moved his family to "Ferny Coombe," some twenty miles below Hope, where he had acquired a large property by purchase and pre-emption. He died at Acre, Syria, in 1880, while returning to British Columbia via an eastern route from a visit to England. For further biographical details, see Goodfellow, *Memories of a Pioneer Life*.

19:23 *Cregie.* The chief constable at Hope (1860–63), who acquired a pack train and went to Cariboo.

19:29 *Florence . . . James.* The Agassiz children were: Florence Eliza Margaret (1854–1940), the wife of John Goodfellow, who lived most of her life in the United States; Lewis Arthur (1853–1941), who acquired property adjoining his father's, some of which he sold for the Dominion Experimental Farm; Jane Vaudine Caroline (1856–1916), who married Ewen McPherson; and James Burwell (1858–1923), who, according to Mrs. Goodfellow, acted as "bridesmaid" at Jane Moir's wedding (*Memories of a Pioneer Life*, p. 14).

20:10 *property of Bishop Hills.* Bishop Hills acquired farm property on a lake near Hope in 1860. "I went over the Lake on my land here with Mr. O'Reilly," he noted in 1861. "The depth is not above 6 feet in the deepest—the channel is from 3 to 4 & the sides shallowed" (Hills' Journal, 6 July 1861).

20:13 *Lakehouse.* A cabin located on the Sumallo River on the Hope Trail.

20:20 *Powder Camp.* In Whipsaw Creek valley, seven miles east of the summit.

20:36 *Hunter.* Henry Hunter, who pre-empted 160 acres on the east bank of the Fraser River seven miles below Hope in January 1866 (Laing, "Colonial Farm Settlers," p. 216).

20:36 *Bristol.* "Captain" William Yale Bristol, "a tall, happy Englishman," who had a farm on Bristol Island, west of Hope, and who for twenty years had an express canoe mail-and-passenger route between Yale and New Westminster. William Yates wrote that "he must have been a cast iron man to stand what he did. He used to come into the hotel here [Hope] wet and worn out—he would have supper and lay down in his blankets and the steam would come off him in clowds [*sic*]. Then he was up in the morning and off with two or three indians through the deep snow—up the road for Yale. It was an eight day journey in the winter to come up [from New Westminster]. There was nothing but a foot path" ("Reminiscences of William Yates," p. 10). See also, Goodfellow, *Memories of a Pioneer Life*, p. 16.

21: 7 *September.* Susan Louisa Moir probably met John Fall Allison in April 1867 when he arrived in Hope to report that there had been severe loss of cattle in the Similkameen because of the hard winter (*Colonist*, 27 April 1867). He was again in Hope and

Yale early in August 1868, when he reported that some fifty men mining on the Similkameen River were doing well, a few of them making four or five dollars a day (*Colonist*, 12 August 1868). On 3 September 1868 they were married at the parsonage by Archdeacon Woods, who had come from New Westminster to perform the ceremony. O'Reilly noted in his diary on that date that the wedding was "Quite private," so it is unlikely that the O'Reillys and Mrs. Landvoight were present.

21:37 *Big Men*. See Appendix 2, pp. 75–79.

22: 2 "*Ogopogo*." The legendary monster of Okanagan Lake obtained the name of "Ogopogo" on the occasion of a luncheon in Vernon on 23 August 1926 when the members of the Vancouver Board of Trade were guests of the Vernon Board of Trade and the Vernon Rotary Club. As on many other occasions, the Kalamalka Players, a group of talented amateurs at Vernon, provided entertainment. The highlight was the singing of a parody of a song written by Davy Burnaby of the English troupe of entertainers, the "Co-optimists." H.F. Beattie's parody, sung by W.H. Brimblecombe, contained the words:

> I'm looking for the Ogopogo
> The bunny-hugging Ogopogo
> His mother was a mutton, his father was a whale,
> I'm going to put a little bit of salt on his tail.

(W.H. Brimblecombe, Okanagan Historical Society, *Fourth Report*, [Armstrong: *Armstrong Advertiser* Press, 1929], pp. 28–29).

22: 9 *the Cedars*. Near the junction of the Skaist and the Skagit rivers.

22:10 *coloured man*. Probably Robinson (not Richardson) from Similkameen who called on O'Reilly at Hope about keeping the Hope trail open during the winter (O'Reilly Diaries, 29 November 1860). Robert Stevenson recounts meeting a coloured man living with the Indians at Wenatchee earlier the same year: "He spoke English with that accent peculiar to the race, and said he had been through a university course. In our party were three university men who at once proceeded to test his knowledge. . . . The coloured man spoke four languages all right, and he knew enough about classics to prove that he probably did have a university education. He would give no account of himself or why he was there, and on being asked if he was a murderer, answered that we wanted to know too much. He was a big powerful fellow, and told us that he was married to the chief's daughter, and that he would be the chief at some time in the future" (Walkem, *Stories of Early British Columbia*, p. 248).

22:12 *Skagit Bluff.* Bluffs east of the junction of the Skagit River and Snass Creek. The Skagit River flows across the Boundary Line east of Chilliwack Lake.

22:17 *rhododendrons.* Pink and deep rose rhododendrons (*Rhododendron Macrophyllum*) grow in compact bushes along the Allison Trail.

22:29 *Spencer Mountain.* When Lieutenant H. Spencer Palmer crossed the Cascades in 1859, he gave a mountain in Manson Ridge the Gaelic name "Stuchd-a-choire," "from a beautiful 'choir' or recess situated about halfway down its eastern slope. . . . On the summit," he wrote, "and invisible except for the rocks immediately surrounding it, lies a pretty sequestered little lake, guarded by one solitary stunted oak, and lower down on the eastern slope is a larger one, on whose banks, there being plenty of firewood, travellers from the eastward frequently camp" ("Report on the Country between Fort Hope . . . and Fort Colville," *BCP* 3: 83). The Gaelic name was soon forgotten, and the mountain acquired Palmer's given name.

22:38 "*Nine Mile.*" This creek was nine miles distant from "Allison's."

23: 2 *Similkameen ford.* The Similkameen River, or Similkameugh, to give it its Indian name, flows south across the Boundary Line to Okanagan River, west of Osoyoos Lake. The ford at the junction of the Tulameen and Similkameen rivers was first known by the name of Red Earth, or Vermilion, Forks, from the red clay or ochre found in that region. Here a townsite was surveyed in 1860 and named Princeton in honour of the Prince of Wales, later King Edward VII (see Introduction, p. xx). Allison's, as the place was more commonly known, was two miles below the forks.

23: 8 *Hayes.* Fitzgerald has not been identified, and little is known about Hayes apart from the fact that he was an American. He is frequently referred to in directories of the period as J. Hayes, partner of Allison, stock rancher and general trader, but Mrs. Allison refers to him as S.W. Hayes. Hayes Creek (Five Mile) takes its name from him.

23:13 *Marsden.* John Marston, a miner near Grave Yard Creek (One Mile). Bishop Hills, who met Marston at Hope in 1860, found his wife "a nice person, comes from Bungery in Suffolk" (Hills' Journal, 4 June 1860). Mrs. Marston was the first European woman to cross the Cascades, but, unlike Mrs. Allison, she crossed the mountains on foot. Though Marston filed a pre-emption claim for 160 acres at the extreme point of Similkameen Forks, he and his wife did not stay at Princeton long (Laing, "Colonial Farm Settlers," p. 434).

23:14 *Young.* Presumably William C. Young, who in 1862 was placed in charge of the Similkameen Customs House by J.C. Haynes after W.G. Cox had appointed him on the recommendation of Peter O'Reilly (J.C. Haynes to W.A.G. Young, 31 March 1862, J.C. Haynes Correspondence, PABC). Young resigned his government appointment in 1865 to go mining.

23:16 *Rock Creek.* Gold was discovered on Rock Creek, which flows into Kettle River, in October 1859 by a Canadian, Adam Beam, who was travelling from Colvile to Similkameen. Beam started work on 6 May 1860 and in the next six weeks took out $977. When Douglas visited Rock Creek in September, there were five hundred miners, mostly Americans, at work, and by the end of the season gold worth $83,000 was obtained. It was this excitement which caused Douglas to order the building of the Dewdney Trail. By the spring of 1861, however, the camp was almost deserted as the miners flocked to the scene of a new find on Mission Creek (Rivière De L'Anse au Sable) on the east side of Okanagan Lake. For further details, see Stanley, *Mapping the Frontier*, pp. 126–28; and L. Norris, "The Rise and Fall of Rock Creek," Okanagan Historical Society, *Second Report* (Vernon: Wayside Press, 1927), pp. 37–40.

23:30 *virtually alone.* On 21 September, O'Reilly arrived at Allison's on official business, only to find, "Allison & Wife with pack train about to start for Hope" (O'Reilly Diaries, 21 September 1868). However, Mrs. Allison did not accompany her husband on the trip.

23:31 *Quinisco.* A famous Indian bear hunter, the chief of the Upper Similkameen band of Indians at Chu-chu-ewaa, twenty-five miles southeast of Princeton. Mrs. Allison's note in her introduction to her narrative poem "Quinesco" states that "Quinesco was chief of the Indians of the Upper Similkameen in 1858 and was introduced by Sir James Douglas to Mr. Allison as 'The Famous Bear Hunter.' Sir James said he was known to have hunted grizzlies alone and to kill them with nothing but his knife" (MS in possession of Mrs. Elvie Sisson). Clive Phillipps-Wolley, who hunted big game in the Similkameen Valley in the 1880's, wrote that "bear-stories were rather the fashion in the Similkameen district when I was there last year, two Indians having been killed in the neighbourhood by grizzlies within the month"; and, "Half the legends which do duty as history among the red-men of the Similkameen have for their hero Tumisco [Quinisco], a chief of the tribe which dwells near Princeton, and the immediate predecessor and father of the reigning potentate In-cow-market [In-cow-masket]" (Clive Phillipps-Wolley, *A Sportsman's Eden* [London: Richard Bentley & Son, 1888], pp. 77–78). In 1870, when O'Reilly marked out the Chu-chu-ewaa reserve, he noted, "Quinisco and about a dozen other Indians came down to camp & had a long talk about their reserves before Allison—they went away apparently well satisfied with the land I had marked off for them" (O'Reilly Diaries, 22 September 1870).

24:30 *Trout Creek.* The summer range for Allison's cattle was near Princeton. Then in 1874 he blazed and cut out an ancient Indian trail, shown on Archibald McDonald's map of 1827 and J.W. Trutch's map of 1871, which extended from Princeton to Trout Creek, near the present Summerland, by way of Link, Chain, and Osprey lakes. His cattle were driven over this improved trail to winter range on the west side of Okanagan Lake. It was this trail that G.M. Dawson followed in 1877 when he was making his geological survey of the southern Interior.

24:38 *piano . . . B.C.* See above, p. 131.

25: 4 *Keremeos.* In 1860 the Hudson's Bay Company abandoned Fort Okanogan on the Columbia River and moved its property to a new post at Keremeos, forty-five miles southeast of Princeton. François Deschequette was in charge of this post until his death in 1862. Roderick McLean, who had been with the Boundary Survey party, then took over. When McLean left the Company's service in 1867, Chief Trader John Tait (1832–1911) was put in charge. The Company closed Fort Colvile in 1871 and Keremeos the following year. All goods and stock were transferred to Kamloops where Tait was put in charge. He became chief factor in 1875 and in 1882 retired from the Company to farm on the North Thompson River. Angus McDonald described Tait as "a fine, tall ⅛ Indian, and once a stewart at Vancouver. He speaks good Cree and French and English, has a fine family of daughters. Two of them play a few English but no Scotch tunes on the piano. His wife, a strong muscular woman, fell dead on Christmas night, while preparing supper, with heart disease. She, too, was of same red man's blood. Heart disease is very uncommon to the Indian" ("A Few Items," p. 211).

25:10 *Nicola.* Nicola Valley, which is situated between Spence's Bridge on the Thompson River and the Tulameen Valley, takes its name from the famous Indian Chief Nicola (N'Kuala, Incola, or, as the Hudson's Bay Company men called him, "Nicholas"). Usually friendly to the Hudson's Bay Company, he assisted its men in apprehending the murderers of Samuel Black (A.C. Anderson, "History of the Northwest Coast," typescript copy of original manuscript in the Academy of Pacific Coast History [Bancroft Library], University of California, Berkeley, University of British Columbia Library, Special Collections Division, pp. 35–36). Bancroft states that Chief Nicola led a joint tribal war party against the Lillooets to avenge the death of his father and that later he threatened to attack Fort Kamloops when he was refused gunpowder by John Tod (H.H. Bancroft, *History of British Columbia 1792–1887* [San Francisco: The History Company, 1890], pp. 152–56). Angus McDonald claimed that he had been deeded Grand Prairie [Westwold] by Chief Nicholas, "the master of the whole country of the Okanagan," but years later when he mentioned this fact to Governor Douglas, "he thought for various reasons that it would be difficult to secure it for me. Had I a written deed of it, he said, before the colony was organized I might get it. I remarked that living witnesses should always be as good as writing, but he thought the colony would not agree to it" ("A Few Items," pp. 205–6). For further information on Chief Nicola, see M.S. Wade, *The Thompson Country* (Kamloops: Inland Sentinel Print, 1907), pp. 14–19, 63–66.

25:14 *oregon-grape. Mahonia* (*Berberis*) *aquifolium*, a woody shrub with leathery, spiny-pointed leaves, found in the southern coniferous forests of British Columbia (Garman, *Guide to Trees and Shrubs of British Columbia*, p. 53).

25:16 *Snow berries. Gaultheria humifusa*, a low shrub producing white, fleshy fruit (ibid., pp. 98–99).

26:15 *father's college library*. Marischal College, University of Aberdeen.

26:30 *Osoyoos*. To prevent American economic penetration of the goldfields, Governor Douglas had a customs post established in 1860 at the north end of Osoyoos Lake for the collection of duties on cattle and horses. In March 1862, after Rock Creek was abandoned by the miners, W.G. Cox removed to Sooyoos Station all government property from the Rock Creek Customs House (W. G. Cox to W.A.G. Young, 6 April 1862, W.G. Cox Correspondence, PABC). J.C. Haynes, placed in charge at Sooyoos, moved the customs office in 1865 to The Traverse, where the lake is nearly cut in two by a narrow extension of land from opposite sides.

26:31 *the Chinooks*. The Chinook wind, "the strong sea breeze blowing up the river, called by the Indians the 'Chinook wind' from the direction it came" (Anderson, "History of the Northwest Coast," p. 43).

26:35 *Coldwater*. Coldwater River flows northeast and northwest into the Nicola River at the present Merritt. The original Shuswap name "Tsillatko" means "cold water."

27: 2 *Tatlehasket*. "For at Princetown, 'when the cold north winds blow, and the long howling of the wolves is heard amidst the snow,' when the ribs of the lordly buck which the boys shot in the morning are roasting on the embers, the door opens quietly, and soft-footed old Quilltasket [Tatlehasket] comes in, his brown eyes bright and keen, and his short square figure clothed in deer-skins and fur, his old wrinkled brown face looking quainter than ever in the flickering firelight. He is the historian of his tribe, an historian who tells his legends, not in dead written words, but in lively speech illustrated by appropriate action. From him and others of his tribe Mrs. Allison has collected all that seems to be known of the Similkameen clan" (Phillipps-Wolley, *A Sportsman's Eden*, p. 152).

27: 3 *Incowmasket.* The subject of Mrs. Allison's long narrative poem published in 1900 (see Stratton Moir, *In-Cow-Mas-Ket* [Chicago: Scroll Publishing Company, 1900]).

27: 8 *Topes and Whaylac.* In the poem *In-Cow-Mas-Ket*, Toupes and Whylac are young men sent by their chief to summon "the mighty, wise old doctor" from the Columbia River to treat his sick son, Hosachtem. This medicine man, however, is subdued by the "foul spirit" which has gripped Hosachtem, and they are then sent to the mountains to fetch their kinsman Cos-o-tasket.

28: 2 *one day.* The distance by trail from Hope to Princeton was sixty-one miles, and from there to the Hudson's Bay post at Keremeos, forty-five miles. From the Keremeos post it was eight miles to the Similkameen Customs House, and from there another nine miles to the Osoyoos Customs House (O'Reilly Diaries, 1865).

28:12 *Cole.* Thomas Cole pre-empted 320 acres north of Henry Nicholson's pre-emption at Keremeos in July 1873. Later he shared a claim on Granite Creek with Nicholson (Laing, "Colonial Farm Settlers," p. 442).

28:16 *Similkameen Valley.* Edgar Allison, who became a farmer at Sardis in the Fraser Valley.

30: 2 *coal.* When Allison explored the Similkameen Valley in the summer of 1860, he found coal on the right bank of the Similkameen River. Douglas reported the discovery to London: "valuable outcrops of coal occur on the Shimilkomeen River, but the present value . . . is not sufficient to induce the investment of capital"

(Douglas to the Duke of Newcastle, 25 October 1860, *BCP*, 1862 [Cmd. 2952, 1st series], 4:30).

30:10 *Waterman.* William J. Waterman and his brother Ernest were born in Sheffield, England, and spent some time in mining ventures in California before their arrival in Princeton in 1893. There they took over the property of S.D. Sandes for a townsite. Ernest Waterman became the manager and W.J. Waterman the consulting engineer of the Vermilion Forks Mining and Development Company, an English company formed to mine Princeton coal.

30:12 *Roche River.* Sebastian Lotario, a miner, usually visited the Similkameen area each season. On this occasion he mined on Roche River, also known as the south branch of the Similkameen River. This branch of the river rises in the United States and flows northwest thirty-nine miles to Princeton. Its original name was Semilkameugh, but in 1859, when it was the eastward point attained by the British Boundary Commission, it was named Roche River by Captain R.W. Haig, R.A., assistant astronomer of the British Boundary Commission, in honour of Lieutenant Richard Roche of H.M.S. *Satellite*, who was seconded to the Boundary Commission and who discovered the river just before being recalled to duty because of the occupation of San Juan Island by United States troops. One of the commission's astronomical stations was constructed on this river ("Extract of letter from Lieut.: Col. Hawkins to the Secretary of State for Foreign Affairs [written at the Boundary Commission Camp, The Dalles, Oregon], 31 May 1860, in Otto Klotz, *Certain Correspondence of the Foreign Office and of the Hudson's Bay Company* [Ottawa: King's Printer, 1899], Part III, p. 34). For further information concerning the explorations of the British Boundary Commission in the Okanagan and Similkameen valleys, see Hawkins to the Foreign Secretary, 29 May 1860, ibid., pp. 39–53.

30:31 *Cosotasket.*

Cos-o-tasket, great and powerful;
Cos-o-tasket, wise though young, full
Of strange, weird unearthly knowledge
. . . . His
Nights were spent in eerie vigils

In the dark lonely mountain caves;
Well knew he the powers of nature,
Well knew he the viewless spirits
That throng the mountains' misty peaks;
And well knew he the flitting ghosts
That at still midnight leave their graves.
(*In-Cow-Mas-Ket*, p. 20)

31: 1 *Ellis.* Thomas Ellis (1844–1918) left Dublin with his friend Andy McFarland for Southampton to sail on the Royal Mail Steamship Line on 17 January 1865. They arrived in Victoria on 10 March. Ellis carried a letter of introduction to Peter O'Reilly, who was to become his friend and adviser. Ellis and McFarland crossed the Cascades by the Hope Trail in the company of J.C. Haynes and the Indian packer Tonasket, and Ellis found employment as Dewdney's supervisor of stores during the building of the Kootenay Trail. In 1866 he and McFarland opened a trading post and general store at Penticton. In July 1865 Haynes had received permission to reduce the size of the huge Indian reserve set aside by W.G. Cox at the southern end of Okanagan Lake, and Ellis took advantage of the opportunity to acquire land and cattle. McFarland returned to Ireland in 1870, and two years later Ellis went home to marry Mina Wade. Over the years Ellis increased his holdings of land and his bands of cattle. After he acquired the land of the Haynes Estate in 1895, his property extended from fifteen miles north of Penticton south to Osoyoos. His cattle numbered 4,000 or more, and to this number he added 1,200 head acquired from the Haynes Estate (*Vernon News*, 13 June 1895). As one of the partners of the B.C. Cattle Company founded in 1893, he was also engaged in the business of importing cattle and sheep in great numbers from Oregon and the North-West Territories, pasturing them near Princeton and driving them over the Hope Trail to the Coast. In 1905 the South Okanagan Land Development Company purchased his land and cattle. "Tom tells me that he has sold Penticton," O'Reilly informed John Trutch, who held a mortgage on the property, "he expects the first instalment, $50,000 of the purchase money to be paid on the 15th inst. He does not mention the sum for which he has sold, but from what he has previously told me I believe it to be $400,000 not a bad beginning for 1905" (O'Reilly to John Trutch, 3 January 1905, Trutch Papers). The syndicate laid out a townsite at Penticton, and in 1909 the District of Penticton was incorporated. For further details, see the obituary, *Colonist*, 5 February 1918; Kathleen W. Ellis, "Tom and Mina Ellis," Okanagan Historical Society, *Fourteenth Report*, pp. 98–109; Ormsby, "Some Irish Figures," passim; and Laing, "Colonial Farm Settlers," pp. 486–88.

31: 2 *Haynes.* John Carmichael Haynes (1831–88), the eldest son of Jonas and Hester Carmichael Haynes, was born at Landscape, Co. Cork, Ireland. His uncle, James Carmichael of Hyndford, was a friend of Chartres Brew, who was appointed inspector of police for British Columbia, and perhaps this connection influenced Haynes's decision to emigrate. Supplied with a testimonial by the mayor and magistrates of Cork, he travelled from Panama on the *Sonora* on the same voyage as Colonel Moody, Arthur Bushby, Thomas Elwyn, and Robert Burnaby and arrived in Victoria on 25 December 1858. In January 1859 he was appointed constable, clerk, and revenue officer at Yale, and in March Brew had him collect mining licences between Yale and Hope. In 1860, he was chief constable and deputy collector of customs at Yale until he was transferred to Rock Creek in October. In November 1861 he was transferred to Similkameen, and in 1862 to Osoyoos. In June 1864 he was appointed justice of the peace in the Osoyoos and Kootenay districts, and in July he was sent to Wild Horse Creek. He was a member of the Legislative Council of the colony from 1864 to 1866. In 1866 he served at Big Bend under O'Reilly, and in 1867 he returned to Osoyoos. He had already begun buying land, and he continued to make purchases until he had accumulated 22,000 acres. W.H. Lowe was associated with him in horse and cattle ranching. On 26 September 1868 Haynes married, at Hope, Charlotte, the youngest daughter of William Moresby. Mrs. Haynes died in May 1872, shortly after the birth of their son, Fairfax Moresby Haynes. In January 1875, Haynes married for a second time. His bride was Emily Josephine Pittendreigh. He died at Allison's on 6 July 1888, after being taken ill on the Hope Trail while returning to his home with two of his sons who had been at school in New Westminster. On 14 August 1895 trustees of his estate conveyed to the British Columbia Land and Investment Agency, 20,756 acres of his land at Osoyoos for $65,000. In September the agency conveyed the same acreage for the same price to Thomas Ellis. For further details, see Hester E. White, "John Carmichael Haynes: Pioneer of the Okanagan and Kootenay," *BCHQ* 4 (1940): 183–201; and Ormsby, "Some Irish Figures," passim.

31: 4 *Lowe.* William Hamilton Lowe (1839–82), a Canadian, was appointed constable and collector of customs at Fort Hope in September 1858. He worked under Haynes after 1 April 1862 and took charge at Osoyoos when Haynes was sent to Wild Horse Creek in 1864. In the spring of 1865 Haynes appointed him clerk and chief constable at Osoyoos (Haynes to the Colonial Secretary, 13 May 1865, Haynes Correspondence). He also became a business partner of Haynes in the cattle ranching business. In 1872, Lowe returned to Ontario to marry Ella Simpson of Goderich. He had the misfortune, as the result of a railway accident, to lose a hand and an arm. After his return to British Columbia, he served as sub-collector of customs at New Westminster from 1873 to 1880. He retired to Keremeos, where he died in 1882 (obituary, *Colonist,* 12 January 1882).

31: 7 *McKay.* McKay was engaged in establishing the Hudson's Bay Company's claim to lands at Keremeos at this time. He did not become Indian agent until 1880.

31:11 *Chinaman.* Chinese were present in the mining population from the beginning. In 1861, Douglas reported that 2,000 has wintered in the Yale district (Douglas to the Duke of Newcastle, 28 February 1861, *BCP,* 4: 46). Their continuing presence in the Similkameen mining country is commemorated in the place names "China Creek" and "China Butte."

31:13 *McKillop.* Like the Chinese, William McKillop had remained in the country after the first rush.

31:19 *Richter.* Francis Xavier Richter (1837–1910), born in Friedland, Bohemia, left home at the age of sixteen, sailed to Galveston, Texas, and mined gold and silver at San Antonio for two years. He then went to Arizona to work in the silver mines. In 1862, he moved on to Lewiston to prospect for gold, and from there he went to Colvile, where he formed a partnership with a Swiss named King who had packed for the Hudson's Bay Company. In 1864 they purchased forty-two head of cattle in Oregon, drove them across Washington, and crossed the boundary at Osoyoos. Richter pre-empted land in the Similkameen Valley in 1865 at the site of the present town of Cawston. This land was sold in 1885 to R.L. Cawston and Mrs. Ella Lowe, widow of W.H. Lowe. Richter then took up a pre-emption in Boundary Valley, and in 1895 he bought a ranch near Keremeos from François Suprenant. There in 1897 he planted the first commercial orchard in Similkameen (see Sam B. Manery, "Keremeos Chronicles," Okanagan Historical Society, *Twelfth Report* [Penticton: *Penticton Herald*, 1948], pp. 115–20; and Kathleen S. Dewdney, "Francis Xavier Richter," Okanagan Historical Society, *Twenty-Fifth Report* [Penticton: *Penticton Herald*, 1961], pp. 78-101).

31:20 *Kruger.* Theodore Kruger (1829–99), born at Hanover, then a British possession, came to British Columbia in 1858 to mine on the Fraser River. In 1860 he went to Cariboo and from there to Similkameen. He managed the Hudson's Bay Company's store at Osoyoos from 1866 until 1872 when it was bought by Barrington Price. Price soon sold it to Kruger. Like Ellis, Kruger acquired extensive holdings of property in the south Okanagan Valley (see Mrs. Chrestenza Kruger, "Early Days at Osoyoos," Okanagan Historical Society, *Sixth Report* [Vancouver: Wrigley Printing Co., 1936], pp. 76–80).

31:24 *Dolly Vardens.* Dolly Varden char, *Salvelinus malma* (H.J. Parham, *A Nature Lover in British Columbia* [London: H.F. & G. Witherby Ltd., 1937], p. 260).

31:24 *Greyling.* Mountain trout, *Salmo gairdnerii whitehousei* (ibid.).

31:25 *Saskatoons.* Service berry, *Amelanchier Alnifolia. Nutt.* (ibid., p. 263).

31:29 *Phillipps-Wolley.* (Sir) Clive Phillipps-Wolley (1854–1918), F.R. G.S., was born at Wimborne, Dorsetshire, the eldest son of R.A.L. Phillipps. He was educated at Rossall College, and after serving as vice-consul at Kertch, he read law and was called to the bar of the Middle Temple. In 1876 he assumed the name of Wolley on inheriting the estates of the Wolley family of Woodhall, Shropshire. He first came to British Columbia on a big game hunting expedition. His letters describing this adventure became the basis of *A Sportsman's Eden*, published in 1888. In 1896 he returned to British Columbia to reside. He served as sanitary inspector in the mining districts and became the owner of the *Nelson Miner*. In 1914 he was made a Knight Bachelor in recognition of his contribution to Canadian literature. His works include *Songs from a Young Man's Land*, *Gold*, *Gold in Cariboo*, *One of the Broken Brigade*, *Sport in the Crimea and Caucasus*, and *Big Game Hunting*. An "imperialist of imperialists," he was active in the Navy League and was strongly opposed to Chinese immigration into British Columbia.

32: 3 *the "Big Hill."* Copper Mountain.

33:29 *Manuel Barcelo.* (Em) Manuel Barcelo was a Mexican who went to Texas and from there drove a herd of cattle to California in 1850. He was attracted to British Columbia by the gold rush and became a packer for the Hudson's Bay Company from Fort Hope to Similkameen and on to Kootenay. In 1873 he pre-empted land at Keremeos and acquired a large band of cattle (Manery, "Keremeos Chronicles," pp. 115–20).

33:35 *Good's Mission.* Mrs. Allison is probably referring to the Indian mission at Lytton, established in November 1870 by Rev. John Booth Good, the founder of the Indian Industrial Schools (*Report of the Columbia Mission* [London: Rivington's, 1871], p. 45).

34:22 *Ashnola John.* An Indian chief, possibly a Colvile Indian, after whom Ashnola Creek was named. Sam Manery describes him as "tall, gaunt, with straggly hair, and wearing a long buckskin shirt" and states that he was a familiar figure riding his pony down the road as late as 1912. He was said to "have had in his possession and hanging in his cabin, the scalps of several whites" ("Keremeos Chronicles," p. 115).

35: 2 *Vowell.* Arthur Wellesley Vowell (1841–1918), born at Clonmel, Co. Tipperary, Ireland, the twelfth child of Richard Prendergast Vowell, a lawyer. Vowell obtained a commission in the Irish militia in 1858 and retired as senior lieutenant in 1860. He reached Victoria in February 1862, travelling by way of Panama and San Francisco. After mining in Cariboo, he entered government service in 1864, serving for a while as jailer at New Westminster.

In April 1865 he went to Kootenay as constable, and in 1866 he was appointed chief constable at Big Bend. After Confederation he was appointed gold commissioner and stipendiary magistrate of Kootenay, but the following year he was transferred to Omineca. In 1874 he was moved to Cassiar. In 1875 he was elected to represent Kootenay in the Legislative Assembly, but he resigned the next year and returned to Cassiar as gold commissioner. In 1884 he went back to Kootenay.

On his way to Ottawa in 1886 to seek a better appointment, Vowell visited the Dewdneys at Government House, Regina. Jane Dewdney wrote at that time to Mrs. O'Reilly: "I have come to the conclusion (whether right or wrong remains to be seen), that he really is not quite right in his head; flighty & odd he always was, but now it is very marked" (Jane Shaw Dewdney to Mrs. Peter O'Reilly, 1 March 1886, Jane Shaw Dewdney Correspondence). Something did come of the Ottawa visit: in 1889 Vowell was appointed superintendent of Indian affairs for British Columbia. He served in this capacity until 1910. At the age of seventy-seven, he committed suicide.

36:26 *Wardle.* James Wardle, born in Nottinghamshire, left England in 1862 to mine in Cariboo. Subsequently he mined on the Similkameen and Columbia rivers. After Confederation he obtained the contract for carrying the mail from Hope to Wild Horse Creek. His "Reminiscences" contain a vivid account of his round trips of 1,300 miles through Colvile Valley, Spokane Prairie, Pend d'Oreille, and across Bonners Ferry and up the Moyie River into British Columbia. The summer trip took from thirty-five to forty days. In winter he left Hope on snowshoes and followed the Hope Trail to Princeton, carrying fifty pounds of mail and express. He packed only half a blanket for bedding and built his campfires on top of the snow. "I used to get $5 a pound for packing opium in," he wrote. "This was for Chinamen who nearly all were on Wild Horse Creek." Hope was his headquarters, and when Phillipps-Wolley knew him in 1887, he was magistrate there and ran a large store. For further information, see James Wardle, "Reminiscences," typescript, PABC; and Phillipps-Wolley, *A Sportsman's Eden*, pp. 49–50.

36:28 *met his death.* February 1878 (*Colonist*, 10 February 1878), see also p. 119.

36:36 *little Wilfrid.* Robert Wilfrid Allison, who became a farmer in the Princeton district.

37: 7 *Younger.* Colonel Henry Washington Younger, father of Thomas Coleman ("Cole") Younger (1844–1916). During the Civil War, Colonel Younger was a Unionist sympathizer, and his son a Confederate who became a guerilla fighter. Cole Younger is supposed to have been responsible after the war for organizing with Frank James the group of desperadoes under Jesse James which engaged in bank robberies and train holdups. For further information, see the biography of Cole Younger by W.J. Ghent, in *DAB* 10, p. 636.

37:25 *bushtail rats.* The bushy-tailed rat (pack rat), *Neotoma cinerea occidentalis* (Parham, *A Nature Lover in British Columbia,* p. 259).

38: 4 *Red Oak.* On 26 September 1872, the *Colonist* noted that "Mr. J.F. Allison of Rock Creek [*sic*], yesterday brought from California 'Red Oak,' a magnificent short-horn yearling [Durham] bull, bred by the famous stock-raiser, Coleman [*sic*] Younger of San Jose, California, and got by 'Glencoe' out of 'Lady of the Lake.' "

38:17 *McLean.* Roderick McLean, who was made chief factor at the Hudson's Bay Company's post at Keremeos in 1863 and who was succeeded by John Tait in 1867. McLean left the service of the Company and opened a store at Rock Creek; from there he went to Cariboo, where he remained for ten years. He then went to Kelowna and later to Okanagan Falls where to took up land. It must have been Tait, rather than McLean, who rented the Hudson's Bay property to Lowe.

38:21 *Beatrice.* Beatrice Allison, who became a teacher and went to Wonsam, Korea. From there she proceeded to Japan where she married C.E. Bruce-Mitford of Madras.

39:17 *Scuse.* An Indian shaman, described by Phillipps-Wolley as "the mighty doctor, from Loo-loo-loo-loo, the Hollow Land, who will pick out the eyes of the evil one with the eagle's beak, tear him with the claws of a bear, and make him writhe with the poison of toad and rattlesnake" (*A Sportsman's Eden*, pp. 164–65). Scuse fought the evil spirit which was destroying Chief Quinisco, but his efforts to save the man failed. Buffalo robes were then piled over the chief's head, and he was smothered. His funeral was followed by the usual feast, and the final burial was carried out according to Similkameen custom.

39:35 *unrest stirring across the line.* The reference is to the unrest in 1877 among the Nez Percés, who, under the leadership of Chief Joseph, objected to being put on a reservation.

40:16 *McDougal.* Johnny McDougal, a "mixed blood," born in 1827, the son of a mill owner at Red River. He is believed to have served Donald Smith as a guide. For twenty years McDougal was a packer with the Hudson's Bay Company, taking trains into the Okanagan Valley as early as 1840. On his retirement from the Company he staked land in 1861 near Kelowna. This property later became the Guisachan Ranch, owned by Lord Aberdeen. In 1890 McDougal moved to the west side of Okanagan Lake. The property he took up there he sold to Joseph Brent.

40:28 *Dog Lake.* Lac Du Chien on A.C. Anderson's map of 1867 and also on J.W. Trutch's maps of 1866 and 1871. The name was changed in 1930 to Skaha Lake.

40:36 *Trout Creek.* Trout Creek enters Okanagan Lake south of Summerland. Its name appears at Trout River on Archibald McDonald's map of 1827.

41: 7 *Indian hemp. Apocynum cannabinum.* The stems of the Indian hemp were gathered in the autumn by the Indians, and the fibres were used for fishing lines and ropes. The Similkameen Indians traded the hemp with the Coast Indians for salmon-bellies and baskets.

41: 8 *Rattle Snake weed. Goodyeara Repens,* a creeping plantain about six inches high.

41:16 *swans.* The whistling swan, *Cygnus columbianus,* which flies through the Okanagan Valley on its way to the breeding grounds in the Arctic.

41:17 *wild rye grass. Elymus canadensis.* It is found on the river and lake banks in the Interior of British Columbia.

42: 1 *Vernon.* Forbes George Vernon (1843–1911), third son of John E.V. Vernon, J.P., Clontarf Castle, Co. Dublin, Ireland, who, after holding a commission in the 21st Fusiliers, came to British Columbia in 1863, accompanied by his older brother, Charles Albert Vernon, who had resigned a lieutenancy in the 20th Regiment, and by a friend, Colonel C.F. Houghton, formerly of the 20th Regiment and a Crimean veteran. All three went to the northern end of the Okanagan Valley where Houghton expected to receive a military grant. Vernon mined at Cherry Creek in 1864 and in 1866 pre-empted land between Priests' Valley and Okanagan Landing. This property he turned over in 1869 to Houghton, and in 1873 he purchased from Houghton the Coldstream Ranch. Land was also purchased from his brother, and eventually Forbes Vernon held 13,000 acres. The Coldstream Ranch was sold in 1894 to Lord Aberdeen.

In 1875 Vernon was elected to the Legislative Assembly, and in 1876 he became chief commissioner of lands and works in the Elliott government. He was re-elected in 1878, did not run in 1882, and was again elected in 1886. He served as chief commissioner of lands and works in both the Davie and Robson cabinets. He was defeated in the 1894 election, and on 8 January was appointed agent-general for British Columbia in London. From this office he was dismissed on 30 September 1898.

With F.S. Barnard, J.A. Mara, and Moses Lumby, he was one of the chief shareholders in the Shuswap and Okanagan Railway, built in 1892. For further information, see Ormsby, "Some Irish Figures," passim; and obituaries of Vernon in the *Victoria Times,* 20 January 1911, *Colonist,* 21 January 1911; and *Vernon News,* 26 January 1911.

42:24 *Chief's wife and Theresa.* The wife of Chief François of the Indian village below Penticton. One of their daughters married Roderick McLean. Father Pandosy died in the arms of Chief François on 9 February 1891. Chief François lived to the age of 108, dying 10 June 1908.

Theresa (Thérèse) was a Flathead woman, the wife of Cyprian Laurence, who accompanied Father Pandosy when the priest was packed into the Okanagan Valley by William Peon, the brother of Baptiste Peon of Peon's Prairie near Spokane.

42:26 *Chapeau Blanc.* The uncle of Thérèse, who was opposed to the priests' coming but who later was converted and became a devout Christian. As a very old man, he died near Okanagan Mission.

42:30 *the Mission.* Okanagan Mission, established in 1859 by Father Pierre Richard, Father Charles Pandosy, and Brother Surel of the order of the Oblates of Mary the Immaculate. The first site was at the southern end of Duck Lake, but the following year the mission was moved to Rivière De L'Anse au Sable (Mission Creek). The first church was built in 1861.

43: 2 *Silletoe.* Rt. Rev. Acton Windeyer Sillitoe (1840-94), first bishop of New Westminster, came to British Columbia in 1879 after Bishop Hills divided the diocese of British Columbia into three: Vancouver Island (Columbia), Caledonia, and New Westminster. Bishop Sillitoe was born at Sydney, New South Wales, and educated at King's College School, London, and Pembroke College, Cambridge. He was ordained in 1870. He was chaplain at Geneva in 1876–77, and from 1877 until 1879, chaplain to Princess Alice and the British Legation at Darmstadt. He arrived in the diocese of New Westminster on 18 June 1880 and soon organized an interior mission centred on Kamloops. For further information, see Violet E. Sillitoe, *Pioneer Days in British Columbia* (Vancouver: privately printed, n.d.); and H.H. Gowen, *Church Work in British Columbia* . . . (London: Longmans Green, 1899).

43: 4 *Lequime's trading post.* Eli Lequime (1811–98) was born at Bordeaux and left an orphan at the age of two years. Raised by an uncle, he ran away to sea when he was fourteen and obtained work as a cabin boy on a windjammer. He was at sea for twenty-seven years, during the course of which he made four voyages round the world. He deserted his ship at San Francisco to go to the California goldfields in 1852. Two years later he returned to France to fight in the Crimean War. He returned to San Francisco in 1856. There he was joined by a French girl whom he had met in France at the end of the war, and they married. The Leguimes came to British Columbia in 1858. Lequime mined at Strawberry Island, half way between Hope and Yale. In 1860 he walked over the Hope Trail to Rock Creek, and there he remained until October 1861, when he walked to Okanagan Mission. At Okanagan Mission he became a successful storekeeper, cattle rancher, and sawmill operator. He sold his properties in 1888 and retired to San Francisco. He was the father of Bernard Lequime, who founded Kelowna in 1892. For further information, see F.M. Buckland, "Mr. and Mrs. Eli Lequime," Okanagan Historical Society, *Seventeenth Report*, pp. 87–91.

43:14 *Laurence*. Cyprian Laurence, a French Canadian, accompanied the priests to the Okanagan Valley and in 1860 pre-empted land at Okanagan Mission.

43:15 *Brent*. Brent, a former United States cavalryman and Indian scout, came to Okanagan Mission in 1865 and in 1871 established the first stone grist mill between the Columbia and Thompson rivers. On 26 November 1868, O'Reilly noted in his diary: "At Houghton's. Fred Christof Christian Brent took the oath of allegiance. Reserved 160 acres of land for him at the south end of Dog Lake." For further information, see Joseph Brent, "The First Stone Grist Mill," Okanagan Historical Society, *Sixth Report*, p. 27.

43:16 *Christian Bros*. Joseph Christian (b. 1829), one of seven brothers who were natives of St. Anicet, Québec, came to British Columbia in 1858 and to Okanagan Mission with Eli Lequime in 1861 and took up land. Joseph's brother Louis, who had mined in California, joined him in 1862 and in 1865 took up land at Coldstream Meadows, Lumby. Thomas Christian, another brother, also took up land in this vicinity.

43:17 *Bushrey*. Isadore Boucherie, an early miner on Mission Creek, who in 1888 settled on the west side of Okanagan Lake. The mountain which Mrs. Allison had named "Mount Edgar" became, in the course of time, "Mount Boucherie."

43:22 *Louisa*. Susan Louisa Allison, later Mrs. Albert E. Johnston of Princeton.

44:16 *Michelle*. Indian guides with this name served O'Reilly and other gold commissioners, and a guide with the same name accompanied the Sillitoes on their early tours of the Interior (Sillitoe, *Early Days in British Columbia*, pp. 28–29).

43:33 *Joseph.* For information on Chief Joseph and the Nez Percé War of 1877, see Merrill D. Beal, "*I Will Fight No More Forever*": *Chief Joseph and the Nez Percé War* (Seattle: University of Washington Press, 1963); and Alvin M. Josephy, *The Nez Percé Indians and the Opening of the Northwest* (New Haven: Yale University Press, 1965). For the unrest among the Okanagan Indians at this time, see Robert E. Cail, *Land, Man and the Law* (Vancouver: University of British Columbia Press, 1973).

46:17 *McLean boys.* Allan, Charles, and Archibald McLean, sons of Chief Trader Donald McLean, who was stationed at Kamloops from 1855 to 1860, and his second wife, Sophie, daughter of Chief Louis. McLean, a man of violent temper, was killed by Indians during the "Chilcotin War" in 1864. Three of his sons, with Alex (Alexander Joseph) Hare became a nuisance in the Kamloops district in 1879 (not 1875) as horse thieves and rabble-rousers. After their escape from the Kamloops jail, they were named outlaws, and John Ussher, government agent, and two constables with warrants were sent after them. When Ussher found them in the Nicola mountains, they refused to surrender, opened fire, and killed Ussher and one of the constables. Then, in roaming the countryside, they killed a shepherd, Peter Kelly. They were eventually captured by a posse. In November 1880, they were tried at New Westminster, found guilty of murder, and on 31 January 1881 they were hanged at one scaffold at New Westminster. For further details, see Mary Balf, *Kamloops: A History of the District up to 1914* (Kamloops: Clow Printing Ltd., 1969), p. 72; and Mel Rothenburger, "*We've Killed Johnny Ussher!*" *The Story of the Wild McLean Boys and Alex Hare* (Vancouver: Mitchell Press, 1973).

46:24 *Hector.* Another son of McLean, Hector, was not associated with the activities of his brothers.

46:28 *Kamloops Louie.* Chief Louis (Hli-hleh-Kan) (d. 1905) was for over sixty years chief of the Kamloops band. His daughter Sophie married Donald McLean in 1859, and it was the seduction of her daughter Anne by a prominent Kamloops businessman that was believed to have caused the wild McLean boys, her brothers, to avenge her shame by starting an Indian uprising.

47:35 *the youngest fifteen.* Allan McLean was twenty-four years old, his brother Archie, fourteen.

48:20 *kikenees.* Kokanee, *Oncorhynchus nerka kennerlyi* (Parham, *A Nature Lover in British Columbia*, p. 260).

48:31 *that year.* Allison was made a justice of the peace in 1876 when there was unrest among the Okanagan Indians.

48:34 *Cawston.* Richard Lowe Cawston (1849–1923), a native of Stratford, Ontario, and nephew of W.H. Lowe. Cawston came to the Okanagan in 1875 to work for his uncle as a ranch hand. In 1884, with his aunt, Mrs. Ella Lowe, he purchased 5,341 acres on the lower Similkameen River from Richter and also leased land at Osoyoos and Penticton. He was appointed justice of the peace for the county of Yale in 1889. In 1910 his extensive holdings were sold to the Similkameen Fruit Land Company. A village and post office were officially named Cawston in his honour in 1916.

48:35 *O'Keefe and Greenhow.* Cornelius O'Keefe (1842-1919), a native of Ottawa, went to Cariboo in 1862, obtained work on the Cariboo Road, and laid out fifty miles of the road between Clinton and Bridge Creek. In 1867, accompanied by Thomas Greenhow (who became his partner) and Thomas Wood, he drove from Oregon 180 head of cattle for the market at the Big Bend mines. All three were impressed with the prospects for cattle ranching in the Okanagan Valley and began to pre-empt land there. In 1868 O'Keefe recorded a claim for 160 acres at the Head of Okanagan Lake. A further 480 acres were acquired by purchase in 1871, and in 1883 he purchased 715 acres from Colonel C.F. Houghton. The property sold by Houghton was the original Vernon property. By 1891 O'Keefe had a herd of 1,000 cattle and extensive lands. In 1907, he sold 5,700 acres to the Land and Agricultural Company of Canada for $184,193. For further details, see the obituary in the *Vernon News*, 29 May 1919.

Thomas Greenhow (d. 1889) acquired property in 1862 near Burnaby Lake, New Westminster District, and at Quesnelmouth in 1863. In 1868 he pre-empted 160 acres two miles north of the Head of Okanagan Lake. By 1885 he had 1,359 acres and 800 head of cattle. After his death, 8,906 acres belonging to his estate were sold for $315,000 to the Land and Agricultural Company of Canada (ibid.).

48:35 *Price Ellison.* Price Ellison (d. 1931) was born at Durham, Cheshire, and as a young man was apprenticed as a whitesmith. He came to the Okanagan Valley in 1876 and eventually acquired the Postill Ranch and the Simpson Ranch, both near Okanagan Mission. He also had property near Swan Lake, meadows near Lumby, and the lease from Thomas Wood of Winfield Ranch. In 1896 he was elected to the provincial legislature. In the McBride governments, he held the portfolio of commissioner of lands in 1909 and of finance and agriculture in 1910. For further details, see Myra K. DeBeck, "Price Ellison. A Memorial by His Daughter," Okanagan Historical Society, *Twelfth Report*, pp. 48–58.

48:37 *Mrs. Postill.* The widow of Edward Postill (1821–73). Edward Postill migrated with his wife and children from Malton, Yorkshire, to Ontario, and from there they moved to British Columbia in 1872. He purchased a large ranch (the "Postill Ranch") at the southern end of Duck Lake. He wintered at New Westminster; then in April 1873, while on his way to his ranch, he was taken ill and died at Priests' Valley (Vernon). His sons Edward (1857–89), Alfred (1852–97), and William made the Postill Ranch famous for stock raising. It was sold to Price Ellison in 1903. For further details, see Primrose Upton, "The Story of the Postill Family," Okanagan Historical Society, *Thirtieth Report* (Penticton: *Penticton Herald*, 1966), pp. 77–85; and Mrs. Robert Lambly, "Early Days at Okanagan Mission," Okanagan Historical Society, *Sixth Report*, pp. 88–89.

48:38 *Lucy.* Lucy Postill, daughter of Edward, later Mrs. Robert Lambly. In 1936 Mrs. Lambly recalled visiting at Sunnyside as a girl and hearing Mrs. Allison "tell of the unidentified creature in the lake which the Indians call Naitaka. She wrote a poem about it about 53 years ago" (ibid., p. 89).

49: 6 *Tamula.* An Indian shaman.

49:35 *Anderson.* A.C. Anderson (1814–84) was born at Calcutta, the son of an army officer who became an indigo planter. Anderson entered the service of the Hudson's Bay Company in 1831 and arrived at Fort Vancouver in November 1832. He was sent to New Caledonia in 1835. He returned to the Columbia in 1840 and in 1841 took charge of Fort Nisqually. In 1846 he was in charge of Fort Alexandria in New Caledonia, and in 1846 and 1847 he carried out explorations for a new brigade route between Kamloops and Fort Langley. He was chief factor in charge of Fort Colvile in 1848 and then was at Fort Vancouver from 1851 to 1853. He retired from the Company in 1854, farmed in Washington Territory for a while, and in 1858 moved to Vancouver Island where he became the first collector of customs for British Columbia and postmaster at Victoria. In 1876 he was appointed by the dominion government to the Indian Land Commission, but this commission was dissolved in May 1878. See the biographical sketch in *The Letters of John McLoughlin . . . Second Series, 1839–44*, ed. E.E. Rich, with an introduction by W. Kaye Lamb ([London]: Hudson's Bay Record Society, 1943), 6: 384–86.

49:35 *Sproat.* Gilbert Malcolm Sproat (1834–1913) was born in Scotland and trained for the Indian civil service. He came to Vancouver Island in 1860 in the employ of Anderson & Co., an English company which established a sawmill at Alberni Canal. Sproat became manager in 1862 and also established an importing, commission, and insurance business. In 1863 he was appointed justice of the peace and stipendiary magistrate for the west coast of Vancouver Island. He returned to England in 1865 and became active in organizing a group of Hudson's Bay Company officials and others who were interested in having the capital of the united colony of British Columbia fixed at Victoria. In 1868 he published *Scenes and Studies of Savage Life*, an important study of the West Coast Indians. From 1872 until 1876 he was agent-general in London for the province of British Columbia. He was appointed to the Indian Land Commission in 1876, and in 1878 he became the sole commissioner. In 1883 the provincial government sent him to the Kootenay. He was stipendiary magistrate at Farwell (Revelstoke) in 1885. In 1886 he became gold commissioner and assistant commissioner of lands and works. He retired in 1889 and remained in the Kootenay until 1898. For further details, see T.A. Rickard "Gilbert Malcolm Sproat," *BCHQ* 1 (1937): 21–32; and Cail, *Land, Man and the Law.*

50: 6 *Dawson.* In 1877 and 1878, Dr. George Mercer Dawson, the famous geologist employed on the Dominion Government Geological Survey, explored along the Paysayten Trail between the Similkameen and Ashnola rivers and also along the Hope Trail. After the Granite Creek rush, he visited the Similkameen again in 1888. No further geological survey was made in the Similkameen until 1907.

51:38 *Mrs. Tommy Christian.* The wife of Thomas Christian, who was a brother of Joseph Christian.

52: 5 *Penextitza.* Gold Commissioner W.G. Cox met this powerful chief, whose name he spelled "Zelahetza," at Rock Creek in 1861 and again in July 1862 when he marked out, at the request of Governor Douglas, an Indian reservation near the Head of Okanagan Lake comprising ten square miles (Cox to W.A.G. Young, 16 January 1861, Cox Correspondence). At Douglas's request, Cox also marked out a reservation at the south end of Okanagan Lake, this one twenty square miles. In 1865 J.C. Haynes reported to New Westminster that incoming settlers objected to the size of these reserves, and he proposed their reduction. To this A.N. Birch agreed (Haynes to Chief Commissioner of Lands and Works, 28 November 1865, Haynes Correspondence). The reduction that was effected made it possible for Haynes and Ellis to obtain land at the south end of the lake and shortly thereafter for O'Keefe and Greenhow to obtain land at the northern end.

52:26 *Winter of 79–80.* This winter was a hard one, but the worst winter since the bitter one of 1862 was the winter of 1880–81.

55: 2 *Phillips.* On the dissolution of the partnership of John Phillips and Hugh Armstrong, a dispute developed over the division of their property. On 20 May 1866 Phillips shot and killed Armstrong (*Colonist*, 3 April 1866). Phillips was arrested and charged with murder, but at his trial he was acquitted on grounds of self-defence. He later moved to Bonaparte Creek in Washington. It was the Phillips–Armstrong property that Boucherie, formerly a squatter, acquired at auction.

55:34 *Carrie and George.* Caroline Elizabeth Allison, later Mrs. William Heald Thomas of Princeton. George Mortimer Allison became a farmer, prospector, and packer. He lived at Keremeos for some time.

56:23 *Barrington Price.* Barrington Price, an Englishman, bought the Hudson's Bay Company's store at Osoyoos in 1871 and disposed of it to Kruger in 1873. Price then pre-empted 320 acres at Keremeos on 26 March 1873 and a further 320 acres in July. In 1885 he obtained 374 acres, the southern portion of the present townsite of Keremeos. In September 1884 he transferred 640 acres to T.A. Daly (Laing, "Colonial Farm Settlers," p. 441). Price had both a cattle ranch and a grist mill, built in 1877. His success with the mill promoted the transition in the Similkameen Valley from cattle ranching to wheat growing. Henry Nicholson, his nearest neighbour, who became his partner, farmed near the Kettle River in the early 1870's and in September 1872 arrived at the Hudson's Bay post at Keremeos. In addition to his land at Keremeos, Nicholson had land at the southern end of Richter Pass on the International Boundary. At the time of the Granite Creek rush, he and Thomas Cole, who had pre-empted 320 acres north of Nicholson's pre-emption at Keremeos in 1873, shared a gold claim. Cf. P.L. Trout, *Prospector's Manual: Being a full and complete History and Description of the newly discovered Gold Mines on Granite Creek, the Canyon of the Tulameen River, and other new mineral discoveries in the Similkameen country* (n.p., 1886), p. 30: "Henry Nicholson is the Recorder for the Granite Creek district, and, until recently, was the owner, along with Thomas Cole, of a claim about half a mile from the mouth of the creek." Price, who had private means, and Nicholson may have attended Oxford University as Mrs. Allison states, but there is no evidence that they were awarded degrees.

56:29 *Pequinac* (*Princess Julia*). The last hereditary chieftain of the Similkameen Indians.

57:13 *Col. Luard.* Captain Luard returned with the Royal Engineers to

England in November 1863 and died there in 1870. The property that Allison purchased was Luard's pre-emption of 1860.

57:13 *Sinnet or Lindsay property*. Corporal Charles Sinnet, R.E., who edited the *Emigrant Soldiers' Gazette and Cape Horn Chronicle* during the voyage of the main detachment of the Royal Engineers on board the *Thames City* in 1859, had pre-empted land at Princeton in 1860. He returned to England in 1863. Sergeant James Lindsay, R.E., remained in the colony and took over Sinnet's preemption.

57:16 *townsite of Princeton*. The old townsite was cancelled by Vernon, as chief commissioner of lands, in 1883.

57:18 *Greaves*. Joseph Blackburn Greaves (1831–1915), of Irish descent, was born at Putsey, Yorkshire. At the age of fourteen he sailed to New York and later joined an emigrant train to California. He came to British Columbia in 1862, spent a year in Cariboo, returned to California, and then bought sheep in Oregon which he shipped to Yale and drove to 150 Mile House. This venture being a success, he went to Oregon for cattle and drove them to Thompson River. In 1882, with Ben Van Valkenberg, he organized in Victoria a cattle-buying syndicate to supply construction gangs of the Canadian Pacific Railway. The following year, with C. Beak of Chapeau Lake (eleven miles east of Douglas Lake), he bought all the property of the Douglas family. He was the largest partner and the manager of the Douglas Lake Cattle Company, incorporated in 1886. The ranch grew to 120,000 acres and supported 20,000 head of cattle. Half of the interest of Greaves and Beak had been transferred to C.W.R. Thompson and W.C. Ward of Victoria, and in 1910 Greaves sold his share in the company to W.C. Ward (see Scholefield and Howay, *British Columbia from the Earliest Times*, 4:880–81).

58: 7 *that spring*. The reference is to Dawson's 1888 visit. Mrs. Allison refers to Professor Dawson, Junior, to distinguish G.M. Dawson from his father who was principal of McGill University. For further details on G.M. Dawson, see the biographical sketch by B.J. Harrington in Royal Society of Canada, *Proceedings and Transactions*, 2nd series, 8 (1902): section iv, pp. 183–92. For Dawson's impression of the Similkameen country in 1888, see

George M. Dawson, *The Mineral Wealth of British Columbia*, Geological and Natural History Survey of Canada (Montreal: Dawson Bros., 1889).

61:10 *Elfreda.* Elfreda Flora Allison, later Mrs. G.H. Holmes of Epsom, England.

62:24 *Jack.* John Stratton Allison, killed in an accident in 1908.

64: 3 *Tavernier.* Jules Tavernier (1844–99), born in Paris, studied with Barrias. After the Franco-Prussian War, he emigrated to the United States in 1871 and joined *Harper's Magazine* as an illustrator. After taking up residence in San Francisco, he made trips to British Columbia to do pastel paintings of Indian life (J. Russell Harper, *Early Painters and Engravers in Canada* [Toronto: University of Toronto Press, 1970], p. 304).

64:10 *Hesketh.* Sir Thomas George Fermor Fermor-Hesketh, 7th Baronet, born in 1849, succeeded to the title in 1876. He married Lady Fermor-Hesketh. He must have had investments in western railways and possibly mines. Two references to him occur in the Trutch Papers. In 1882, when the O'Reillys were on their way to England via San Francisco, Kathleen O'Reilly wrote to her uncle, John Trutch, from the Palace Hotel on 15 April 1882: "Papa has just come in with very good news. Sir Thomas Hesketh and wife are to arrive here to-day in a special Pullman Dining Car, and we are to start back in it to-morrow so that it will do away with a lunch basket and the different changes on the way." After the O'Reillys arrived in England, Cary O'Reilly wrote to John Trutch on 23 May 1882: "We had the advantage of travelling in a Pullman dining car the whole way to Chicago!"

64:16 *Howse.* Albert E. Howse (1855–1938), born in Lincoln County, Ontario, and educated at Smithsville. In 1872, when he was in poor health, he was sent to an American sanitarium. He went to San Francisco in 1876 and from there to British Columbia in 1877. In 1878 he pre-empted land in the Nicola Valley, bought cattle, and went into partnership with E. O'Rourke. In 1880 he visited Ottawa and was made Indian agent for the Nicola agency, including the Nicola, Similkameen, and Okanagan valleys, by Sir

John A. Macdonald. He held this position until 1884 when he resigned. He later owned a chain of stores, a lumber mill, and a flour mill. In 1905 he became manager of the *Similkameen Star*, which had commenced publication in March 1900, and from 1906 until 1911 he was the sole owner of the paper.

64:25 *Joe Linton's ranch.* Linton commenced cattle ranching in the Chopaka Valley about 1882.

65: 1 *Nichols . . . Ferguson . . . George Reynolds.* No doubt these men were interested in the claim of the B.C. Copper Company, in which Allison was the main shareholder.

65: 2 *discovered in '58.* Allison's first trip to Similkameen was in 1860, not 1858.

65:12 *Prior.* Lieutenant Colonel Edward Gawlor Prior, (1853–1920), born near Ripon, Yorkshire, the son of a clergyman. After being trained as a mining engineer, Prior came to British Columbia in 1873 and became assistant manager of the Vancouver Coal and Mining Co. Ltd. He resigned this position in 1878 and was appointed inspector of mines. He gave up this position in 1880 to go into the hardware business. Prior represented Victoria in the Legislative Assembly from 1886 until 16 January 1888, when he resigned to run for the House of Commons. He represented Victoria in that house until 1896. In 1900 he re-entered provincial politics and was elected to the Legislative Assembly. For a short period from November 1902 until June 1903 he was premier. He held the portfolio of minister of mines from November 1900 until June 1903. Appointed lieutenant-governor in 1919, he died one year later.

65:12 *Jones.* T.H. Jones of the Similkameen Mining Company.

65:14 *Mitchells.* The Mitchells went to the Summit to mine in 1889.

65:15 *Coulthards.* A.M. Coulthard applied on 9 September 1889 to purchase 294 acres at Keremeos, the property originally pre-empted by Roderick McLean (Laing, "Colonial Farm Settlers," p. 439). J.H. Coulthard staked "Roonie" claim near Granite Creek in 1887 and "Kingston" claim on Nickel Plate Mountain in 1894. He had bought some of Price's holdings and improved his mill.

65:38 *Premier.* John Robson became premier in 1889.

66: 3 *Mr. Tunstall.* George Christie Tunstall (1836–1911), one of the Overlanders of 1862. Tunstall left Montreal on 5 May 1862 with six companions, travelling by rail to La Crosse, and from there by steamboat to St. Paul. After completing his journey to the goldfields, he mined for a while in Cariboo. In 1879 he was appointed government agent at Kamloops, and on 1 December 1885, gold commissioner at Granite Creek (British Columbia, *Government Gazette*, 1885). He became registrar of the county court for the district of Yale on 29 July 1886 (ibid., 1886). He was gold commissioner at Revelstoke in 1890 and then returned to Kamloops to be gold commissioner and government agent (Mark S. Wade, *The Overlanders of '62*, Archives Memoir no. 9 (Victoria: King's Printer, 1931), p. 169.

66: 9 *Oroville.* A town in the north central part of Okanogan County, Washington, originally called Oro because of its placer mines, but named Oroville when a post office was established in 1892.

66:13 *Jenkins.* William Jenkins, a Virginian who was said to carry an ivory-handled revolver with four notches filed in it, was one of the four men who staked the discovery claim on Granite Creek. In 1886 he took up land on the west side of Okanagan Lake, just north of the present Peachland. He soon sold this property and on 5 July recorded 320 acres at the mouth of Meyers Creek. This property he also soon sold. He moved to the United States, settling just south of Grand Forks. There, he shot and killed an outlaw in a dispute and wounded another man. He died in prison. A.J. Splawn refers to Jenkins as one of the half-dozen "squaw-men" who sometimes frequented Brewster, Washington. "They had purchased their women for about two ounces of gold per head and were for many years the lords of that part of the Columbia" (A.J. Splawn, *Ka-Mi-a-Kin: The Last Hero of the Yakimas* [Portland: Kilham Stationery and Printing Co., 1917], pp. 184–85). For Jenkins, and also his imitator, William McLoughlin, a second "Wild Goose Bill," see Dorothy H. Gellatly,

A Bit of Okanagan History (Kelowna: *Kelowna Courier,* 1932), pp. 37–38.

66:21 *Chance.* John M. Chance, according to legend the discoverer of gold at Granite Creek, is described by Phillipps-Wolley as "an old trapper" (*A Sportsman's Eden,* pp. 55–56). William Briggs, Mike Sullivan, and John Bromley had discovered gold in the fall of 1884, but they were prevented from mining by heavy rains which caused high water. They showed the gold to Allison and told him they would stake in the spring. That winter, Chance, Jenkins, Thomas Curry, William McCain, and Harry Hobbes heard of the discovery while they were camping at Allison's. Chance died at Republic, Washington, a pauper.

66:32 *Cooper.* Rev. Canon W.H. Cooper, F.R.G.S., after serving the church in Australia, Manitoba, and the North-West Territories, was sent to the Kamloops missionary district in 1887. He immediately set out on a three-week horseback trip to Penticton, Keremeos, and Princeton, returning to Kamloops by the Nicola Valley. It was after his visit with the Allisons that Phillipps-Wolley found three of the Allison boys shingling a log hut and "doing their work smartly and well" to convert it into a schoolhouse (*A Sportsman's Eden,* p. 77). Canon Cooper returned to England in 1890. Mrs. Allison gives 24 April 1888 as the date of Canon Cooper's visit (Allison Family Papers).

66:32 *Father Pat.* Rev. Henry Irwin, an Irishman, came to British Columbia in 1885 and was stationed at the Kamloops missionary district. He soon became Bishop Sillitoe's secretary and chaplain. The death of Mrs. Irwin (Frances Stuart Innes) left Irwin very depressed, and in 1894 he went back to Ireland. He later returned to British Columbia, this time to work in the Kootenay, where he became a beloved figure. He died tragically in 1902, when, near Montreal, he alighted from a train and was exposed to intense cold. For further information, see Sillitoe, *Pioneer Days,* pp. 24–30; and Mrs. Jerome [Anne] Mercier, *Father Pat: A Hero of the Far West* (Gloucester, Mass.: Minchin & Gibbs [for SPCK], 1911).

66:36 *Settle.* A.J. Settle (1861–1949), born at Great Sturton, Lincolnshire, studied at Lincoln Theological College for three years before coming to Canada to work for the Anglican Church. He arrived in the Okanagan in January 1888 and for several months conducted services at Enderby, Vernon, and other points. He then took a position as tutor at the Allison Ranch for six of the boys. In September 1888 he gave up this position and moved to Kamloops, where he was employed by the Canadian Pacific Railway. In 1889 he moved to Salmon Arm, squatting on property until it was surveyed (see the obituary, Salmon Arm *Observer*, 22 December 1949).

66:38 *Lauren College.* Lorne College, a boys' school at New Westminster, supported by the Anglican Church and opened by Bishop Sillitoe in 1883. The school, which had a short life, was probably named after the Marquis of Lorne, who visited New Westminster in 1882 and whose wife, Princess Louise, was a sister of Princess Alice, whom Sillitoe had served as chaplain at Darmstadt.

67: 8 *Sherman.* The visit of General William Tecumseh Sherman occurred in 1883. Sherman (1820–91), the Unionist general famed for his Atlanta campaign in the spring of 1864, his march to the sea, and his campaign in the Carolinas, succeeded General Grant to the command of the United States Army on Grant's inauguration as president of the United States in 1869. He retired from the army in 1883, the year of his visit to Allison's.

67:26 *Miles.* Nelson Appleton Miles served in the Army of the Potomac during the Civil War. After the war he entered the regular army as colonel in 1866, became brigadier-general in 1880, major-general in 1890, and lieutenant-general in 1900. He was engaged in many wars against the Indians, including the war against the Nez Percés in 1877.

67:26 *King.* A Charles King served in the United States Army from 1866 until 1879 when he was put on the retired list because of a wound received in the Apache campaign of 1874. It is unlikely that he was a member of Sherman's party, since he served in the Wisconsin national guard from 1882 until 1895.

67:27 *Mallory.* In an article in the *Princeton Star* on 19 January 1923, Mrs. Allison describes Mallory as "a young Southerner who was always uneasy that his men might try and desert, which they did in spite of his watchful care."

68: 7 *Sands.* Samuel Dickenson Sandes, who married Rose Allison in May 1898. Sandes had pre-empted 320 acres at Osoyoos in 1891, and on 14 December 1897 he received the crown grant for 331 acres, the present townsite of Princeton. This had been Allison's pre-emption, but the title to it had never been completed (Laing, "Colonial Farm Settlers," p. 434). In 1899 Sandes sold the property to W.J. Waterman. Sandes then took a position as draughtsman for the Vananda Copper Company on Texada Island. After his wife's death, he took his child to his family in England and went to Rhodesia.

68:13 *Cook.* Foxcrowle Percival Cook (d. 1918) came to British Columbia in the 1870's and was the pioneer merchant at Granite Creek. Subsequently he had stores at Coalmont and Princeton.

68:13 *Mrs. Cawston.* Mrs. Richard Lowe Cawston (d. 1933), formerly Mary Ann Pearson of Stratford, Ontario. On her wedding trip to Keremeos, she travelled on horseback from Colvile to Osoyoos over the "Little Mountain Trail." For further information, see Verna B. Cawston, "Pioneers of the Similkameen: Mr. and Mrs. R.L. Cawston," Okanagan Historical Society, *Thirteenth Report* (Vernon: *Vernon News*, 1948), pp. 109–16.

68:13 *Mrs. Daly.* In 1884, Thomas Daly, who had been engaged under Andrew Onderdonk on the construction of the Canadian Pacific Railway, acquired two parcels of land, one of 356 acres and the other of 320 acres, on the west side of Keremeos, which Barrington Price had pre-empted and which he called "The Willows" (Laing, "Colonial Farm Settlers," pp. 433, 441). Mrs. Daly came over the Hope Trail in August 1885. When a post office was opened at Keremeos in 1886, she was appointed postmaster (see her reminiscences, "Pioneer Days in the Similkameen," Okanagan Historical Society, *Twenty-Seventh Report* [Vernon: *Vernon News*, 1963], pp. 131–35).

68:14 *Pearce ... Asp.* Sam Pearce had a property on Tulameen River adjoining that of Charles Asp. Asp's property was on China Creek, just west of Princeton. Asp, a miner, went to Granite Creek and died there in 1933. He is described by John C. Goodfellow as a "tough hombre, who looked like the picture of Father Time without his scythe," (A.G. Harvey, File on British Columbia Place Names, MS, PABC).

Acknowledgements

My first acknowledgement must be to the descendants of Mrs. John Fall Allison who supplied me with the materials out of which this book has been created. A daughter of Mrs. Allison, the late Mrs. Alice O. Wright of Summerland, B.C., provided the typescript of "Some Recollections of a Pioneer of the Sixties." This typescript was compared with other typescripts of the same work, one deposited in the Vancouver City Archives and the other in the Provincial Archives of British Columbia, and with the holograph which was entrusted to the late Major J.S. Matthews and deposited by him in Vancouver City Archives soon after Mrs. Allison's death in 1937.

A daughter of Mrs. Wright, Mrs. Elvie Sisson of North Vancouver lent me the original John Fall Allison Letters in her possession and, in addition, made available a miscellaneous collection of family records, letters, account books, newspaper clippings and photographs, classified together as the Allison Family Papers. Through Mrs. Sisson's efforts, further information concerning Mrs. Allison, largely in the form of notes and memoranda, was obtained from Mrs. Allison's surviving daughters, and in particular from Mrs. A. Johnstone (Susan Louisa Allison) of Princeton, B.C. Mrs. Sisson provided the portrait of Susan Louisa Moir which is reproduced in the book. She was also kind enough to lend me the manuscripts of Mrs. Allison's unpublished short stories, her sketches of Similkameen Indian women, a lengthy narrative poem "Quinesco," and stories about the Similkameen Indians entitled "Tales from Tam-tu-sa-list." Furthermore, in sessions which she spent with me Mrs. Sisson enlarged my knowledge of Mrs. Allison's social and cultural background and conveyed to me a sense of Mrs. Allison's strength of character, the keenness of her intelligence, and not by any means least, the sprightliness of her nature. For all the insights which Mrs. Sisson provided, I am deeply grateful.

Likewise I am grateful to those who provided me with information concerning Mrs. Allison's progenitors. Mr. Colin A. McLaren, Archivist and Keeper of Manuscripts, Aberdeen University Library, supplied information concerning William Moir's attendance at Aberdeen University, and Stratton Moir's attendance at Marischal College and graduation from Aberdeen University. Mrs. V. de Souza, Librarian, University of Ceylon, Sri Lanka, and Mr. J.R. Sinnatamby, Reader, University of Ceylon Library and Deputy Surveyor General (retired), Ceylon, were most helpful. Mr. Sinnatamby was kind enough to examine the baptismal register at St. Peter's Church, Colombo, and thereby verify the date of Mrs. Allison's birth. Mr. Ian Baxter, India Office Library and Records, London, supplied information concerning two members of a Moir family from Aberdeenshire who served in the Indian Medical Service. Information concerning four Moir Brothers from Laurencekirk, possibly cousins of Stratton Moir, who became coffee planters in Ceylon, was provided by Dr. T.J. Barron, Department of History, University of Edinburgh.

My indebtedness to Dr. Barron goes far beyond the supplying of this latter information. Dr. Barron gave me a fund of information concerning the circumstances under which coffee planting in Ceylon was commenced, the setbacks that the planters incurred, and the later development of tea planting. In the light of this information, the story spread by Edgar Dewdney that Stratton Moir was the first tea planter in Ceylon seems hardly credible.

In addition to the assistance mentioned above, one of Mrs. Allison's grandsons, Mr. R.L.S. Bruce-Mitford, Department of Medieval and Later Antiquities, the British Museum, was able to supply some information concerning his own mother (Beatrice Allison) and her mother's connection with the Mortimer family.

Closer at hand, I am indebted to a number of archivists. Mr. Robert Watt, while he was Vancouver City Archivist, supplied me with a xerox copy of the holograph copy of Mrs. Allison's reminiscences. His successor, Mr. Lynn Ogden, conducted a further search in the same archives for additional Allison material. At the Provincial Archives of British Columbia, Mr. Willard E. Ireland, and his successor, Mr. Allan Turner, lent their co-operation. Miss Frances Gundry and other members of the manuscript division provided answers to specific questions. Mrs. Anne

Yandle and the staff of Special Collections Department, University of British Columbia Library, assisted in many ways, and in particular with making available the Trutch Papers. I must also thank the Reverend Cyril Williams, Archivist of the Ecclesiastical Province of British Columbia, Vancouver School of Theology, for permission to consult the Journal of Bishop George Hills. At Calgary, the staff of the Glenbow-Alberta Institute granted access to the Edgar Dewdney Collection.

At the early stages of research, Mrs. Jacqueline Gresko conducted at the Provincial Archives of British Columbia a preliminary scouting for relevant materials. Her industry resulted in the production of much useful information relating to obscure events and to persons of minor importance among the early settlers of the Mainland of British Columbia.

Finally, I am indebted to two friends, Dr. Dorothy Blakey Smith and Dr. Jane Fredeman. Dr. Blakey Smith, though engaged in her own research on, and the editing of, the Reminiscences of Doctor John Sebastian Helmcken, found time to obtain information for me on little known facts and details of British Columbia's history, advise on editorial matters, and offer the companionship of another writer. Dr. Fredeman, Senior Editor of the University of British Columbia Press, never allowed her interest in my work to flag and provided me with the most expert editorial advice and criticism. Any oversights in text and in detail which may still exist in the present work betray my own deficiences and are not in any sense to be charged to lack of care and scrutiny on her part.

Index